Montroville Wilson Dickeson

The American numismatical manual of the currency or money of the aborigines and colonial, state, and United States coins

With historical and descriptive notices of each coin or series. Second Edition

Montroville Wilson Dickeson

The American numismatical manual of the currency or money of the aborigines and colonial, state, and United States coins
With historical and descriptive notices of each coin or series. Second Edition

ISBN/EAN: 9783337152291

Printed in Europe, USA, Canada, Australia, Japan

Cover: Foto ©Suzi / pixelio.de

More available books at **www.hansebooks.com**

THE

AMERICAN

NUMISMATIC MANUAL.

OF THE

CURRENCY OR MONEY OF THE ABORIGINES,

AND

COLONIAL, STATE, AND UNITED STATES COINS.

WITH

HISTORICAL AND DESCRIPTIVE

NOTICES OF EACH COIN OR SERIES.

BY

MONTROVILLE WILSON DICKESON, M.D.,

MEMBER OF THE AMERICAN ASSOCIATION FOR THE PROMOTION OF SCIENCE, THE HISTORICAL SOCIETY OF PENNSYLVANIA, THE ACADEMY OF NATURAL SCIENCES OF PHILADELPHIA, AND THE ETHNOLOGICAL SOCIETY OF NEW YORK; FELLOW OF THE ROYAL SOCIETY OF ANTIQUARIES OF COPENHAGEN, ETC. ETC.

ILLUSTRATED BY TWENTY PLATES OF FAC-SIMILES.

SECOND EDITION.

PHILADELPHIA:
J. B. LIPPINCOTT & CO.
1860.

Entered, according to Act of Congress, in the year 1860, by
MONTROVILLE WILSON DICKESON,
in the Clerk's Office of the District Court of the United States for the Eastern District of Pennsylvania.

STEREOTYPED BY J. FAGAN.

DEDICATION.

To the People of the American Union.

In publishing this work, the basis of which is the Anglo-American Colonial coins, I have endeavored to rescue from the graves of modern antiquity those original, and, in many cases, rude representatives of value, which, to the early colonists and their successors for many years, possessed an importance in developing, conducting, and advancing their agricultural industry, trade, and commerce, equal in magnitude and purpose, relatively, with the more extended and perfect appliances of the present day.

Contrasting the coinage of our infant colonies with that of the present time; their struggles against kingly prerogative for its existence, with the undisturbed authority of the people over the same subject now, is an instructive commentary relative to their triumphs and our progress as freemen since, which is calculated to excite our wonder and induce our gratitude.

It shows that our fathers were so constituted, that though they might be worn out, they could not be crushed in their contests for ultimate freedom. In their weakness, full of diplomacy without compromising principle, principle was their bulwark in all their contests for self-government. Learning from dear-bought experience, that local security and national prosperity could neither be attained nor maintained by a legislation of foreign dictation, and that a fair but just independence of any authority

DEDICATION.

but their own could not be achieved but by making themselves sovereigns instead of remaining subjects, they early planted the seeds of liberty in every practicable form; among the earliest acts of which was the establishment of the Mint at Boston, whose fruits, meeting the popular taste, so excited the colonial appetite for more, that it laid the foundation for wants, which the open declaration of independence in 1776, and its acknowledgment in 1783, could only appease.

The full fruition of early purposes and struggles having been long since confirmed, may our country still further exemplify its progressive character; and through the patriotism and vigilance of its *sovereigns*, occupy, to the remotest period of time, its present exalted position among the nations of the earth; and may the people fail not to refresh their love of country by frequently contemplating the feeble sources of their origin — seeing that the neglect of the lessons of the past leaves no certain guide for the future.

THE AUTHOR.

PREFACE.

Coin or money is the medium which mankind has adopted to facilitate the exchange of one commodity for another, and, consequently, it is now inseparable from the trade, commerce, and exchanges of the world.

The history of money, in our own country, dates from the lignite, shells, wampum, &c., &c., of the aborigines, down to the present very highly artistic coins of the United States Mint. Thus, in coins or money, as in the arts generally, and also in agriculture and commerce, the advancement, from great rudeness to comparative perfection, excites our wonder; so effective, for improvement and progress under Providential arrangement and guidance, has been man's intellect, which, in its further achievements and victories, it is not gifted with the prescience to unfold or determine.

To trace the progress of any art, from its rude origin up to the period of its present perfection, is an agreeable task, and it induces self-gratulation, and merits public approval and support in proportion to its utility. It is peculiarly gratifying to be able to contemplate the results of the inventiveness and ingenuity of mankind, gradually progressing, and finally triumphing over all obstacles to complete success.

The coins of the colonies have been involved in much obscurity, and the facts in relation to them have been chiefly derived from the specimens, and such history in regard to them, as the curious and scientific have collected and preserved.

The specimens are more numerous, and have been better taken care of than those of any other art; so natural is it, and ever has it been, for mankind in all ages to cling to the representatives of value.

It is the purpose of this work, as far as practicable, to establish the origin, and faithfully describe the coins and coinage of our country, from the dawn of the period when the pioneers of discovery, settlement, and civilization, experienced the necessity, and adopted the measures, for founding some commercial standard or representative of value in their commerce, and also trade, with one another, down to the present very enlightened era in our history; thus forming a metallic chain, the description and history of the links of which will embrace every feature relevant to a thorough knowledge — so far as I have been able to acquire it — of the whole and its parts;

PREFACE.

and thereby imparting to the student, or the gentleman of leisure, the proper relation of coins to the chronological and historical events therewith connected.

The attention paid to numismatics in other countries has elicited much useful information, and induced numerous publications upon that subject. In our own country, the aboriginal — so far as it can be classed under that head — and the colonial coins — the main purpose of my effort — have been peculiarly neglected in every work of the kind. In collating and presenting, therefore, as perfect a history of them, as is practicable, I have expended much labor and time, and incurred great expense. I hope the result will impart much pleasure to my patrons, and contribute something to their stock of information, though it may not be of the kind that adds to the hoards of their metallic treasures.

In the present age, the subject of money can be no intrusive one; as it certainly has lost none of the attraction or interest, which the fondness for its acquisition or possession has heretofore given to it. In fact, every advancing stage of civilization or progress, with its increased refinements and luxuries, has but enhanced its importance in the practical estimation of mankind, till it has become a lever in the movement of the world, totally eclipsing the conceptions of an Archimedes, or any other physical or mental teacher in regard to power, except the modern disciple of gold.

The fac-similes of this work — numerous and expensive — are of themselves such a collection for the general observer, and the young collector of coins, as has never before been produced.

Feeling, as I do, that every department of science has claims to the public consideration and understanding, this volume is presented with the hope that it may meet with the popular approbation; it being my purpose, if it should be approved, to prepare an edition for the use of schools; where certainly no harm could arise from proper information being imparted relative to the origin and progress of our metallic currency — occupying as it has, and now does, a paramount relation to everything that has made us a successful agricultural, manufacturing, and commercial people, and without which we should not yet have emerged from our infancy as a nation.

In this work, I am indebted to the REV. JOSEPH FELT, on the "Massachusetts Currency;" HENRY NOEL HUMPHREYS, "on the coinage of the British Empire;" LLOYD P. SMITH, ESQ., Librarian of Philadelphia Library; JOSEPH MICKLEY, ESQ., of Philadelphia, for access to his fine and extensive cabinet of coins; the "Manual" and "Supplement" thereto, by JACOB R. ECKFELDT and WILLIAM E. DU BOIS, Assayers of the U. S. Mint; HON. JAMES ROSS SNOWDEN, Director of the Mint; other officers of that institution, and to numerous private individuals; to all of whom I present my thanks.

THE AUTHOR.

DESCRIPTION OF PLATES.

Portrait of the Author .... To Face Title-page.
Frontispiece .... " Page 11.

ABORIGINAL COINS.

Plate I.	Lignite	Figures 1, 2, 3, 4, 5, 6, 7, 8, 9, 12.
"	Coal	" 10, 11, 16, 17, 19.
"	" (Ancient Britain)	" 13, 14, 15.
II.	Lignite	" 1.
"	Coal (Ancient Britain)	" 8, 9, 14.
"	Stone	" 2, 13, 15.
"	Stone Hatchets	" 8, 10.
"	Jasper, &c., Darts	" 4, 5, 11, 12.
"	Lily Encrinite	" 6, 7, 16, 17, 18, 19.
III.	Terra-Cotta	" 1, 2, 3, 4, 5, 6, 7, 8, 9, 10, 11, 12, 13.
IV.	Gold	" 1, 2.
"	Galena	" 6, 7, 8, 9, 10, 11.
"	Copper	" 12, 13, 14, 15, 21.
"	Stone	" 3, 4, 5, 16.
"	Copper Beads and Tubes	" 17, 18, 19, 20.
V.	Wampum.	

COLONIAL COINS.

VI.	Sommers' Islands	" 1.
"	Massachusetts Pattern-shilling	" 2.
"	New England Shilling and Six-pence	" 3, 4.
"	Pine-tree Shilling, Six-pence, and Three-pence ..	" 5, 6, 7.
"	Oak-Tree Shilling, Six-pence, Three-pence, and Two-pence ..	" 8, 9, 10, 11.
"	Good Samaritan Shilling	" 12.
"	Lord Baltimore Shilling, Six-pence, Groat, and Penny ..	" 13, 14, 15, 16.
VII.	Tin Piece — King James II.	" 1.
"	Carolina Half-Penny	" 2.
"	Louisiana Copper	" 3.
"	Rosa-Americana Pennies, Half-Pennies, and Farthing ..	" 4, 5, 6, 7, 8, 9, 10.
"	Granby Coppers	" 11, 12.

DESCRIPTION OF PLATES.

PLATE VIII.		Florida Piece — Charles III., Spain	Figure	1.
"		Pitt Piece	"	2.
"		Louisiana Copper	"	3.
"		Virginia Half-Pennies — Copper and Silver	"	4, 5.
"		"Washington Piece"	"	6.
"		Continental Currency	"	7.
"		Janus Copper	"	8.
"		Massachusetts Coppers	"	9, 10.
"		Pine-Tree Copper	"	11.
"		U. S. A. Copper	"	12.
"		Non Dependens Status	"	13.
	IX.	Nova Constellatio — Gold	"	1.
"		" " Silver	"	2, 3.
"		" " " Immune Columbia	"	4.
"		" " Copper	"	5, 6.
"		Georgius Triumpho	"	7.
"		Anapolis Shilling, Six-pence, and Three-pence	"	8, 9, 10.
"		Confederatio Copper	"	11.
"		Vermonts Res Publica	"	12.
"		Vermontensium Res Publica	"	13.
"		Vermon Auctori — Immune Columbia	"	14.
"		" "	"	15.
	X.	George III. — Immune Columbia	"	1.
"		Auctori Plebis	"	2.
"		Georgius III. Rex	"	3.
"		Auctori Connec.	"	4, 5, 6, 7, 8, 9, 10.
"		Nova Cæsarea	"	11, 12, 13, 14, 15, 16, 17, 18, 19, 20.
"		Immune Columbia — New Jersey	"	21.
	XI.	Neo Eboracensis	"	1.
"		New York Gold Coin	"	2.
"		Immunis Columbia	"	3.
"		Nova Eborac.	"	4.
"		Liber Natus Libertate Defendo	"	5, 6.
"		First United States Cent	"	7.
"		Kentucky Coppers	"	8, 12.
"		Massachusetts Cent and Half-Cent	"	9, 10.
"		New York Cent	"	11.
"		Castorland Half-Dollar	"	13.
"		North American Token	"	14.
"		De Dansk Americ	"	15.
	XII.	Washington Cents	"	1, 3, 4, 5, 6, 7, 9.
"		" Tokens	"	2, 10.
"		" Half-Dollar	"	8.
	XIII.	" Token	"	1.
"		" Cent	"	2.
"		" Copper	"	3.
"		" Half-Penny	"	4.
"		" Medalet	"	5.
"		Liverpool Half-Pennies	"	4, 6.

DESCRIPTION OF PLATES. ix

PATTERN PIECES.

PLATE XIII.	Cent, 1792...............................	Figure 7.
"	" — Eagle volant, 1855...............	" 8.
"	Disme, 1792	" 9.
"	Cent, 1792...............................	" 10.
"	" "	" 11.
"	" — Eagle, 1792.......................	" 12.
"	" " "	" 13.
"	Half-Dollar — Trial, 1858	" 14.
"	Cent — Eagle	" 15.
"	" — Liberty-Cap — Composition, 1854	" 16.
"	" — Composition, 1835.................	" 17.
"	" — Indian Princess, 1858	" 18.
"	" — Feuchtwanger, 1837...............	" 19.
"	" — Composition, 1851................	" 20.
"	" — Ring, 1850.......................	" 21.
"	Three-Cent Pieces	" 22, 23, 24.

UNITED STATES' COINS.

XIV.	Eagle, 1795............................	" 1.
"	" Half-, 1795	" 2.
"	" " 1798	" 3.
"	" 1797	" 4.
"	" Quarter-, 1796...................	" 5.
"	" Double-, 1849	" 6.
"	" Quarter-, 1808...................	" 7.
"	" " 1834...................	" 8.
"	" Half-, 1834	" 9.
"	" 1838	" 10.
"	" Half-, 1838	" 11.
"	" Quarter-, 1838...................	" 12.
"	" Half-, 1808	" 13.
"	Dollar, Gold, 1849.......................	" 14.
"	" " Indian Princess, 1854...........	" 15.
"	" Three- Piece, Indian Princess, 1854	" 16.

PATTERN PIECES.

"	Gold Ring-Dollars and Half-Dollar, 1852............	" 17, 18, 19.
"	" Dollar, Liberty-cap, 1836..................	" 20.
XV.	Dollars, Silver, 1794, 1796, 1798, 1840............	" 1, 2, 3, 4.
"	Half-Dollars, Silver, 1794, 1803, 1808, 1837, 1840........	" 5, 6, 7, 8, 9.
XVI.	Quarter-Dollars, 1796, 1815, 1831, 1843, 1853............	" 1, 4, 7, 10, 15.
"	Dimes, 1796, 1798, 1809, 1837, 1838..................	" 18, 2, 5, 8, 11.
"	Half-Dimes, 1792, 1795, 1796, 1829, 1837, 1839............	" 3, 6, 9, 13, 12, 14
"	Dollar — Trial, 1836	" 19.
"	Three-Cent Pieces	" 16, 17.

DESCRIPTION OF PLATES.

PLATE XVII.	Cents, Chain, 1793			Figures	1, 2.
"	"	Wreath, 1793		"	3, 4.
"	"	Liberty-Cap, 1793, 1794, 1795, 1796		"	5, 6, 7, 8.
"	Cent, Cue, 1796			"	9.
"	"	Turban, 1808		"	10.
"	"	Fillet, 1816		"	11.
"	"	" —fifteen stars, 1817		"	12.
"	"	" —Three Types, 1839		"	13, 14, 15.
"	"	Nickel, 1856		"	16.
"	Half-Cent, Liberty-Cap, 1793, 1794, 1795, 1797			".	17, 18, 19, 20.
"	"	Cue, 1800		"	21.
"	"	Turban, 1809		"	22.
"	"	" —twelve stars, 1828		"	23.
"	"	Fillet, 1840		"	24.
XVIII.	Half-Eagle, N. G. & N., Cal.			"	7.
"	Ten and Five-Dollar Pieces, Oregon Ex. Co., Cal.			"	1, 8.
"	"	"	Moffatt & Co.	"	2, 12.
"	"	"	Cinn. Mining and Trading Co., Cal.	"	4.
"	"	"	Pacific Co.	"	3.
"	"	"	Massachusetts and California Co.	"	6.
"	"	"	Baldwin & Co.	"	10
"	"	"	Dubosq & Co.	"	9.
"	"	"	Shultz & Co.	"	11.
"	"	"	Mormon, Utah	"	5, 14.
"	"	"	Dunbar & Co.	"	13.
"	Ten-Dollar Pieces, U. S. Assay Office at S. Francisco, Moffatt & Co.			"	18.
"	Ingots, Moffatt & Co.			"	20, 21.
"	Bars, F. D. Kohler, Assayer of the State of California			"	19.
"	Five and One-Dollar Pieces, North Carolina			"	15, 16, 17.
XIX.	Ten-dollar Pieces, Miners' Bank, San Francisco, California			"	12.
"	"	"	J. S. O.	"	10.
"	Twenty-five and Ten-Dollar Pieces, Templeton Reed			"	2, 7.
"	Ten-Dollar Pieces, Cincinnati Mining and Trading Co.			"	4.
"	"	"	Pacific Co.	"	6.
"	Tens and Twenty-Dollar Pieces, Baldwin & Co.			"	8, 3, 13.
"	Ten-Dollar Piece, Dubosq & Co.			"	11.
"	Twenty and Two-and-a-half-Dollar Pieces, Mormon, Utah			"	5, 9.
"	Fifty-Dollar Piece, U. S. Assay Office, San Francisco, California.			"	1.
"	Gold Dollar, Half, and Quarter, California			"	14, 15, 16.

TO COMMEMORATE THE TRIUMPH
OF
AMERICAN INDEPENDENCE.

Device.—The bust of the Goddess of Liberty: the liberty-pole, surmounted by the cap, rests against the right shoulder, and the hair is blown back, as if by the wind against which the goddess appears to be running, to announce to the world the tidings of her victory.

Legend.—LIBERTAS AMERICANA 4 JUIL, 1776.

Reverse.—Pallas, holding in her left hand a shield with three fleur de lis — the arms of France — and opposing it to a leopard — England — which is springing toward it: her right hand is drawn back and holds a barbed javelin, as if in the act of plunging it into the leopard. Under the shield is an infant in a stooping posture, strangling a serpent with each hand, and, apparently, contemplating the same act upon another at its feet.

Legend.—NON SINE DIIS ANIMOSUS INFANS.[1]

Exergue.—17 Oct. 1777
19   1781

According to ancient mythology, Hercules, under the protection of Pallas, is said to have strangled two serpents which had assaulted him in his cradle. Infant America, like Hercules in his cradle, had destroyed two armies — Burgoyne's, which surrendered at Saratoga, Oct. 17, 1777, and Cornwallis', at Yorktown, Oct. 19, 1781. — *Mease's Description of American Medals.*

The embellishments and illustrations in this work, by Rosenthal Brothers, of Philadelphia, are, of themselves, sufficient encomium upon their taste and skill as lithographers. I cannot, however, forego the expression of my personal appreciation of, and indebtedness to them for, the zeal with which they entered into the work, and prosecuted it to completion — evidencing not only pre-eminence in their art, but a corresponding interest in whatever is useful or beautiful. M. W. D.

---

[1] The infant's strength was dependent upon the gods. — HORACE, Ode IV., Book III., Verse 20

THE

AMERICAN NUMISMATICAL MANUAL.

INTRODUCTION.

HAVING no parentage in the arts, except from our famous old mother, England — our predecessors, the aborigines, when we came among them upon this continent, being armed with, and possessed of no traces of civilization, not since exhumed from their mounds, and they superseded in value by the progress of the arts of other nations — we not only trace our lineage to her, but in our connection, otherwise, as scion and pupil so long, look to her records and acts. Hence, to begin where she did in coinage, and follow it up to the period when, having set up for ourselves, we adopted a national coinage of our own, cannot but be both entertaining and instructive.

Temples, statues, triumphal arches, or any monuments of art, have been of vast importance in elucidating and testing the chronicles and histories of past times, and often in bringing to light important events in the history of the world, of which no written record existed. Coins, similarly applied, become the more positive evidence.

A coin, find it where we may, is an index to the people who originally issued it, and truly indicative of their state of civilization. The date of the foundation of Rome, as accepted by the Romans themselves, is proved by a coin struck by the Emperor Philip II., to commemorate the millennium of the city. The inscription of this coin states it was issued in the year of his third consulship, the period of which being known, the foundation of Rome is fixed at one thousand years before that event. Other Roman coins, where triumphal arches have crumbled to dust, and statues have been overthrown, record such great historical facts as "Judæa Capta," "Victoriæ Brittanicæ," "Aegypto Capta," and others of equal importance.

Astronomy acquires evidence from the device on a coin of Augustus Cæsar, of the appearance of a great comet at a certain period. This comet was supposed by the

INTRODUCTION.

populace of Rome to have been the spirit of Julius Cæsar after his apotheosis. Sir Isaac Newton availed himself of the use of coins, in testing the dates of his great work on ancient chronology; and through these means, the names of upwards of two thousand places, provinces, and princes, have been preserved — many of them having no other record. In portraiture, coins are of the greatest interest; the Greek and Roman series furnishing accurate representations of the features of Alexander the Great, the Ptolemies, Cæsar, Augustus, Homer, Sappho, and Cicero; who, though not placed upon the public coinage during their lives, were afterwards engraved on the public money of different States, in honor of their memory. Ancient works upon portraiture are chiefly indebted for their value to the portraits found upon coins.

Lost history has been revealed through the medium of recently-discovered coins. I refer to the series of "Græco Bactrian" and "Græco Indian" coins. After the death of Alexander the Great, his powerful lieutenants divided up his empire among themselves, each erecting for himself an independent sovereignty out of the conquered provinces; but, of the names of the rulers in north-western India, only eight of the immediate successors of Alexander were preserved. The discovery of these coins has extended the number to twenty, and the coins of their more barbarous successors disclose a series extending from the third century before, to the twelfth century after, the Christian era.

The earliest money transaction on record, is that in which it is related that Abraham weighed to Ephron "four hundred shekels of silver, current money with the merchant," in payment for the field of Machpelah. These were, doubtless, mere pieces of silver without stamp or mark, which passed by weight only, as the term *shekel*, to weigh, fully implies. The term used in the book of Job for money is not shekel, but "kesitah," a lamb, from the image of that animal having been stamped on the pieces of the weight of a shekel, as the image of an ox was subsequently placed on the Roman pound weight of copper. The shekel, when long afterwards issued in the form of a positive coin, was of the weight of two Greek drachms, and equal to about fifty-six cents, or about the value of a lamb at that period. On the obverse of this coin, was the sacred cup of manna, and on the reverse, the rod of Aaron, on which three flowers are perceptible. The inscriptions were, on the obverse, "Shekel of Israel," and the reverse, "Jerusalem the Holy." Some have such inscriptions as "Saviour Prince of Israel," "the first year of the deliverance of Israel," &c. &c.

As commerce increased, from the time of Abraham to that of Micah, who lived about 1500 B. C., commercial wants increased, and the pieces of silver used in trade were largely augmented at the expense of their size; for a transaction of Micah with his mother refers to a thousand pieces of silver; and similar sums are mentioned three centuries later, in the transaction of the five lords of the Philistines and Delilah; and that they were very small pieces, is evident from the statement, that the lords brought the money in their hands—probably in sealed bags, each containing a certain weight.

The Jews, it is said, did not adopt the use of positive coins till long after their introduction into other countries. From the time of Abraham, however, to that of the Maccabees, about 144 years B. C., they had, like other oriental nations, in addition to common money, formed of small pieces of silver, a kind of jewel-money, consisting of personal ornaments adjusted to a certain weight, which, if occasion required, might be used as money. Such are the jewels mentioned in Genesis xxiv. 22, as given by Abraham's servant to Rebekah. "The man took a golden ear-ring of half a shekel in weight, and two bracelets for her hands, of ten shekels' weight of gold." They also had ring-money, such, undoubtedly, as was used by the Celtic nations of the West. This ring-money of the East appears to have been formed of wire, so attached together — not being fastened — that portions could be detached at pleasure from the chain. Representations of this kind of money are found in hieroglyphic sculptures, where men are represented as weighing rings, and a scribe is taking an account of their number and value. Similar rings are still current as money in Nubia, and the portion of this work devoted to the aboriginal currency of North America, will show that they were in use as such among the Indians. The bags of silver given by Naaman to Gehazi, 2 Kings, v. 23, may or may not have contained the ring-money, their weight probably being a talent; among the Hebrews, a weight and denomination of money equivalent to 3000 shekels. As a weight, therefore, it was equal to about 93¾ lbs. avoirdupois; as a denomination of silver, it has been variously estimated at from £340 to £396 sterling, or from about $1500 to $1800. Other kinds of money of a ruder character also existed, such as engraved stones, like the Egyptian *scarebei*, pieces of cloth, slices of salt of an estimated value, the remnants of patriarchal times and customs, which still form the currency of some parts of northern Africa.

To the Greeks, that once noble people, to whom the world is so largely indebted for so many features of civilization, we must ascribe the first invention of positive coins as money. As it is natural that the honor of origin of any creation in art, conferring either individual or national distinction, should be contested, some have given precedence, in time, to the Persian daric of gold and silver — coins equal to our five-dollar and quarter-dollar pieces. Others place, as first, the Phœnician coins struck in the island of Malta; and others, again, the brass money of Italy. In neither of which, however, except the Greek, has there been that gradual development of the art of coining, from the stamping of the simple lump of metal, through all its phases, to that of the perfect coin.

The first species of money that was circulated by tale instead of weight, of which we have any account, consisted of spikes, in shape, of brass or iron; six of these being as many as the hand could grasp. From this rude money were derived the words *obolus* and *drachma*, meaning spike and handfull, which continued to be the names of two well-known pieces of Greek money; the latter of which had a value equal to six of the former. Drachma is the name of the principal coin now in use in Greece.

The date of the change in Greek money from weight to positive coins, of specific and guaranteed value, cannot be determined; but as Homer states, that an ox was exchanged for a "bar of brass of certain size;" that a woman who understood several useful arts was of the value of four oxen; that the brazen armor of Diomedes was of that of nine oxen, and the golden armor of Glaucus of that of one hundred oxen, we must conclude that a positive coinage did not exist in his time; while the allusion in the laws of Lycurgus to gold and silver coins prove that they were then in use; and hence, then, between these two epochs, we must place the invention of coined money.

Herodotus states that the Lydians were the first to issue gold coins. The first appearance of gold coins, however, whether Greek or Lydian, is determined to have taken place about eight hundred years before the Christian era, and to have been followed by an issue of silver coins, of a similar character, in the island of Ægina, about fifty years later, by Phidon, prince of Argos. The first symbol placed upon these coins was of a sacred character — emblems referring to protective gods, and images of the gods themselves; but not till after the age of Alexander, were portraits of sovereigns either allowed or introduced.

The principles of the Greek coinage were rapidly extended through the north of Greece into transalpine Gaul, and, radiating from another centre of Greek civilization, the ancient colony of Massitia, now Marseilles, extended northward even to the then remote island of Britain, where imitations of the coins issued by Philip of Macedon and Alexander, began to supersede the Celtic ring-money.

Asia Minor being rich in gold—the fabulous richness of the sands of Pactolus being known to every school-boy—its first coinage was of gold. Italy and Sicily abounding in copper, their first emissions were of that material, or rather a mixture of copper and other metals termed Æs, a term, perhaps, for *bronze*. The *litra*, in Sicily, and the *libra*, in Italy, was the unit upon which this bronze coinage was founded. The pound weight of copper first received a State impress in Rome, to pass as coin, in the reign of Servius Tullius, about 578 B. C. These coins, from being impressed with the images of cattle, such as oxen, sheep, &c., were called *pecunia*, from the Latin *pecus*, cattle, which has now been so long translated money. The Romans did not issue a silver coinage till the year 281 B. C., when its standard was based upon that of the Greek drachma. The *drachma* being, at that time, of the value of ten Roman *æses*, the new silver coin was denominated a *Denarius*, or piece of ten *æses*. This piece became the parent of the silver pennies of the Anglo-Saxon coinage, and of those of France, where the silver pieces corresponding to English pennies are still called *Deniers*, particularly in the provincial districts of that country. The Romans coined gold in 207 B. C. Their standard gold coin was called the *Aureus*, and was worth twenty-five Denarii.

Such was the state of the Roman coinage at the time of their conquest of Britain, where their coins soon superseded those of the natives.

Cæsar states that the Gauls used for money gold and iron rings of a certain weight. The lowest denomination of the ring-money was found to be exactly one-half pennyweight, which was the unit from which the larger sizes were graduated. The gradations of value existed up to 13 oz. 7 dwts. The system of ring-money in Ireland was about as perfect as real coins. This ring-money not only existed in England and Scotland, but probably continued in use as currency till it was superseded by the more convenient coinage of the Roman empire. The Britons, from their proximity to Gaul, received thence the coined money of the Greeks at an early day, which was displacing the ring-money very rapidly, even before the conquest of the Romans.

Cæsar, in speaking of the civilization of the Britons, says, "They had both lozenge and gold money; or, instead of money, rings adjusted to a certain weight." There were, also, rude coins of tin, evidently of native workmanship. Tin, the ancient staple of the island of Britain, establishes the truth of the existence and the antiquity of these coins. Following these, then, were coins of Greek form and style; then came coins bearing the names of British districts or cities; and next came those bearing the names of chiefs or rulers. Cæsar also speaks of Comius as possessing considerable influence, and of coins bearing the name Epillus, son of Comius, which may be attributed to him.

The British prince, Cunobeline — the Cymbeline of Shakspeare — whose dominions extended over Norfolk, Suffolk, and Essex, and much of the country west of the Severn, issued coins bearing his own effigy and name, Cunobelinus, in full. He is said to have visited Rome in the reign of Augustus, and to have brought back with him Roman artists to superintend his coinage. Taciovanus, supposed to have been of Gallic origin, but holding dominion in Britain, had coins also bearing his name.

In the 42d year of the era of Britain, the southern parts of the island were subjugated by the Emperor Claudius, and the Roman coinage soon after gained the

INTRODUCTION.

ascendent. The first allusion to Britain on a Roman coin, occurs in those issued under that emperor — followed by those issued under Britannicus, the son of Claudius; Septimus Severus, who died in York, Eng., A. D. 211; Caracalla, Geta, Postumus, Victorinius, Marius; *British coins* of the usurper Carausius, under the reign of Maximianus; Allectus, his treacherous successor, Constantine the Great, Crispus, and Constantius. Roman coin thus circulated in Britain till the final abandonment of the country, about A. D. 414.

The Saxons now succeeded the Romans in Britain, and as their money is totally different from that of the Romans, it must have been brought into the island with them, along with a new set of weights, values and measures. Their coins were called Skeattæ — Latinized Scatta — a term which Ruding derives from a Saxon word meaning a portion; and which he illustrates, by supposing that these coins were a portion of some merely nominal sum, by which large amounts were calculated. They were mentioned after the adoption of the Saxon silver penny, in the laws of Æthelstan, where it is stated that 30,000 skeattæ are equal to £120, which would make them about one twenty-fifth part less in value than a penny sterling. Of the origin of the word penny, Ruding says: "It is variously spelled as peneg, peninc, &c., and some derive it from the Latin word *pendo*, to weigh, while others consider pecunia as the parent word." The penny, with occasional half-pennies, constituted the only money of the country up to the reign of Edward III. It was intended that a pound Tower should make 240 pennies, giving 24 grains to each; but this weight was gradually decreased by successive princes, 22½ grains being afterwards deemed full weight, and 20 grains being about the average weight down to Henry III. Their standard purity seems to have been 11 oz. 2 dwt. fine, and 11 dwt. alloy. The name of the moneyer or mint-master of the district in which the piece was coined, was now — about 700 A. D. — generally placed on the reverse of the coin with some ornament, and afterwards the name of the place of mintage.

Next followed the coins of the Saxon Heptarchy — those of the kings of Kent, from the accession of Ethelbert in A. D. 568, to the end of the reign of Baldred, A. D. 823, under whom the first silver penny was coined; of the kings of Mercia, from the penny of Eadwald or Ethelwald to that of Burgred in A. D. 874, the last of the Mercian princes; of the kings of the East Angles, the earliest emission of coins by whom, were by Beruna in A. D. 750; they were of the form and size of skeattæ. Guthram, a Dane, succeeded to the throne, who, being converted to Christianity, was baptized by the name of Ethelstan in A. D. 878. His name is found on his coins with Re or Rex, and Rex Ang.—Angliæ — the first time the title of "King of England" appears on any coin.

THE COINS OF THE KINGS OF NORTHUMBERLAND. — The distinctive feature in the Northumbrian coins is their metal, a composition containing in a hundred parts, 60 to 70 of copper, about 20 of zinc, 5 to 11 of silver, with minute portions of gold, lead and tin. These coins were termed *stycas*, two being equal to a farthing. There were also skeattœ of the usual purity of silver. The first styca was by Egfrith, from A. D. 671 to 685. Eric, the son of Harold of Norway, slain A. D. 951, was the last king. His coins were silver pennies. Coins of saints also were issued under his reign; those of St. Peter having been called "Peter Pence," and erroneously supposed to have been coined for the purpose of paying to Rome the tribute known by that name; they were silver pennies, coined at York. There were others bearing the name of St. Martin, St. Edmund, &c.

The dignitaries of the Church, soon after the firm establishment of Christianity in the island, had authority to strike money, and enjoy the profits of mintage. Archbishops alone, however, had the privilege of stamping these coins with portraits and names. This privilege was withdrawn by Æthelstan in A. D. 924. Subsequently, the prelatical coinage was distinguished from the royal by peculiar mint-marks, and these terminated in the reign of Henry VIII. The coins of the Archbishops of York were stycas, till they became, by the edict of Æthelstan, assimilated to the coins of the realm. Ulphere or Vulphere, who held this See from A. D. 854 to 892, is the last prelate whose name occurs on coins of the Episcopal mint.

Next in order are the coins of the Saxon and Danish sole, monarchs of England; the coins of Egbert do not differ in general from those of the kings of the Heptarchy. Some bear the king's profile with his name, as "Ecgbeorht Rex," with a cross and the moneyer's name; the style the same under Ethelwlf, Æthelbearht, Æthelred, Ælfred the Great, Edward the Elder, Æthelstan, Ædmund, Eadred, Eading, Eadgar, Edward the Martyr, Æthelred, the son of Elfrida, Edmund Ironside; Cnut, whose coins were very numerous, and distinguished by 340 variations of moneyer's names, and more places of mintage than any other. Harold I., whose coins resemble those of the preceding reign; Harthacnut, of whose coins, both English and Danish are found; Edward the Confessor, whose pennies were various in design, but differing only from those of his predecessors by being larger, though of the same nominal value; half-pence and farthings being produced by cutting the penny into two or four pieces. Harold II., who issued coins, but with nothing new in regard to them.

At the period of the Roman conquest of England, the old Celtic ring-money was still used in many parts of Ireland, though the Danish invaders, who had subdued the southern part of the island, had introduced a coinage of silver pennies, similar to that of England. The Irish had no other money than ring-money, till the Danish invasion, as no other coins have been discovered, except the series of Hiberno-Danish coins, which extend from that period down to its subjection by the Norman-Anglo princes of England, in the reign of Henry II., A. D. 1154 to 1189. After the subjection of Ireland to the Anglo-Norman princes, the first coins — pennies, half-pennies, and farthings — were those issued by John, who was created Lord of Ireland.

ANGLO-NORMAN KINGS. — Great changes in the coinage might have been expected from this succession to the throne of England; but in that we are disappointed. No improvement took place, and the Saxon types were still adhered to, as well as the standard and weight. The emissions were all silver pennies; and half-pennies and farthings were obtained by cutting them into two and four pieces. William Rufus, Henry I., Stephen, Henry II., and Richard I., so far as the coinage is concerned, did not deviate, except for the worse, from the precedent of their illustrious predecessor. Henry III. is said to have issued a coinage of half-pennies and farthings, which were afterwards recalled. He also issued what were called gold pennies, which circulated but for a short time. Ruding describes this gold coin as one called gold pennies, and weighing two sterlings, and coined to pass for twenty pennies of silver; but that it afterwards passed for twenty-four, or two shillings of 12 pence. He says, this piece, properly a *royal*, was the first of the sort coined in modern Europe.

Henry III. also issued an Irish coinage similar to the English coinage — the long double cross on the reverse, and the legend, on the obverse, HERICUS REX III. The coins of Edward I. exhibit the head of the king, designed, for the first time, in a manner that was to continue without alteration for eight successive reigns, including that of Henry VIII. It was, in fact, a new conventional king's head — a kind of head which, in colonial times in America, answered for George III., Washington, Pitt, or any other distinguished person for whom an effigy was wanted. Edward I. had the credit of coining the first groats, or fourteen-penny pieces. EDWARD III., 1327 to 1377. — The silver coinage of this reign was groats, half-groats, pennies, half-pennies, and farthings. The words "Dei Gratia" were adopted for the first time, on English coins, during this reign; first on the gold coins, and afterwards on the groats; though it had appeared on the great seal since William I., and on the coins of France since the time of Charlemagne, who seems to have adopted Christianity as his watchword. The great feature, however, of this reign, was the coinage of gold; and the attempt of Henry III. being too partial, it may be considered England's first gold coinage. Three denominations of gold were coined, to be current at 6s., 3s., and 1s. 6d., being called florins, half-florins, and quarter-florins — derived from the celebrated gold coin of Florence. It was the name only that was adopted, the devices and values being original and national. The *noble* being rated too high, this gold coinage was recalled. The gold nobles were then determined on; these were nobles, half-nobles, and quarter-nobles; the first denomination passing at 6s. 8d. RICHARD II., 1377 to 1399, issued, without change, groats, half-groats, pennies, halfpence, farthings, and gold nobles. Henry IV. reduced the pennies from 18 to 15 grains. Nothing new under Henry V., except some further improvement in the style of coinage. Henry VI. ordered a groat of 45 grains to be struck; also, two coins of base metal, an Irelande d'argent, to pass for a penny, and a Patrick, to pass for one-eighth of a penny, for Ireland. EDWARD IV. — His silver coins were exactly like those of preceding reigns. The gold nobles were increased in value to 8s. 4d., the value of the precious metals being enhanced. It was this king who encouraged and invoked the aid of the Alchymists, announcing, with confidence, that he should soon be able to pay his debts with gold and silver produced by "the stone." Notwithstanding this, however, gold rose; the additional price procured gold faster than "the stone," and a new issue of nobles took place — fifty to the pound weight. Shortly this proportion was changed, and then forty-five were issued to the pound. The angels and half-angels, a new coin, having the archangel Michael piercing a dragon with a spear, on the reverse a ship with a large cross for a mast, made their appearance. There is no record of Edward V. having done anything in the way of coinage. Richard III. issued a considerable coinage, similar to that of his predecessors.

COINS OF THE ENGLISH SOVEREIGNS. HENRY VII., 1485 to 1509. — The eighteenth year of this reign was marked by an entirely new coinage; for the first time, some attention was directed to the artistic execution of silver coins. The shield for the royal arms was now first adopted for the reverse. This was the most florid and decorative period of mediæval art, and it is not surprising that the coinage should partake of it; hence the rich device of the great seals was transferred to the "sovereign," the principal gold coin of this reign. The shilling, also, made its appearance, and, in the new coinage, groats, half-groats, and pennies, were minted; but the great feature was the issue of the gold royal, or *royal*, twenty-two and a half such pieces to be coined out of the pound weight, Tower.

HENRY VIII., 1509 to 1547. — In this reign, the penny was reduced to ten grains, and other silver coins in proportion. The gold coinage was debased to make it accord in value with the coins of the continent—the old sovereigns to pass for 22s., and afterwards for 22s. 6d. St. George and the Dragon formed the type of the obverse of the *noble* issued and called the George noble — a device not repeated till adopted by George III., as the reverse of the sovereigns and the silver five-shilling pieces. The angel was still coined, and crowns and half-crowns of gold were now added for the first time. In this reign, the pound Troy superseded the pound Tower, in the mint, and the standard of gold was settled, which has ever since been termed crown gold. It was debased in the latter years of the reign; but the standard, termed crown gold, was 22 carats fine to 2 carats alloy. In the thirty-sixth year of this reign, pieces of the denomination of sixpence, threepence, and three-half-pence, were first struck in Ireland, similar to the English coinage.

EDWARD VI., 1547 to 1553.—Under this king, no change worth noticing.

MARY, 1553 to 1558, declared her intention of restoring the old standard in the silver coinage, 11 oz. 2 dwt. fine, and 18 dwt. alloy; but, instead of that, the coinage fell 1 dwt. lower than the last of Edward VI. Sovereigns were issued, to be current at 30s.; half-sovereigns, to be called ryals of gold, at 15s.; the angel to be current at 10s., and the half-angel at 5s. Shillings, groats, half-groats, and pennies were struck for Ireland.

ELIZABETH, 1558 to 1602.— The complete restoration of the integrity of the currency is due to her. She ascertained the amount of silver in the base money, and caused it to be stamped and to pass for its true value — a loss to the nation and a gain to the government, which received back at $2\frac{1}{4}d.$ what was issued for 12d. She afterwards produced a coinage scrupulously corresponding in weight and purity with its nominal value, excepting the just rate of profit or seignorage. The great event of the coinage of this period, was the temporary introduction of the mill and screw, instead of the hammer and punch, by which coins, in their mechanical production, were much improved. The regularity of the process, combined with placing the date on the coins, resulted in the discontinuance of the mint-marks. It is said, the originator and maker of milled money was one Philip Mastrelle, a Frenchman, who finally got to counterfeiting, was convicted and executed at Tyburn on the 27th of January, 1569. In 1601 and 1602, very handsome half-crowns were issued. During this reign, there were coined of silver, including the base money of Ireland, £4,718,579 2s. $8\frac{1}{2}d.$; of gold, £440,552 8s. $9\frac{3}{4}d.$ Copper pence and half-pence, the first struck by a British sovereign, were issued in Ireland in 1601.

COINAGE OF SCOTLAND BEFORE THE UNION.—The earliest coins attributed to Scotland were those of William the Lion, A. D. 1165. A few coins have been attributed to princes of the Hebrides, which are not of earlier date than the eleventh century; to Donald VIII. A. D. 1093, to Alexander I. 1107, and to Alexander II. and III.—all of very rude execution. Those of Baliol and Bruce are in some respects inferior to the English contemporary coinage. Coins were issued by Robert II. of a national character —the arms of Scotland on the obverse, and St. Andrew and the Cross on the reverse; by David II., in whose reign the first gold coinage was issued — A. D. 1371 — in imitation of the *nobles* of Edward III., differing only in the substitution of the arms of

Scotland for those of England on the shield, and the name and titles of the Scottish king in the legend; Robert III., James I. and II.—1390 to 1460—issued similar coins to those of Robert II. The silver coins of James I., II., and III., were like those of preceding reigns, very closely copied from the English. *Billon* coins were issued, and attributed to Robert III. These base coins were pennies, and afterwards, when still baser coins were issued, they were termed "white pennies," to distinguish them from the baser, or "black pennies." In the reign of James IV., the types of the coinage were modified, he issued a groat of equal weight of the English, which was ordered to pass for 14 pennies Scotch, also a gold coin with a new type, of which there were two or three sizes — the king armed on a galloping horse on the obverse. James V. issued coins of gold to pass for 20s., and also gold pennies of several kinds; but the finest coin of his reign is the gold "bonnet piece," so called from cap or *beret*, termed in Scotland a bonnet which the king wears. Of this piece there were two-third and one-third pieces issued at the same time.

MARY — 1542 to 1587 — issued the testoon, 3s. Scotch, and also the half-testoon. During her union with Darnley, the fine large silver royal was struck, and the twenty and ten shilling pieces. The *bawbees* — half-penny — of Mary, as they were styled, were issued in the following reign. The gold coins issued were numerous, and among them was the royal, one of the best wrought coins of her reign.

JAMES VI., 1587 to 1625.— The first silver coins of this reign were issued by authority of the Lord Regent. They were of thirty, twenty, and ten shillings. Various other moneys of silver were coined, among which was the two-mark piece. Up to this time, the arms of Scotland crowned, &c., formed the type of the obverse of the silver coinage of this reign; but in 1582, forty, thirty, twenty, and ten shilling pieces were issued, bearing the king's portrait on the obverse; the balance-mark and half-mark were next coined. His gold coinage was large; among it, the "Sceptre" being a fine large coin of the size of a double English sovereign.

SCOTLAND HAD BEEN MERGED IN THE "UNITED KINGDOM," &C. — JAMES I. — 1602 to 1625 — issued crowns, half-crowns, shillings, half-shillings, pieces of two pennies, pennies, and half-pennies. Subsequently, the term Great Britain for the United Kingdom was adopted in the coinage. The shillings bore the king's bust instead of the figure on horseback; the two-penny pieces had a rose on one side, and a thistle crowned on the other; the pennies had the rose and the thistle without the crown, and the half-pennies the same, without mottoes. The first gold coins of this reign were the sovereigns and half-sovereigns, having the king in armor, holding the orb and sceptre. The pound weight of gold, 23¾ carats fine, and one-half carat alloy, was next coined into 27 rose-rials of 30s. each, or 54 spurrials of 15s. each. The first gold coinage of

James was of the same standard as that of the last of Elizabeth — the pound weight of gold, 22 carats fine and 2 of alloy, to make thirty-three sovereigns and a half of 20s. each. Next, the pound weight of the same gold was coined into thirty-seven units of 20s. each, and a thistle crown of four shillings, because the English gold coin had long been of more value than those of other nations, and was exported for melting, from the true proportion of the relative value of gold and silver not having been properly understood in England. The Irish coinage received attention during this reign, and steps were taken to restore its intrinsic value and purity. Shillings and sixpences 9 oz. fine, to 3 oz. alloy, were issued; the base money of the previous reign being ordered to be received at one-third of its original value — the shilling for fourpence, &c. They were subsequently reduced to one-fourth. The Irish sixpences and shillings bore the portrait of James in armor, same as the English shillings, and on the reverse the Irish harp crowned. Copper farthings were issued for Ireland as well as England.

CHARLES I., 1625 to 1649.—A coinage was soon issued in this reign, of the same weight and purity as that of the last — $7\frac{3}{4}$ grains to the silver penny, which had been eight grains in the beginning of the reign of Elizabeth, but which was reduced to the above weight by her. Notwithstanding the waste of resources in the civil wars during this reign, no debasement in the coinage took place; the very rudest of the coins of Charles, and even his *siege-pieces*, being of the proper purity and weight. The first silver coins of this reign were of the same denomination and value as those of James, viz.: crowns, half-crowns, shillings, half-shillings, two-pences, pennies, and half-pennies. The shillings and sixpences represent the king in the dress of the day. First, the stiff ruff like that of the reigns of Elizabeth and James, then in a limber or falling one, and, lastly, in a simple falling collar edged with lace, as he is seen in most portraits by Van Dyke. On some of his pieces he appears in his parliamentary robes. The crowns and half-crowns have the king pretty generally on horseback, in armor. None of the pieces coined in the Tower were dated, but the mint-marks afford sure indications of the dates. To January, 1625, they are marked with the trefoil; to January, 1626, with the fleur de lis, and so on. This refers to the London coinage; but in his reign there were extensive coinages of silver in various parts of the kingdom. The coins of the York Mint are beautifully executed, and have a lion passant guardant for mint-mark, also the word "Ebor," York. It is supposed the York Mint was established when Stafford was President of the North, and some money was probably coined when the king was there, during his magnificent progress to Scotland. There was also a permanent mint at Aberystwith, for refining and coining the silver produced from the Welsh lead mines. The coins of this mint bear the Welsh feathers. The coins of this reign, milled at the edge, were produced by the mill and screw, under the direction of Nicholas Briot, who had been chief engraver of French moneys. He also coined money for Charles I., for Scotland. He subsequently returned to France, but left in disgust, in consequence of some regulations that displeased him. His return to France at the time prevented the permanent establishment of the mill and screw.

The king, 1642, removed to Shrewsbury, when the Master of the Mint, Mr. Bushell, was ordered to join him, and money was coined there. After the defeat of Edgehill, the king removed the mint of Aberystwith to Oxford, to coin there, in the New-Inn Hall, under the direction of Mr. Bushell and Sir William Parkhurst, all the remaining plate of the colleges—a large loan having been previously made to him in 1642, while he was at Nottingham, by the Universities. In this mint a large quantity was coined of both gold and silver. The silver, twenty and ten shilling pieces, are peculiar to this mint, and to this period, for no other such pieces occur in the annals of the English coinage. The best executed of these pieces have the king on horseback, crowned and in armor, the horse trampling upon arms and trophies, surrounded by the usual titles; the reverse has the motto " Exurgat Deus," &c., with " Relig. prot. leg. aug. liber. par.," dated 1644; alluding to his declaration at the breaking out of the war, that he would protect "the Protestant religion, the laws and liberties of his subjects, and the privileges of Parliament."

This coining down the plate of the colleges, caused the barbarous destruction of many rare and interesting relics of the highest antiquity; but such are the inevitable consequences of civil war; for in 1644, the Commons, House of Parliament, with equal recklessness, ordered all the king's plate in the Tower to be melted down and coined, notwithstanding a remonstrance from the Lords, alleging that the curious workmanship of the ancient pieces was worth more than the metal.

On many occasions, during the disastrous fortunes of the king, his partizans were under the necessity of striking off money in a rude manner, by coining down their own plate for the relief of the soldiers. By which course, as many magnificent family, as national, monuments of arts, perished. The first examples of this kind of money were coined at Dublin; they were merely weighed pieces of plate, simply stamped with numerals to denote their value — some having on the obverse, C. R. under a crown. In 1645, when Carlisle was defended by Sir Thomas Glenham for the king, he coined down plate into shillings, &c., with the king's head very rudely executed. Some of these siege pieces are stamped with a castle, and numerals to denote their value; for instance, those struck during the siege of the Castle of Scarborough. During the defence of Pontefract Castle, coin were stamped there with the motto, "Dum spiro spero." This place was defended seven weeks after the execution of the king, by Colonel John Morris; and after that event, this staunch royalist struck the coin he issued in the name of Charles II. The shillings so struck are of an octagonal shape, with "Carlos Secundus, 1648," round the figure of the castle, and the reverse had, "Mortem patris pro filio." Of these irregular coins there was a great variety, both of gold and silver.

The first Scottish coinage in this reign consisted of crowns and half-crowns. But the pieces coined by Briot, who was sent there for that purpose, were surpassingly well executed; they consisted of crowns, half-crowns, shillings, and sixpences. Some coins were also issued of a more specially Scottish character — small silver pieces, size of an English penny, but of the value of twenty Scottish pence, having the king's head and XX. on the obverse, and the crowned thistle on the reverse; also two-shilling pieces, Scotch, and the noble or half-mark, with the head and title as usual on the obverse, and the arms of Scotland, legend, &c., on the reverse, with $\frac{VI}{8}$. to denote the value — 6s. 8d. Scottish money. All these coins were the work of Briot.

It was ordered in this reign that the name, Irish money, should be abolished, and that thereafter all accounts should be kept in Sterling or English money. No silver money was issued in regular form for Ireland by Charles I.; but his troubles induced the irregular coinage struck in Dublin.

The gold coinage of this reign was not various. The fine old sovereigns or ryals, and the nobles, were abandoned soon after the beginning of the reign, and a small coinage of angels was issued. The principal coins in the early part of the reign were the units or broad pieces of 20s. each, with halves and quarters; the gold pieces struck at Oxford were £3, £1, and 10s. There was an issue of *sceptres* in Scotland, coined for £12 pieces, Scotch, but passed on account of their weight at £13. 13s.; also crowns, half-crowns, &c.

THE COMMONWEALTH — 1648 to 1660 — with Cromwell at its head, proceeded at once to make great changes in the coinage. The royal arms were thrown aside, and the simple cross of St. George, as a suitable badge for Puritanical England, was adopted. It was placed within a palm and an olive branch, and had for legend, in good plain English, "The Commonwealth of England." On the reverse were two joined shields, one having the cross of St. George, the other the harp of Ireland, and the motto also in English, "God with us," and the date; that of the first issued being 1649. The issue consisted of crowns, half-crowns, shillings, half-shillings, and pieces of two-pence, a penny, and half-penny. The smaller pieces had no mottoes.

Pierre Blondeau, a Frenchman, who had carried to perfection the stamping of coin by the mill and screw, was invited to England. His first pattern half-crown bore on the edge, "Truth and Peace," 1651, Petrus Blondeus; another, "In the third year of freedom, by God's blessing restored." The established rival workers in the mint sent in rival patterns; one with the double shield, supported by winged figures, with the motto, "Guarded by Angels." The opposition finally frustrated the plans of Blondeau. The screw process was, however, adopted without Blondeau's immediate aid, who was thus shabbily treated by the new saints. In the latter part of the protectorate, Cromwell issued coins bearing his bust, which were laureated, with "OLIVAR. D. G. R. P. Ang. Sco. ET HIB. ETC. PRO." Oliver, protector of the Republic of England, Ireland, and Scotland, and substituting "Ect." for France. The gold coins bore the same devices and mottoes as the silver coins, and were simply 20s., 10s., and 5s. pieces. The silver standard adopted by the Commonwealth was 11 oz. 2 dwt. fine, and 18 dwt. alloy. No coins were struck in Scotland. In Ireland, as in England, great numbers of town tokens were struck off and circulated.

CHARLES II., 1660 to 1684. — On his accession to the throne, silver coins, from half-crowns downwards, except groats and quarter-shillings, which soon followed, were issued. They were struck like the earliest of his father's coins, with the view of restoring the ancient monarchical feeling, with the old shield, traversed by the cross, *fleurie*, and the same mottoes. The new improvement of the mill and screw, also, being abandoned, the coins were again produced by the old process of the hammer. This prejudice against an important improvement was of short duration; for, in 1662, Peter Blondeau was again employed to direct the mint, upon the new principle of the mill and screw.

Great competition arose, at this time, between the celebrated Simon, who had engraved the dies for the Protector's last coins, and John Roeter, of Antwerp, which was unfairly decided in favor of the latter. Simon afterwards produced a pattern-crown, exquisitely engraved. On the edge of this famous coin is inscribed his petition to the king, against the previous unjust decision in favor of his opponent, which was unheeded. The petition is, "Thomas Simon most humbly prays your Majesty to compare this, his tryal piece, with the Dutch, and if more truly drawn and embossed, more gracefully ordered, and more accurately engraven, to relieve him." After this, it is said, he was discharged from the mint; and, we may add, that he had been probably a very ardent supporter of Cromwell.

In 1663, the first milled coinage took place, consisting of crowns, half-crowns, and shillings. In Ireland, no silver money was issued in this reign, except crowns and half-crowns, irregularly formed, which came under the head of money of necessity, rather than of that of regular coinage.

The gold coins were not various in this reign. In 1664, a gold coinage by the new process was issued. This coinage consisted of £5 pieces, and forty and twenty shilling pieces; the latter called "guineas," from being made of gold brought from

Guinea; there were also half-guineas. The term guinea, for a twenty-shilling piece, continued down to the reign of George III. The English gold coins being still above the value of other nations, the nominal value, and the old unit of 20s., was raised to 22s., and other coins in proportion. In 1670, the weight of the gold coins was again reduced, the pound of gold — 22 carats fine — being coined into £44 10s. Copper was first issued in bulk in this reign. As early as the reign of Henry IV., V., and VI., the black or base money of the continent circulated in England. These pieces were known as "Abbey pieces." In the reign of Henry VIII., or even earlier, many traders, for want of small change, coined for themselves leaden tokens, to pass as half-pennies and farthings; but as these rested upon the personal liability of those issuing them, great loss was caused to the poor. In order to put a stop to this kind of coinage, it was proposed to Elizabeth to issue a small copper coinage. About this time — 1594 — the city of Bristol struck copper farthings, by authority, and, afterwards, some other towns were allowed to do the same. In the reign of James I., in order to put a stop to these town and private tokens, it was determined to issue a small copper currency. The royal repugnance to it was so great, however, that it was not coined at the royal mints; but patents were granted to private persons, the first being to Lord Hamilton. These copper farthings bore, on the reverse, a *harp*, which shows they were intended chiefly for Ireland — the destination of all discreditable coin — though they were, by royal proclamation, current in England. They were, also, issued by Charles I. and II., and have become a permanent currency. After the Revolution, in 1688, a proclamation was issued by James, in Ireland, for coining sixpences and shillings of mixed metal. They were made from old pieces of ordnance, and known as the "gun-money."

WILLIAM AND MARY, AND WILLIAM III., 1688 to 1702. — The same style of coinage was continued at the commencement of these reigns. The profiles of the king and queen are shown, one over the other, on the obverse of all the coins, surrounded with "Gulielmus et Maria Dei." The general coinage had fallen into a bad state, but, after the death of the queen, in 1695, the king, who continued to reign by the title of William III., determined to restore its general character. A tax was imposed upon dwelling-houses, to raise the sum of £1,200,000, to supply the deficiency of clipped money; and to prevent delay, and to carry into effect a complete new coinage, mints were established at York, Bristol, Norwich, Exeter, and Chester. The new coinage was completed in two years. The pride of the king upon this subject, and the determination that it should be ably managed, were exemplified by the appointment of the illustrious Newton to the position of Master of the Mint. Nearly £7,000,000 of silver money were coined during the years 1696 and 1697. But the silver coinage was still insufficient, and continued so for twenty years afterwards; for, in 1717, in the reign of George I., Sir Isaac Newton, who was still in office, stated, in his report, "If silver money became a little scarcer, people would, in a little time, refuse to make payments in silver, without a premium."

In Scotland, in the reign of William and Mary, sixty, forty, twenty, ten, and five shilling pieces were coined. William III. duplicated this issue. The gold coins of William and Mary, and William III., consisted of £5 and £2 pieces, guineas, and half-guineas. The last Scottish gold was issued during the reign of William III., and consisted of a small issue of pistoles and half-pistoles. These pieces were about the size of guineas and half-guineas, resembling them in type, and were coined from gold sent over from the colony of Darien by the Scottish African company. Notwithstanding all the emissions, the precious metals were scarce, and guineas, at one time, rose to the value of 30s. An enactment reduced them, subsequently, to 26s., and, afterwards, to 22s.

ANNE, 1702 to 1714. — The coins of this reign were of the same denominations, weight, and fineness, as those of the last. After this reign, the English coins circulated in Scotland as in England — no difference of type being made for the former. During the short reign of Anne, the coins marked another epoch in the improvement of English money. The gold coins of Anne were £5 and £2, guineas and half-guineas. No copper coin was issued in this reign, either for England, Scotland, or Ireland.

GEORGE I, 1714 to 1727. — The coinage of this reign remained the same in weight and value as the preceding; the bust of the king was executed in the conventional style of the times, with Roman mantle and armor. The legend on the obverse contains the titles as well as the name, with, for the first time, as a permanent addition, "Fidei Defensor," "Defender of the Faith," abbreviated, Georgius D. C. M. BR. FR. ET HIB. REX F. D. On the reverse, his German titles appear, as, "Brunsvicensis et Lunenbergensis Dux, Sacra Romani Imperii Archithesaurius et Elector," abbreviated, Brun. et L. Dux S. R. L. A. T. H. ET EL. His own arms not being placed in the centre, like those of William III., but occupying the fourth shield.

The copper coinage was much extended in this reign, above £46,000 worth having been issued in 1717, when the pound avoirdupois was coined into twenty-eight pence.

GEORGE II., 1729 to 1760. — No change took place in the weight, value, &c., of the coinage during this reign. The coins bore the titles, "GEORGIUS II. DEI GRATIA," as in the reign of his father; on the reverse a change took place in the arrangement of the titles, which stands thus: M. B. F. ET H. REX F. D. B. ET L. D. S. R. I. A. T. ET E., being merely a new abbreviation of the English titles, followed by a still more close abbreviation of the German ones. Of the gold coins, the quarter-guineas were omitted in this reign. The principal gold coins minted were guineas and half-guineas, only a few £5 and £2 pieces being struck. The guinea was, by proclamation in 1737, raised to 22s. 9d. The reverse of the gold coins was changed in this reign, and the old garnished shield, somewhat varied, was adopted in place of the four shields disposed in a cross. This change of arms did not extend to silver coins, which were continued as before. The first coinage of copper half-pence and farthings in this reign was under warrant of Queen Caroline in 1738, for the time guardian of the realm. There were forty-six half-pence coined out of the pound avoirdupois. There was also a great quantity of false copper money now put into circulation. Birmingham was the chief seat of these illegal mints, though destined afterwards to become the legitimate seat of the whole copper coinage of the country, in the great works at Soho. The copper coinage of George II. presents no remarkable features.

GEORGE III., 1760 to 1820. — This prince, in succeeding to the throne, did not attempt to issue a silver coinage, although the currency was limited in amount, and of diminished value from wear and tear. In 1762 and 1763, £5791 only were issued, but of what denomination is not stated. In this coinage, and until 1787, one pound of silver, of 11 oz. 2 dwt. fine to 18 dwt. alloy, was coined into sixty-two shillings. In 1780, a proposal was made, but without success, to take the coinage out of the hands of the sovereign, abolishing the mint establishment, and vesting the power of coining in the Bank of England. After such a proposition, it seems almost incredible that no serious issue of silver money took place till 1787, twenty-seven years after the accession of the king, and more than the average length of a long reign. 1787 was marked by an issue of £55,459 in shillings and sixpences. Some years afterwards, the bad condition of the silver coinage was somewhat alleviated by the sanction of bank tokens of 5s., &c., which were well executed. They had on the obverse, the king's head, and on the reverse, the words BANK TOKEN in a wreath of oak and bay, with the value. The tokens of the Bank of Ireland were similarly gotten up, and they consisted of three-shilling pieces and ten-pences, resembling an English shilling. The wretched condition of the national coinage was permitted to go on, getting to be gradually worse till 1803, when the attempt was made to patch up the grievance by stamping Spanish dollars for circulation, with such a mark as is used at Goldsmith's Hall for stamping silver plate. In the following year, the stamp was changed for a small octagon containing the king's head; and about the same time, an arrangement was made with Mr. Boulton, of Soho, to stamp the entire face of the dollar with a device by means of machinery, the result of the great inventions in the application of steam-power by Watt.

In 1798, Messrs. Dorrien & Co. endeavored to remedy the scarcity of silver money to some extent, by sending bullion to the Tower to be coined on their own account, according to the act of Charles II., "upon payment of certain dues." But after it was coined, the Government of this unfortunate period — destined ever to be obstructive — caused it to be melted down, on the plea that a coinage could not be lawful without a proclamation; so that this attempt of private enterprise to remove the grievance, was rendered futile through the obstinacy or stupidity of the Government. These coins were dated 1787, and only a few specimens escaped the crucible.

The gold coinage was not quite so flagrantly neglected as the silver; but, nevertheless, the issues were small and insufficient. In the year of the king's accession a gold coinage occurred, and there are guineas of every year from 1760 to 1774. In 1770, there was a coinage, when forty-four guineas and a half were coined out of every pound of gold, twenty-two carats fine to two carats of alloy. In 1787, a new gold coinage took place, and the guineas, known as the "spade guineas," appeared. They were so called, from the shield on the reverse, which is in the form of a pointed spade.

Having been relieved, by our own act, of all dependence upon George III., in 1776, having had our capabilities for self-government acknowledged in 1783, and having adopted the Federal Constitution in 1787, we happily avoided the balance of a reign, that terminated in 1820.

PART I.

MEASURE, WEIGHT, STANDARD, STERLING, COINS, AND COINING.

WE have deemed it important to present the following *data*, under its proper heads, viz.: MEASURE, WEIGHT, STANDARD, STERLING, COINS, and COINING, as being relevant, in a work of this kind, because bearing, either directly or indirectly, upon the subject-matter of the origin and details of a metallic currency.

MEASURE.

Measure, in a commercial sense, signifies the dimensions of anything bought, sold, or estimated. It is of three kinds, viz.: linear, or long measure; square, or superficial measure; and solid, or cubic measure.

1. Linear Measure is applied to lines; as roads and distances of all kinds.
2. Square Measure is applied to superfices, having both length and breadth; as land, flooring, &c.
3. Solid Measure determines the contents of bodies that have length, breadth, thickness or depth; as marble, timber, &c.

Linear measure is the element of all other measures. Square measure is determined by multiplying length and breadth together; and solid measure, by multiplying length, breadth and depth together.

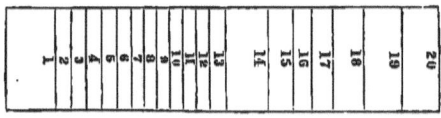

Scale of Sizes, or Measure, of Medals and Coins.

(30)

WEIGHT—STANDARD.

It is from measure that weight is properly deduced. Coins are adjusted by weight; and imaginary moneys, whether of account or exchange, are valued from their established relation to coin.

WEIGHT.

Weight may be defined as a natural property of matter, proportioned to its bulk and the density of its parts. It is determined by being balanced in a scale, against some known or acknowledged weight, placed in the opposite side. The following are the chief properties of weight, as demonstrated by Sir Isaac Newton, viz.:

1. The weight of all bodies, at equal distances from the centre of the earth, is directly proportioned to the quantity of matter that each contains.
2. On different parts of the earth's surface, the weight of the same body is different; increasing from the equator to the pole in proportion to the *sine* of the latitude.
3. That the weight of the same body, at different distances from the earth, is inversely as the squares of the distances from the centre of the same.
4. That, at different distances within the earth, or below its surface, the weight of the same body is directly as is the distance from the earth's centre; so that, half way toward the centre of the earth, a body would weigh but half as much as at the surface, and at the exact centre it would have no weight at all.
5. That a body, immersed in a fluid which is specifically lighter than itself, loses so much of its weight as is equal to the weight of the quantity of the fluid displaced.

STANDARD.

Standard signifies any measure or weight of established authority, by which others are sized or adjusted. It is distinguished as being arbitrary, from human sources; or, invariable, from nature or God. The former is that which is almost universally adopted, and the latter is intended to restore the former, if lost, and, hence, serve as a model or guide to new systems of meterology.

From the highly intrinsic value of the materials which have been adopted for the formation of money, and from the necessity of adding to them materials of inferior worth for their preservation, has been derived the practice of reducing such mixtures to a fixed proportion, which is denominated the standard, or fineness.

From the indefinite account which Cæsar has left us in relation to the brazen and iron money in use among the ancient Britons, no positive conclusion can be reached relative to any standard having been adopted by them, as he has only said, "They adjusted their brazen masses and iron rings to a fixed weight." In 1266, it was enacted — 51 Edward III. — "That an English penny, called a sterling round, and without clipping, shall weigh thirty-two wheat-corns from the middle of the ear; twenty pence to make one ounce, twelve ounces one pound, eight pounds one gallon of wine, and eight gallons of wine one London bushel." Soon after, the weight of the penny was represented by metallic grains, which are supposed to have been the same as the modern Troy grains.

STERLING.

Though this word is now an established one, and familiar to us in its application, its origin or derivation is considered by some to be uncertain and unsettled. The opinion of writers relative to it is various; but the most probable is that which deduces it from the Easterlings, who were said to have been expert refiners from the eastern part of Germany, and who came into England, and first established the standard properties of silver, viz. : 11 oz. 2 dwt. fine silver and 18 dwt. alloy. Ruding fixes the time between the year 1086, when the great survey of the kingdom was completed in the reign of William I., and the 4th of Henry II., A. D. 1158, when it first came into use. Whatever may be the etymology of the word, or the period of its introduction, it is certain that it has been in use all over the world, as particularly designating the money of England; and it is a marked feature in the history of coinage, that the fineness of silver money, expressed by the term *sterling*, has preserved its integrity and the confidence of commercial nations uninterruptedly, from the reign of Henry II. down to the present time, fully seven hundred years.

COINS.

Coins are pieces of metal, in shape round and flat, generally stamped by authority of Government with certain impressions, designed to give them a legal and, hence, current value, and also a guarantee for a particular weight and fineness. Gold, silver, and copper, are the most desirable metals for coins. Of all the metals, gold is the most valuable, and the most difficult of imitation, being remarkable for its rich color, the beauty of its polish, and its slight liability to change. It is so malleable, that gold leaf can be reduced to the thickness of the 300-1000 part of an inch, and gold gilding to the ten-millionth part of the same. Silver follows next in value, and can be reduced to 170-1000 part of an inch in thickness; its density, compared with that of gold, being as 170 to 300, and their specific gravity nearly in the same proportion; that is, as 105 to 193. The value of gold and silver, commercially, they being the subjects of purchase and sale, is fluctuating. At the present day, 15½ oz. of silver are equal to one of gold.

In all regular governments, a standard for coins has been fixed by law; that is, a certain proportion between the quantity of pure metal and alloy. The fineness of gold is generally expressed in carats — twenty-two of which are of pure metal, and two alloy. Hence, the standard of gold is said to be twenty-two carats fine. Lately, the gold and silver of our own mint, and the mints of most other countries, are alloyed in the proportion of one to ten, which seems to afford a sufficient degree of resistance to abrasion. The alloy of silver is generally copper, and that of gold, both silver and copper. In the computation of the value of coins, the alloy is not included. In England, France, and Germany, the theory now is, to dispense with the silver as alloy in the gold coins, and use copper only. In our own country, to retain the gold color, both silver and copper are used, and the proportions are — 900 parts gold, 25 silver, and 75 copper — 1000. Beside the standard of fineness of coins, there is a legal weight fixed "of rates of coinage"— a mint regulation. In the mint regulations of most countries, there is an allowance for deviation from the standard weights and fineness of coins, which is termed "the remedy of the mint." In some, the "remedy" is applied in the weight, and in others, in the fineness. Sometimes it is made a source of emolument, and when the government issues coins at a rate above their intrinsic value, or the market price of the metals, the gain is called seignorage, and the charges for mint expenses are denominated brassage.

COINAGE.

MONEYER — "a reponsible and authorized manufacturer of coin"— appears to have been at one time an important personage, and very naturally so when the art of coining was so little understood. In the 33d year of Henry II., the moneyers of York were expressly exempted from the payment of the *donum*, which was assessed upon the population. In the 18th year of Henry III., the mayor of the city of London was commanded not to interfere with the liberty of the king's moneyers, by exacting *talliage* from them. The cut in the margin represents a moneyer jubilant at the king's favor.

In less than eight years thereafter, this exemption or favor to the moneyers was extended to all the officers of the mint.

The office of Cuneator — from L. cuncus, a wedge — or coiner, was held in high repute, and descended by inheritance, even into the female line; and it was construed so strictly as a right or property, as to be the subject of alienation or transfer.[1] In

---

[1] Doughdale's Baronage, vol. ii. p. 31.

the 18th year of Edward III., the widow of the former possessor of the office sold it to William Lord Talimer, for himself and his heirs, which office he held till his death, which occured in the 4th year of Richard II.

The mode of coining was very rude, the means employed being to fix one die firmly into a wooden block, the other into a puncheon, which, being applied to the prepared metal, and struck by hand with a mallet, made the impression. This method was probably coeval with the first regular attempts at coining. See Cut.

The new coins that made their appearance in the 18th year of Edward I., were made by the following process, viz.: the metal was cast into bars from the melting-pot; these were cut by shears into square pieces of exact weight; then with tongs and hammer they were forged into a round shape; after which they were blanched by nealing or boiling, and afterwards stamped or impressed with a hammer.[1] The next improvement in coining is best exhibited by the annexed cut, into the faces

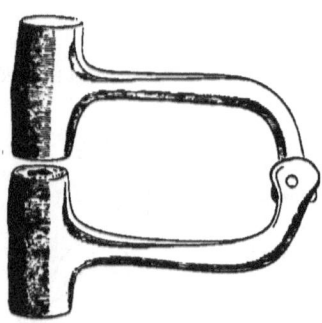

of which were inserted the obverse and reverse die. This contrivance was worked by hand, with the aid of a pulley.

Though peculiar, it is nevertheless true, that no improvement of any importance upon this machine was made till the power of the screw was applied to coinage, in their mint, about the middle of the sixteenth century;[2] and which was introduced into the English mint about the year 1561, when it was worked in conjunction with the old process, till the latter was wholly abandoned in the 14th year of Charles II., 1662. From that time, till some few years ago, only very slight improvements have been made in the machinery of the English mint, which consisted of a lever, to which the upper die was attached, worked by a fly, which forced it down upon the stationary die beneath. This machine was known by the term, mill and screw, and was a material improvement, in power, over *the hand and the pulley*, as it made the impression by a single application, and hence was a great saving of time and labor.

---

[1] Leak, p. 76; quoting the Red-Book.   [2] La Blanc, Historique de Monnage France, p. 68.

In 1787, Mr. Boulton, of France, invented a powerful machine, concentrating, in one operation, all the requirements of a mint; such as rolling the metal, cutting the blanks, shaking them together to wear down the edges, and working at the same time any number of stamping machines, a single movement of which made a perfect impression upon both faces of the metal, and milled or stamped its edges — thus forming a perfect coin.[1]

The earliest specimens of milled money appeared in the reign of Queen Elizabeth; legends upon the edges of coins, date from 1651, as they occur upon those made by the process of Blondeau and Ramage at the time of the Commonwealth. This process was by impressing the letters upon the edge of the coin, by enclosing the blanks in a collar which contained the letters, of the same diameter as the pieces to be impressed, but of less thickness. The blank, thus placed, being struck with the die, expanded under it, and received the impression of what might have been placed in the collar, which opened by means of four joints, and permitted the coin to escape. The operation, which is known by the name of milling, was first applied to coins in 1663, the strokes having been given at that time at right angles across the edge; in 1669, diagonal strokes were introduced, but still not meeting the requirement against counterfeiting, angular strokes were substituted in 1739, which increased the protection.[2]

In 1685, however, the invention by Monsieur Casting for milling, made its appearance, and then the impression given to the edge of coins was by passing them between two plates — one stationary, the other movable by a pinion which worked in teeth on the back edge of the same. By this process, one-half of the legend was cut in each of the pieces, so that when the coins had been impressed or engraved by the movable plate to the end of that which was stationary, the impression upon the edge of the coin was complete.

---

[1] Shaw's History of Staffordshire, vol. ii. p. 118. See the Account of the Mint at Soho.
[2] Vallarine's Observations on the Current Coin, p. 17.

PART II.

ABORIGINAL COINS, OR MONEY.

All nations or peoples have possessed something — relatively of more value than anything else — for the acquisition of which they have energetically taxed their faculties. This, whatever it may have been, whether a shell, a bead, a piece of lead, silver or gold, has been the standard or measure of value. No matter how rude or savage a people may be, the love of gain or accumulation, in some form, is a predominant feature in their character; and to gratify it, their energy and ingenuity have been zealously exerted. It is not peculiar or strange, then, that the aborigines of this continent should have originated and used coins or money as a measure of value, or a medium of exchange, in their dealings with one another.

The earliest knowledge we have of aboriginal coins or money in this country, is derived from the evidences of it exhumed from the mounds that skirt the waters of the Mississippi and its tributaries. In these mounds have been found relics which, similar to those of ancient Egypt, as represented by paintings in her tombs, are as demonstrative of the measure of art and civilization, at the time they were deposited, as were the subjects of those paintings when they were committed for execution to the hands of the artist.

The specimens of aboriginal coins or money, found in the *tumuli*, were composed of lignite, coal, bone, shell, terra-cotta, mica, pearl, cornelian, chalcedony, agate, jasper, native gold, silver, copper, lead, and iron, which were fashioned into forms, evincing a skill in art to which the descendants of the aborigines now surviving are strangers.

Here we find shells from the sea-side; mica from the primitive formation; coal and lignite from the secondary; gold and silver from the Carolinas — perhaps from California; native copper from the shores of Lake Superior; lead from Missouri, &c. &c.; showing, to some extent, the intelligence, energy, and communication with the distant

PLATE I.

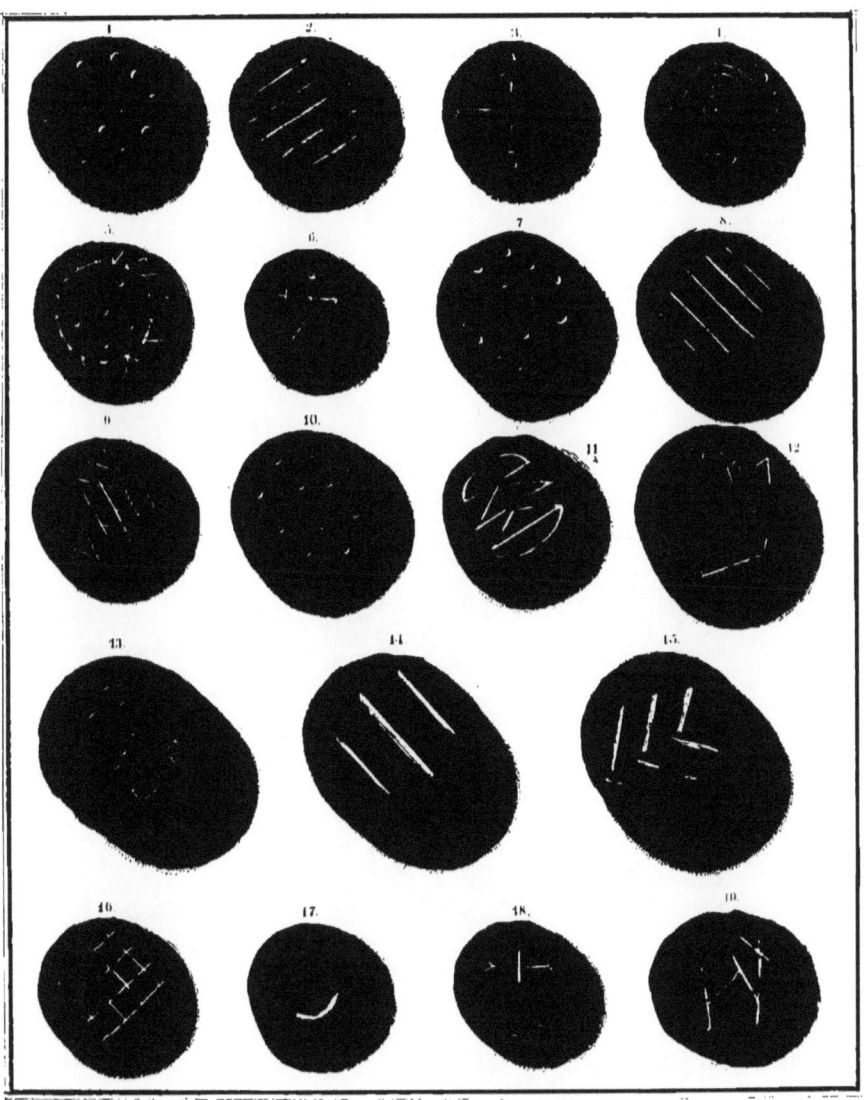

ABORIGINAL COINS.

parts of our country, by those who heaped up these monuments over treasures — unwritten histories — for our instruction and enlightenment.

Many of these specimens of American aboriginal art — such as they are — in many cases very rude, and in others of very good workmanship, present a striking analogy, in form and design, to the ancient Egyptian; agreeing, as they do, in shape and ornament with the Egyptian and Etruscan relics exhumed from their sepulchral homes.

The first medium of circulation, as money, among the aborigines, is believed, by antiquarians, to have been formed from lignite, coal, shell, bones, and terra-cotta. These specimens are frequently found now, upon opening the small oblong-oval mounds in the valley of the Mississippi. The Scripture injunction, "to put no money in thy scrip," being farthest from the practice of the aborigines, who supplied even the dead with the wherewith for a long journey.

The first specimens of this kind which we — Thomas Mitchell, Esq., and myself — met with, in our, *at that time*, aboriginal researches, were from a small mound upon the plantation of William Ferriday, Esq., in Vidalia, Concordia Parish, Louisiana, in 1844. We removed from around the bones of a male aborigine, of very large size, forty-three small pieces — round and flat — of lignite, coal, shell, and jasper. These specimens were mostly entire, but the bone and shell crumbled to pieces from exposure to the air. The lignite and coal pieces were of two sizes, which would measure, by the scale in this work, 9 and 6. They were mostly plain on both sides. In two of the largest, however, we found rude figures, composed of lines and depressions, which see in Plate I., figs. 1 and 2. Occasionally, what are represented as depressions in the fac-simile extended entirely through the piece.

Judging from the anatomical conformation of the crania, we believe these mounds to have been the burial-places of the Tensaw tribe of Indians, as the heads are flattened in an upward or conical direction.

The next collection we will describe was taken from a small mound upon the plantation of Charles Chamberlain, Esq., in the same year, 1844, located about six miles above Natchez, Mississippi. They were found in a small vase, which was elaborately carved around the bulbous portion of it, filled with light-colored ashes. Numerous vases of this description are often found placed near the neck of a skeleton. These pieces are now in our collection. See Plate I., Figs. 3, 4, 5, and 6.

A great number of lignite and coal pieces were found, some twenty years since, in a small mound, on the border of the Miami River, in Ohio, the largest of which was about the size of our old cent, but much thicker. There were two other sizes, which were smaller. The largest of these coins, or money, was perforated with sixteen small holes; the faces of others were indented with from five to eight parallel lines, and on one specimen the lines were crossed, forming diamond-shaped figures. See fac-similes, Plate I., Figs. 7, 8, and 9.

These specimens were taken to Cincinnati, Ohio, and distributed among the lovers of the curious. Some few were deposited in the Dorfeul Museum there, where we had the pleasure of examining them in 1844, and taking drawings from them.

In July, 1845, we opened a small mound on the plantation of General Quitman, situated on the margin of the Mississippi River, eight miles above Natchez. Near the bottom of this structure, we found a small vase, finely ornamented, and composed of an unusually fine material. The ornaments were painted vermilion color, relieved by a dark red, and it contained very fine white ashes. See figure in the margin.

Near this vase we found two oval masses of conglomerated burnt bones, mixed with ashes and coal. Breaking open these peculiar masses, we found, in the centre of one of them, a small cup of coarse material, not ornamented, and within it a small hornstone model of an axe or hatchet, pierced at its upper extremity with a hole, and evidently designed to be suspended from the neck as an ornament or symbol of war; possibly to denote to the denizens of another world that the possessor — presumed to carry all the buried paraphernalia with him — was a chief of the first class. We also found four unfinished jasper beads, two of them partly drilled through the centre; and at the bottom of the cup lay a coin-like mass of lignite, the size of a twenty-five cent piece, with rude figures upon both sides, and evidently designed for a coin of much value, being the solitary pecuniary deposit or resource for a long journey. See fac-simile, Plate I., Fig. 12.

A similar vase to that previously described, was found a short time afterwards in the upper stratum of a small mound, on the premises of Mrs. Posthlethwait at Natchez, Miss., containing ashes and a similar lignite coin, more elaborately ornamented. See fac-simile. Plate II Figure 1.

Such coins as we have been describing, were undoubtedly as highly prized by their aboriginal possessors, as are those of the present day by us; and they were, unquestionably, as subservient to the laws of value and exchange, as is a more modern coinage now.

The coal specimens of coin or money are quite as frequently found in the mounds as the lignite, but they are not as well preserved. Subjected to the action of the air, they become very dry, soon become disintegrated, and crumble to pieces. They are also less elaborately carved, owing to the difference in material, though the designs are similar lines and cross-lines, with occasionally an effigy of a man or bird upon them, and on one specimen we have seen, the extended hand. In shape and size they also

PLATE II.

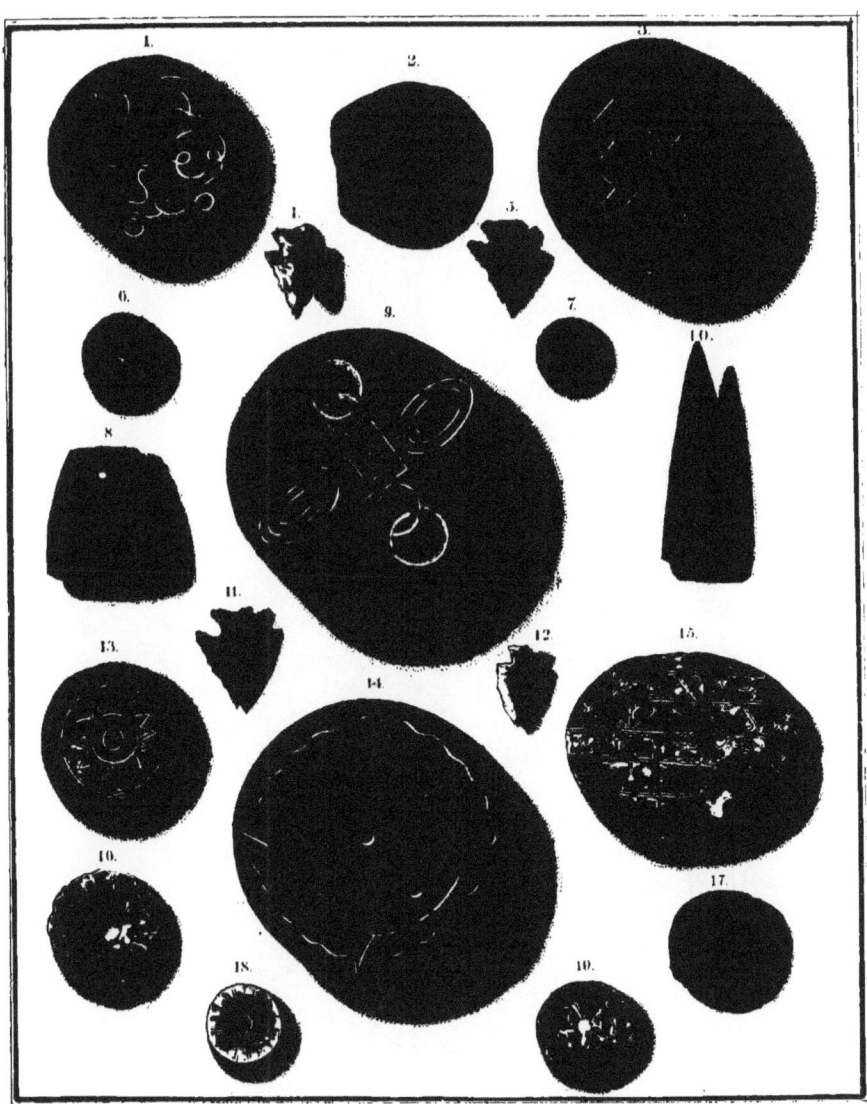

agree with the lignite, except in being about double their thickness. We have met with several hundreds of specimens in our explorations, but have been unable to preserve but few of them, some with figures. See fac-similes. Plate I, Figures 10, 11, 16, 17, 18 and 19.

The similarity of barbarous or semi-barbarous people is much greater than would be supposed, without *data* or reflection upon the subject; as the human mind in its natural condition seems to have been directed by the same impulses, and to have adopted the same means for the attainment of the same ends. For we find that what we term coal-money among the aborigines of America, is denominated the same by transatlantic antiquarians, and is found in the barrows or sepulchres of the ancient Britons. The Britons had also—found in the same localities—what was composed of the Kimmeridge clay of the coal formations, which was strongly impregnated with bitumen. These coins or money are circular in form, varying from one inch to three inches in diameter, and from an eighth to half an inch in thickness. They appear to have been wrought into form with much precision, and they exhibit devices of circles and angles turned with much exactness.

It appears to be peculiar that the aborigines of America, and the ancient Egyptians and Britians should have selected the sepulchres of the dead for the absolute depository of representations of art, value, and instruction. Such is, nevertheless, the truth; and hence it confirms our previously expressed opinion of the sameness of the human mind in its first efforts in the direction of civilization.

The opinion entertained by Sir Richard Hoare was, that these pieces were used as the representatives of money; that is, not for circulation, but as symbols of value, and that they were introduced into Briton by the Carthagenians and Phœnicians, who traded with the ancient Britons for lead, tin, copper, and other metallic substances. This theory does not appear to be reasonable to us, for the reason that the very materials of which it is composed are indigenous to Briton, and that the ancient Britons could have fashioned it themselves, seeing that they made tin and iron money; and why not money of coal and clay? See fac-similes of the coal money of the ancient Britians which will show its resemblance to that of the aborigines of America, and for which purpose we have introduced it into Plate I, Figures 13, 14 and 15. Plate II, Figures 8, 9, and 14.

BONE MONEY.—Some of the specimens of this kind of money are in their composition strange indeed. They are about the size of an old cent, and were wrought out of the interior and exterior tables of the human skull, also of the bones of the thigh, the *scapula* and *patella* of human subjects — probably, relics of enemies slain in battle, or prisoners subsequently tortured at the stake, and symbols of revenge, the most exalted virtue among the aborigines.

This money is also made from the tusks and ribs of the mastodon gigantium, the enamelled portion of the teeth of the alligator, and from the bones of the gar and cat-fish. Great quantities of the last two named, which must have been of the least valuable denomination of money, were found in the mounds; in some instances, amounting in quantity to bushels — it being the custom of some of the aboriginal tribes to bury all the treasures of a deceased with him. As with other specimens, we found them around the necks of the occupants of the mounds, punctured and strung, and also in terra-cotta vases and cups.

Mr. A. B. Tomlinson, in a letter describing the opening of the Grave Creek Mound, on the border of the Ohio river, below Wheeling, Va., says: "One of the skeletons was surrounded by six hundred and fifty ivory pieces, resembling button moles, and varying in diameter from three to five-eighths of an inch, and in thickness, from pasteboard to a fourth of an inch. In another mound, were found upwards of seventeen hundred ivory pieces, five hundred shells of the involute species, and five copper bracelets that were around the wrist-bones of the skeleton."

SHELL MONEY. — The specimens of shell coins or currency, occur in large quantities in every aboriginal mound. They are made of shells, from the Unio or fresh-water clam up to the huge sea-conch. The pieces most common are from small spiral shells, taken from the fresh-water lakes or streams; their colors are various, and when manufactured, they make beautiful pieces. We found large quantities of the Venus species, formed of the pearly portion of the shells, very highly polished, and about the size of a twenty-five cent piece, with eccentric lines carved upon them, and in some cases figures. Some pieces we found were as large as two and a half inches in diameter.

Nothing more rational than that an aborigine should give half a dozen or more of such pieces, as we have been describing, for a tomahawk, a terra-cotta cup, or anything else he might want or covet; nor is it strange that an aborigine's wealth should have been estimated by such accumulations as this money — the fruit of labor and tact with them, as is our money with us.

Pearls are a fruitful subject. A passage in Suetonius reports Cæsar's invasion of Britain, as incited by the hope of finding pearls. We think the ambition of conquest had much more to do with it. Pliny informs us that Cæsar dedicated a breast-plate to Venus, ornamented with pearls, which he pretended to have found in Britain. Cleopatra fed Anthony upon pearls; yet with all this true or fabulous account of them, the number would sink into insignificance, compared with the immense quantities that

PLATE. III.

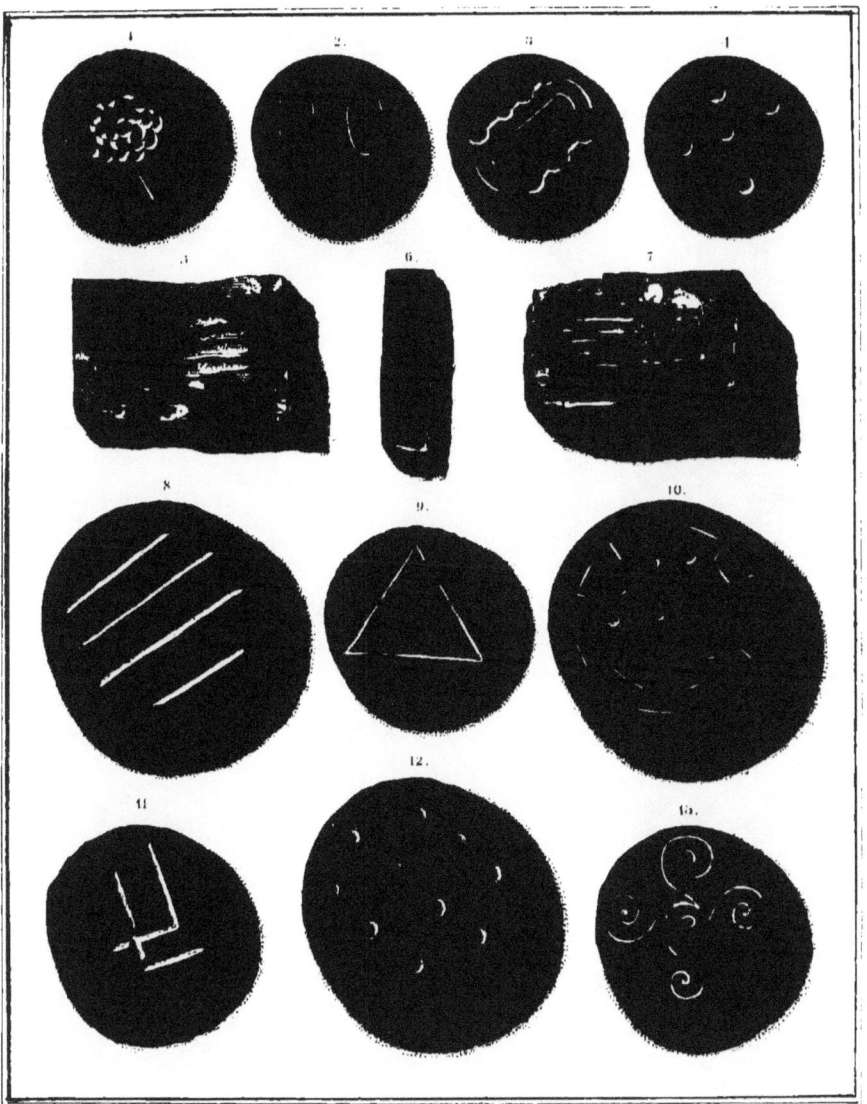

ABORIGINAL COINS.

greeted the eyes of De Soto, when he first made his appearance among the aborigines in the Valley of the Mississippi. The quantities found in the temples and villages, as related by Spanish and Portuguese historians, almost exceeds belief.

Among the sepulchral graves of the aborigines, the plow-share turns up human relics, and also brings to light large quantities of pearls; and the broken vases at the same time disclose what were their depositories. The pearls found are rarely perfect; alas! time and exposure to the damps of the earth have rendered them very fragile, and hence they are easily peeled into lamina, sometimes, however, reaching a kernel by this process, which is sound and brilliant. We have a number in our possession, from which we scaled off the lamina, till they became perfect. Finding them as we have, carefully deposited in vases and mortars with the dead, we must conclude that they were among the things of value, which were exchanged or hoarded by the aborigines, as circumstances or choice dictated.

TERRA-COTTA.—This money is formed from clay and tempered with bone, and also ferruginous matter. Some of its varieties are of a beautiful red color, which, upon analysis, were found to be composed of, viz.: silex, 51, aluminum, 19, lime, 9, and iron, 21 parts.

The devices upon these pieces are numerous, generally on one side, but occasionally upon both. They consist of the heart, the extended hand, leg, birds, frogs, snakes, and many curious figures formed of lines, dots, and circles.

The extended hand, as we have illustrated it from the originals, frequently appears, according to Stephens, upon the bricks and stones found in Central America, and upon the dressed skins forming the robes of the present Indians, thus establishing an affinity of ideas between the aborigines of the Isthmus, and those of the Valley of the Mississippi.

It is not improbable that it was a symbol referring to a Supreme power, and designed to keep in constant remembrance Deity, to which the aborigines, equally with the Christians of more enlightened times, were disposed to defer; and to whom their rude, but natural, devotion was undoubtedly sincere, if not profound. See Plate III, Figures 1, 2, 3, 4, 5, 6, 7, 8, 9, 10, 11, 12, and 13.

It is a peculiarity also, that the extended hand was an emblem upon *quadrans*, a coin, among the ancient Romans, which was the fourth of an *as* or *æs*; the value of which was estimated with reference to the *denarius*, which contained or was equal to ten *asses*; and the *as*, four quadrans. Thus, as the denarius, in the time of our Saviour, was equal to about seventeen cents of our money, the *as* was equal to three farthings, English, and the quadran being the fourth of that sum, was a little less in value than a half cent. The two *mites*, which the widow threw into the Temple treasury, were of the value of a quadran.

Though, in both the Roman and aboriginal coins, the idea was undoubtedly distinct and original — there having been no communication between the Old and the New World — the extended hand, as an emblem, might have been designed to suggest openheartedness, liberality, a disregard of money, or grasping selfishness. It might have been dictated as an emblem of confidence or affection; or, as we have imagined, in the case of the aborigines, a deference to Deity, in connection with which, by the followers of the Saviour, the hand was symbolized as the "outstretched hand," "mighty to save," &c., or indicative of the power which invites love and confidence, and promises protection. Hence, whether of heathen or Christian application, it has much appropriateness, and in such connection, is not devoid of ideal beauty.

STONE MONEY.—These specimens occur in great quantities in the aboriginal mounds. They are composed of jasper, quartz, agate, chalcedony, and, occasionally, cornelian. The more common specimens found are wrought from sand-stone and slate. Size of this kind of money, from eight inches in diameter down to half an inch; in many instances, very highly polished, and occasionally figured over with hieroglyphics and other devices. See Plate II, Figures 2 and 13. Plate IV, Figures 3, 4, 5, and 16.

In opening the Grave Creek Mound, previously referred to, a small thin and flat piece of sand-stone was found. See fac-simile for form, size, and the hieroglyphic inscription, Plate II, Figure 15.

Schoolcraft says: "The characters are in the ancient rock alphabet of sixteen right and acute angled single strokes, used by the Pelasgi and other Mediterranean nations, and which is the parent of the modern Punic as well as the Bardic." See fac-similes of stone hatchets, previously referred to, Plate II, Figures 8 and 10. Darts of chalcedony and jasper, Plate II, Figures 4, 5, 11, and 12.

THE LILY ENCRINITE.—This fossil, belonging to the family *Crinoidea*, is found in great numbers in the rocks of the Silurian system, upwards, and occurs plentifully in many of the aboriginal mounds.

This animal petrifaction is formed of long jointed stems, composed of calcareous divisions or plates closely fitting each other. A single fossil of this species contains the enormous number of one hundred and fifty thousand pieces; they are generally found separated, and it is these divisions of the stems which are denominated entrochites and screw-stones; and, in the north of England, fairy-stones and St. Cuthbert's beads.

In this wonderful result of nature, the aborigine had a coin or currency properly fashioned and beautifully ornamented, without the labor of design or workmanship,

PLATE IV.

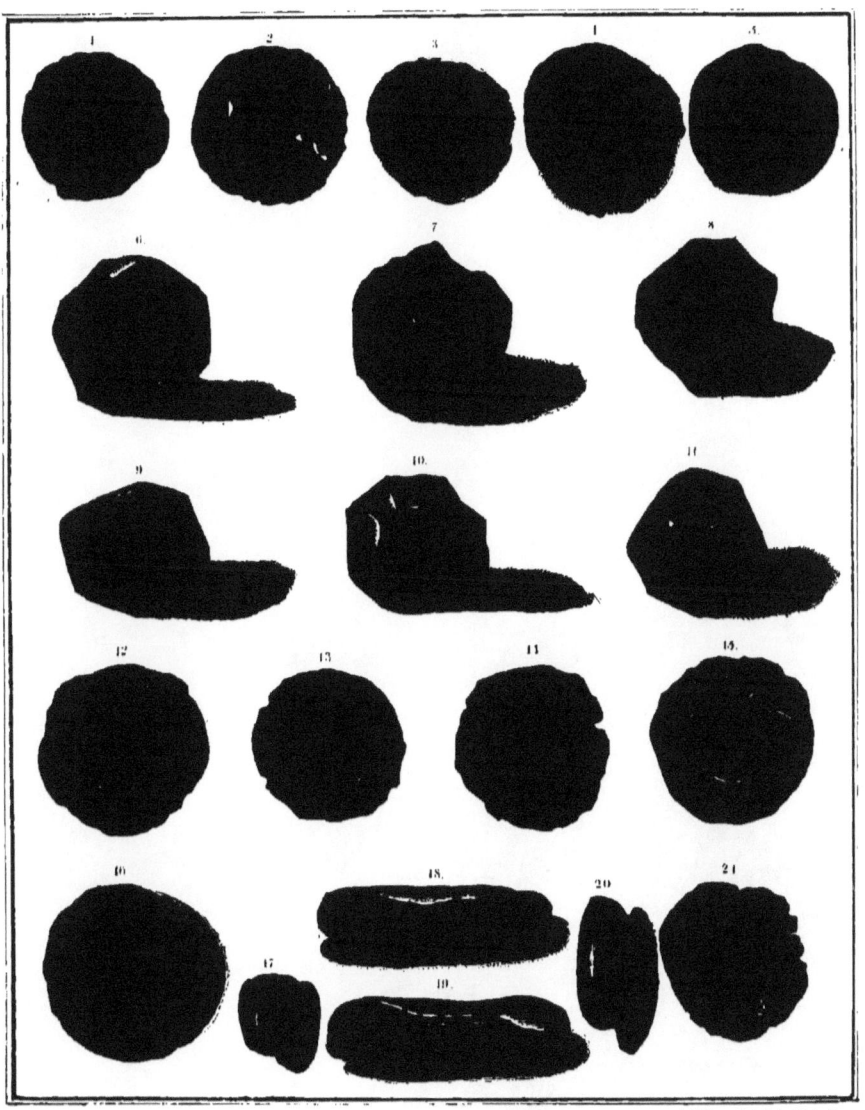

ABORIGINAL COINS.

and from the care with which it was preserved, he must have highly appreciated it. See Plate II, Figures 6, 7, 16, 17, 18, and 19.

GOLD MONEY.— Specimens of this money are occasionally found in the form of small lumps or balls slightly flattened, and irregular on their edges. Several have been found in Louisiana and Mississippi. In the year 1845, in company with Doctors Fox and Benbrooks, we opened a mound at old Fort Rosalie, near Natchez, and the last named gentleman found one of these gold balls, slightly flattened, which weighed upwards of two pennyweights. A similar specimen of very fine gold was found in Ross county, Ohio, lying in the palm of the hand of a skeleton. Subsequently, this piece was presented to Peale's Museum. See fac-simile. Plate IV, Figure 1.

Another specimen was found in Perry county, Ohio, which was in the possession of Mr. Charles Ayres, of Cincinnati, in 1846. The circle of this piece was irregular, and its greatest diameter was about three-fourths of an inch. The face of this piece bore two rude figures — a man and a bird, beside four foot-prints of the latter. Both faces of the piece were alike. See fac-simile, Plate IV, Figure 2.

Two similar pieces of native gold, completely covered with curiously designed figures, were found at Grave Creek Mound. They were sent to the East, and perhaps at this very time adorn some private collection or cabinet.

SILVER MONEY.— Similarly shaped pieces to the gold are found of native silver in the mounds. Generally not so large as the gold, but with similar devices.

GALENA MONEY.— This is found in large quantities in and about the small mounds in the valley of the Mississippi. They are variously ornamented; some, with dots and lines; others, with curious hieroglyphic figures, while others are entirely plain. See fac-similes, Plate IV., Figures 6, 7, 8, 9, 10, and 11.

We have derived from H. Morton, Esq., now publishing a work on the "Rosetta Stone,"— the Key to the interpretation of the Hieroglyphics of Egypt— the following: "That the figure or symbol No. 11, Plate IV., is a sign of very frequent occurrence in the Egyptian sculptures, paintings, and inscriptions. When used as a hieroglyphic sign, it denotes life, as may be seen in the 5th, 6th, 10th and other lines of the Rosetta Stone, and, indeed, in almost every other hieroglyphic inscription. This is the only sign whose value has been transmitted to us by tradition. It is frequently represented in paintings and sculptures as being poured from, by two divinities, over the head of a king, and as held in the left hand by gods and goddesses in general. In the Coptic churches it was frequently substituted for the cross."

This identity of the Egyptian with our own aborigines in originality and idea, opens a wide field for inquiry, occurring, as it does, upon distinct continents, which learned and popular opinion has totally disconnected from the earliest periods of time. Con-

WAMPUM.

The use of wampum as a currency, or subject of barter and exchange, among the aborigines upon the northern portion of this continent, extends back to a very remote period, the antiquity of which we shall not attempt to determine. It was, probably, the first idea of an arbitrary standard of values suggested to the mind of the Indian in the portion of country now occupied by the middle and Eastern States of this Union and the Canadas. In another part of this work, frequent allusion is made to the wampum; and we there find that the first settlers in this part of the continent, for want of something better — which could hardly have been suggested at that time, if we decide from the results — soon accommodated themselves to the currency of the Indian. It soon found its way into the colonial exchequers, those of private institutions, and private hands — its arbitrary value being admitted and sustained for many years.

The primitive wampum consisted of strings of small spiral fresh-water shells. As soon as the Dutch became fairly located in "Manhadoes" — New York — they caught the idea of wampum, and set about improving its manufacture by rendering it more convenient and beautiful. The beads, or constituents of wampum, were purple and white, about a quarter of an inch in length, and an eighth of an inch in diameter, and perforated lengthwise, so as to be conveniently strung. The white bead was manufactured from the sea-conch, and the purple from the muscle-shell, though not confined to those shells.

In the history of that portion of the Indians to which we have alluded, wampum became an "institution," being the medium of love, trade, religious ceremonies, diplomacy, and war. They were woven into belts, used in strings, and singly, and were arranged, by the disposition of colors, into figures, symbolizing objects, events, and acts. In fact, they were the chronicles of the Indian.

So far as they were a currency, they enabled the Dutch settlers to pile up fortunes of peltry; and, could we look into the past, we should, undoubtedly, see the foundation of many a Knickerbocker fortune which has been handed down to our own times. What the Dutch did at "Manhadoes," the English and others did farther east; and their examples were not lost upon their descendants, for gew-gaws have followed the Indian in his retreat before civilization, thus giving him shadows of value in exchange for his substance — the result of the battle and the chase.

"Alas! the poor Indian." He is still the prey of the white man's cupidity; and it is, in all human probability, his destiny so to continue till the last of his race — a wanderer amidst the splendors of civilization — shall have paid the debt to nature.

For wampum and its components, see Plate V.

PART III.

MASSACHUSETTS CURRENCY.

THE Colony of Massachusetts, at the period of which we are writing, embraced what was subsequently the Territory, now the State of, Maine. Anterior to any permanent settlement upon the shores of Maine, there was an active commerce carried on with the Indians by the fleets which annually came from Europe for fish and peltry. The natives were ready, at all times, to barter large quantities of skins for beads, knives, hatchets, and blankets, but particularly for powder, shot, and *strong water*. As the trade increased, the question of providing a medium for currency undoubtedly exercised the minds of the traders; and Felt, in his "Massachusetts Currency," informs us that, in a voyage made by them to Manhadoes — New York — in 1628, they brought back with them the wampum, which subsequently became an important auxiliary for that purpose.

Roger Williams, in his description of the money or currency of the New England Indians, gives the following account: — "It is of two kinds — white, which they make of the stem or stock of the periwinkle, after all the shell is broken off. Of this kind, six of the small beads — which they make with holes to string upon their bracelets — are current, with the English, for a penny. The other kind is a black, inclining to a blue shade, which is made of the shell of a fish, which some of the English call *hens-poquahock;* and of this description, three are equal to an English penny. One fathom of this stringed money is worth five shillings."

1628.

Corn, a generic term for all kinds of grain, including peas, with other productions and live stock, was received at the colonial treasury for taxes, and termed "country pay," which term has been handed down to the present times, being a common one in the rural districts of our country, where it is invited for goods by advertisement, and for newspaper literature, original and selected, by editorial. About this time, the General Court passed a law, that musket-balls, of a full bore, should pass currently for-a farthing each, but that no man should be compelled to take more than twelve-pence of them at any one time. A colonial treasury, plethoric with corn, live-stock, and musket-balls induces ludicrous sensations in contrast with the modern contrivances which now prevail in connection with trade, currency, and revenue.

The earliest metallic currency of the colonies was of the coins of the country by which it was settled. As the settlers were of a class which did not bring much money-wealth with it, and as the shipments of merchandize from the mother-country soon drained the colonies of their coins, the General Court was impressed with the necessity of enacting the following law : — " That, upon any execution for debt *past*, the officers of the law shall take land, houses, corn, cattle, fish, and other commodities"—meaning, undoubtedly, anything personal or real in the shape of property — " and shall deliver it in full satisfaction, to the creditor, at such prices as the same shall be valued at, by three understanding and indifferent men, to be chosen, the one by the creditor, another by the debtor, and the third by the marshal. And the creditor is at liberty to take his choice of what goods he will, and if these are not sufficient to discharge the debt, then he is to take houses and lands, as aforesaid."

The reader will perceive the great difficulties that existed in regard to currency — the public treasury being a recipient of agricultural productions for taxes, and the General Court compelled to arbitrarily prescribe the same, with every other species of property, for the liquidation of debts.

During this year, owing to the failure of the crops in the preceding one, the *currency* of agriculture became very scarce, and hence, together with 1640. *waumpum*, was much appreciated in value. The General Court therefore ordered, "That, while *waumpumpeage* should be current at four for a penny, and the black, two for a penny, no one being compelled to take more than twelvepence of them at a time, except the receiver is willing." This was deemed a necessary measure in aid of the colonists generally.

To increase the facilities of exchange, and aid the cancelling of the public debts, the authorities farmed out the wampum as well as the fur trade to a 1641. company. For this privilege, the company were to pay into the Colonial Treasury one-twentieth of all their peltry, and were also to purchase whatever wampum was received by the college — Harvard — provided it did not exceed £25 at any one time.

"Among the coins in good credit among the colonists were the Holland Ducatoon, which, being worth three guilders, shall be current at six shillings; 1642. the Rix dollar, which, being equal to two and a half guilders, shall be current at five shillings, and the ryal of eight, which shall be current at five shillings, and be receivable at such rates, for all payments within the jurisdiction of the Massachusetts Colony." Though this was the edict in relation to these coins, their very great scarcity prevented much practical benefit from it, for though heard of, they were rarely seen.

1645. During this year, there was a great scarcity of hard money and every other species of exchange; and it was, consequently, productive of serious embarrassment — commerce and confidence being also very much obstructed by the contentions in the mother country, between Parliament and the Royalists. The effect in the colony was to unsettle the population, which led to continual changes or emigration — thus neutralizing both the industry and production of the country. We are thus reminded that financial crises and revulsions are not of modern origin; but that our forefathers were subject to fluctuations and changes in their affairs, which can only be accounted for, in the past, by the lack of perfection and, hence, harmony in the aggregate of the human mind, and for which we can perceive no remedy.

1648. We find the following law or order promulgated by the General Court: "It is ordered for trial till the next court, that all payable or passable *peage*—shell currency — henceforth shall be entire, without breaches — both the white and black without defacing spots, suitably strung in eight known parcels of the following denominations or value, viz.: 1*d*., 3*d*., 12*d*., and 5 shillings in white, and 2*d*., 6*d*., 2-6*d*., and 10 shillings in black." The court also ordered, that *waumpumpeage* should pass current in the payment of debts, to the value of forty shillings — the white at eight for a penny, and the black at four, if they be entire, and without breaches and deforming spots, except in payment of "country rates" to the Treasurer — the Government evidently not desiring the accumulation of shells, beads, &c., as cash in the Treasury.

It was evident, that while coin of any kind was very scarce, the "Indian money," in view of its lack of intrinsic value, and the danger of its accumulation in the colonial treasury, beyond any immediate or prospective reliance for its demand or absorption, was beginning to be felt as a burden by both the Government and the colonists; seeing, as they did, that the time was not very remote, when it must be superseded by a currency bearing a more modern relation to their increasing trade and commerce; and hence the wealth and importance which they must assume toward countries, the currency of which did not partake of the character of conchology.

1650. The period had now arrived when the colonial thought and experience began to be shaped to a somewhat more practically progressive form; as ideas in relation to what should constitute a currency, and the *modus operandi* for attaining it, were seriously entertained.

Finding that their country was continually drained of its specie — a principal source of supply being the Dutch West India Islands — by the European merchants, and that, in their commerce with the West India Islands generally, they were subjected to the imposition of receiving considerable quantities of light Spanish coins, the colonists saw the necessity for establishing a mint of their own, for melting down the coin thus received, and stamping it according to its real weight and value. Governor Hutchinson, relative to their trade with the West Indies, states, "that part of the bullion, taken at this time, by the buccaneers and pirates from the Spaniards, began to find its way into the colonies," thus furnishing an additional necessity for a mint. The colonists were also emboldened in their determination to act for themselves, by its having been proposed in Parliament to substitute a new patent for that under which they were then living, thereby manifesting, from its character, a disposition to subject them more rigidly to its control; and feeling, as they did, justified in assuming that degree of independence of Cromwell that he had observed toward royalty. Hence, without inviting an open rupture with the Dictator, they virtually declined either committing themselves to his authority or policy, and therefore adopted such measures in relation to pecuniary matters, as comported with the interests of their own commonwealth — the unsettled condition of the mother country, and the uncertainty of the result being with them an apology for the treason with which they were charged after the fall of Cromwell. It is evident, however, from the manner in which the colonists subsequently defended themselves against the charge of exercising a right of the throne, by establishing a mint and coining money, that they appreciated their relation of dependence upon the mother country, and that the acts of which they had been guilty were really a violation of the superior power. Had mankind, in all ages, however, been strictly obedient to those who, whether under the forms of government or otherwise, have assumed to be their masters upon the basis of human prerogative, they would have made but limited progress, if any, from the despotism of political slavery, from which they have fully in our own, and measurably in other countries, extricated themselves, by gradually repudiating all authority not clearly delegated to man by the Supreme Governor of all.

A mint once determined upon, the authorities appear to have been actively and vigorously engaged on the subjects of coinage and currency. We find, that in order that the adoption of any new system should not operate prejudiciously upon the interests of the people, that the then existing laws in regard to currency should be in force till September (1652) — "the money hereafter appointed and expressed shall then be the current money of this commonwealth and no other, unless English, except the receivers themselves consent." The court then enacted: "that all persons whatsoever shall have liberty to bring into the mint house, at Boston, all bullion, plate, and Spanish coin, there to be melted, and to be brought to the alloy of sterling silver, by John Hull, master of said mint, and his sworn officers; and by him or them to be coined into twelve-penny, six-penny, and three-penny pieces, which shall be for form flat, and square on the sides, and stamped on the one side with N. E., and on the other, with the denominations XII*d*., VI*d*., and III*d*., according to the value of each piece, together with a privy mark, which shall be appointed every three months by the Governor, and known only to him and the sworn officers of the mint. And, further, the said master of the mint is hereby required to coin all the said money of good silver, of the just alloy of new sterling English money, and for value, to stamp two-pence in a shilling of less value than the present English coin, and the lesser pieces proportionally. And all such coins, as aforesaid, shall be acknowledged to be the current coin of this commonwealth, and pass from man to man, in all payments, accordingly, within this jurisdiction only. And the mint master, for himself and officers, for the labor in melting, refining, and coining, is allowed to take one shilling out of every twenty shillings which he shall stamp. And it shall be in the liberty of any person who brings into the mint house any bullion, plate, or Spanish coin, to be present and see the same melted, refined, and alloyed, and then to take a receipt of the master of the mint for the weight of that which is good silver, alloyed as aforesaid, for which the mint master shall deliver to him the like weight in current money, viz.: every shilling to weigh 3 dwt. Troy weight, and lesser pieces proportionally — deducting allowances as before expressed."

A committee of the General Court was appointed for carrying the foregoing 1652. order into effect, and, at a meeting of that committee, it was decided that there should be a mint house built, and the necessary tools procured at the cost of the commonwealth. Immediate action, on the part of the colonial authorities, followed this decision — the mint house was erected, and very soon thereafter, pattern pieces of coin were prepared. These pattern pieces, bearing upon the obverse a double ring enclosing a tree, with the inscription of Masathvsets around it, and on the reverse New England, with the year of our Lord, 1652, were rejected — the law having specified the design. The first emissions, therefore, accorded very nearly with the prescription of the law — the type being a plain irregular circle of silver, with no other inscription upon it than the letters N. E. on the obverse, and the numerals XII., VI., on the reverse. Shillings and sixpences were only coined at this time — the sizes being 8, 5 — see scale. It has been stated that three-penny pieces were also coined, but as we have never seen them, nor heard of them, otherwise, we may with propriety be permitted to question the truth of any such statement.

It has also been stated, that what we are treating of, and recording as the first coinage of the Massachusetts mint, was struck off in Newcastle, England, or, as Leak has it, in Newark. There can be no doubt, however, but that it was really of domestic manufacture, for beside the law we have given authorizing it, we have the direct testimony of the celebrated numismatologist, Mr. Thornley, to that effect, and who also states that they were familiarly known as the North-Easters, and that the late Earl of Pembroke denominated them New England money in his collection.

The first emissions of coin appear to have been too plain for the colonists, and we have no doubt but that they were generally denounced for their lack of art and beauty; for, at the assembling of the next General Court in the month of October, 1652, it was decreed that the type should be altered, (which was easy, if the types of the pattern pieces we have previously described had been preserved,) and "that instead of N. E. on the obverse, there should be a double ring enclosing a tree, with the inscription of 'Masathvsets' around it, and on the reverse, 'New England,' with the year of our Lord, 1652, and the respective values, XII., VI., III., II., I. The three first denominations only were struck off at this time, and the two-penny pieces followed in 1662, ten years thereafter — the date of which they bear. It is exceedingly doubtful whether the one-penny pieces were ever coined, this being the opinion of numismatologists generally. The coins issued were of the fineness of sterling silver, as prescribed by the colonial mint law, two-pence less in weight and, hence, value, in the shilling than the English coin of the same denomination.

The most perfect specimens extant at this day weigh from 64 to 67 grains, and by assay at our mint, have been proved to be 926-1000 fine — the value of which, therefore, is about seventeen cents. So much opposition was there in England to this colonial coinage, when it first made its appearance there, that it would only pass at a discount of one-fourth of its home value.

The Court, as we learn, finally came to the conclusion, that the contract with John Hull, the mint master, was too lucrative, and an offer was made to him for the release of the same, which he refused. This Mr. Hull accumulated a large fortune from his connection with the mint; and left at his death one of the largest estates in the colony. It is stated that Samuel Sewell, Esq., who married his daughter, received with her the snug sum at that day of 30,000 New England shillings; that he was the son of a poor woman, to whom he was particularly dutiful and kind, and that, in consequence, his minister, the Rev. Mr. Wilson, prophesied that God would bless him, and that though then poor, he should acquire a large estate. This is a very natural incident of those peculiar times, when the mass of mankind in New England believed that God directed the minutest details of everything sublunary, in accordance with human merit.

Although the Massachusetts mint continued to coin its peculiar currency for thirty-six years, up to January 16, 1686, no alteration of date, from the establishment of the mint, except upon the two-penny pieces issued in, and bearing the date of, A. D. 1662, occurred, and though there were, during that time, a great variety of dies, the dates of coinage cannot otherwise be determined.

From a retrospective view of the colony of Massachusetts, we can perceive that her mint was an important institution, as it related to her prosperity; and also as a successful innovation upon kingly authority, which aided to sow the seeds of her future independence; as an isolated and subject people never forget the slightest approximation to practical success in any position they may have assumed, or act undertaken — uniformly increasing, as it does, their self-importance and desire for self-government, against any and every authority not inherent in themselves.

During Governor Andross' administration, endeavors were made to obtain leave from the mother country for the continuance, or, in other words, legalization, of the mint. The matter was submitted to the Master of the Mint in England, who opposed it upon the plea of "prudential considerations." Though the words "royal prerogative" were not used, we have no doubt the answer involved thoughts unfavorable to the continuance of such an assumed privilege in the hands of the colonists.

1662. The following very interesting incident in the history of the colony is well authenticated. Sir Thomas Temple, the Governor of Nova Scotia, and a warm friend of the New England Colonies, while on a visit to London, was permitted an interview with his sovereign, Charles II., who, in conversing with him relative to affairs in the Colony of Massachusetts, evinced great warmth of feeling against the colonists. Among the matters referred to, in the interview, the king said that they had invaded his right by coining money. Governor Temple is said to have replied that the colonists, in view of their isolated condition and necessities, had deemed it no crime to coin money for themselves; and, in the course of conversation, took from his pocket and presented to the king some of the coin. Upon observing the *tree*, he inquired what kind it was. The prompt and happy reply of the Governor was, that is the Royal Oak,[1] that saved your majesty's life. Such an answer restored

---

[1] The defeat of the Scotch army at Worcester, England, by Cromwell — affording to him what he denominated the crowning mercy — compelled Charles to seek safety in flight, attended by a few of his devoted friends. To provide for his safety more certainly, however, it was deemed best for him to separate from them, and without their knowledge. By the advice, therefore, of the Earl of Derby, he went to Boscobel, a lone house on the borders of Staffordshire, inhabited by one Penderell, a farmer. To this man Charles entrusted himself; and, though death was denounced against any one who concealed him, and a large reward was offered for his betrayal, Penderell's honor and loyalty were unshaken. Taking Charles, with his four brothers, having first clothed him in a garb like their own, they retired to the woods, where they were all

the king to good humor, and induced him to listen to the pleas of Governor Temple in behalf of the colonists. The king expressed no further dissatisfaction, but, laughing heartily, called the coiners "honest dogs."

The colonial government was called to account by the royal commissioners who had come hither respecting the mint. The commissioners declared the coining of money to be a royal prerogative, for the commission of which, the act of indemnity was the only *salvo*. They were so dictatorial, that the government refused any further conference with them, and made an appeal to the crown — the usual resort of a subject people to ward off immediate action.

As a step toward softening the asperity of the king, who could ill digest the act of establishing a mint by the colonists, two very large masts were sent to London for his majesty's navy; and, very soon thereafter, a ship-load of smaller sized spars followed. 1666.

The mint-master was ordered, by the government, to stamp N. E. on all foreign coins, as evidence of the proper weight and value. 1672.

Notwithstanding the continued opposition of the royal authority to the mint, it was ordered, that the masters of the mint, John Hull and Robert Saunderson, continue to mint what silver bullion shall come in for seven years, and that they shall receive 12*d*. of every twenty shillings, and 3*d*. for waste in every three ounces of sterling silver — 15*d*. in every twenty shillings coined; and the mint-masters shall pay into the colonial treasury, during the said term of seven years, £20. 1675.

A committee of the Legislature, in an interview with Captain Hull, of the mint, and others, relative to increasing the coinage at the mint, and to prevent the export of specie, decide that there is no other remedy but the raising the values of coin, or making the mint free. 1677.

Still perceiving the finger of royal displeasure pointed at them, on account of their mint, the General Court sent another peace-offering to his majesty, in the form of ten barrels of cranberries, two hogsheads of special good samp, and three thousand codfish. This ought to have softened the heart of his majesty; but subsequent events prove it to have been as obdurate as ever. He had, however, a people to deal with as full of expedients as he was of prerogative, and who, having ultimately acquired strength enough for resistance to prerogative, used it manfully and successfully.

---

employed in cutting fagots. Some nights, the king laid upon the straw; but subsequently, for better security, he climbed an oak, where he sheltered himself among the branches and leaves. From his hiding-place, he saw the soldiers who were in search of him, and heard their earnest expressions in relation to his seizure. Hence the tree that protected him was called the *Royal Oak*, and was regarded with great veneration by many in the neighborhood. — *Hume.*

1680. A free mint was the idea—bullion to be coined at it without charge—it being urged, that foreign coins came from the mint six and a quarter per cent. less in value than they entered it; that the stamp of the mint upon their money added nothing to its real value, a Spanish cross, in all other places, being as much esteemed as a New England pine.

1681. The agents of the government, bound to London, were instructed to be humble suitors to his majesty, for obtaining his royal grant for the remittance of all past errors or deviations from the rules of their charter; and, also, to tender him an annual recognition of the same; and, as an acknowledgment of their thankfulness for his majesty's clemency and forgiveness, twenty or thirty beaver-skins, or any thing the growth or product of the colony, which his majesty might please to demand, *at Boston*.

1682. To prevent the export of specie, the General Court raised the nominal value of a pillar, Mexican or Sevil piece of eight, from 6s. to 6s. 8d., if weighing one ounce of silver, Troy weight, and its parts in like proportion.

1685. The officers of the London Mint report to the commissioners of the Royal Exchequer, relative to the money of Massachusetts, that it was $22\frac{1}{4}$ per cent. lighter than that of England, and that, in consequence, much of it was brought hither. They recommend that, if the king permit the continuance of the Boston Mint, he should order its emissions to be of equal value with his own specie. They add, that the Legislature of Massachusetts have pursued the unwarrantable act of coining money ever since the year 1652, without alteration of date. This was a premonitory symptom of the loss of their charter privileges, and this event they soon experienced.

1686. The long-established form of colonial government had departed, and its remains had been placed in the hands of a better-reputed royalty, to be modified and administered according to direct instructions from the crown. Still the mint survived, and coining was not at an end. It became the occasion, however, of another report, by the Earl of Rochester — Lord High Treasurer of England — in which he gave his reasons why the Mint of Massachusetts should be abolished; which were, that a similar establishment had been refused to Ireland, after being granted in 1662, and, also, in Jamaica in 1679, and that it tended to injure the standard coins adopted by Parliament. This same year, the establishment of a bank, or paper currency, was agitated.

1687. "Country pay" was still permitted. The administration of Sir Edmund Andross was accommodating; as the public demand on the town of Hingham was paid in milk pails, and which we believe are a lawful tender down to this day. The coffers of the treasury were, as it appears, still kept open for the products of the field as well as the mine.

January 1.—Treasury Report, viz.: 1688.

	£.	s.	d.
Corn remaining unsold	938	11	1
Money	1340	10	3

This year, a petition was sent to William and Mary for permission to renew their mint operations. It was received unfavorably, and coining, suspended by authority under the late administration, received its quietus. Thus fell an institution, around which the hopes and fears of the colonists had long clustered, and against which, expressions of rigid dissatisfaction had been often uttered. Though the mint was dead, its products were long current, and down to the Revolution, which resulted in our independence, they were often seen and passed currently with other coin.

Having been forbidden to coin money, they resorted to paper, and empowered a committee to issue £7000 in bills, from 5 shillings to £5. Thus was begun a system of furnishing a paper currency regulated by the Government, which continued down to 1750.   1690.

Paper at this time abundant but irredeemable; an emission having been made of £3000, in denominations of 1d., 2d., 4½d., 6d., 9d., and 18d.   1750.

Unceasing expedients and contests for maintaining the value of paper money, and legislating to effect it, by defining the value of coin.   1751.

Governor Shirley congratulates the colony upon a return to a silver medium, in consequence of Parliament having reimbursed it for expenditures incurred in the reduction of Cape Breton — much of the embarrassment that had existed, having arisen from burdens imposed by the dictation of the mother country for belligerent aggression or defence.   1753.

But little love between Parliament and the colonies. Governor Hutchinson, however, congratulates the province upon the good condition of its treasury, it being free from debt — the tax from last year, with the amount in the treasury, being equal to all of the securities due from the Government, and the current charges for the year. The lovers of liberty in the colony regarded this as but a "gilded pill," which was no antidote for the political diseases incident to either a restricted charter or personal rights; and hence it was not acceptable to them.   1774.

August 23d, the General Court, to supply the wants of the treasury, after several weeks of consideration, authorized an emission of £100,000 in paper. It was also ordered that there shall be on the back of each bill the figure of an American with a sword in his right hand, and the following inscription suspended   1775.

therefrom, viz.: "Ense petit placidum sub libertate quietam."[1] He seeks with his sword for peace and liberty.

The circumstances under which this currency was sent forth, were clothed with serious greatness. It embraced the oppressions, necessities, purposes, perils, hopes, and fears of a people breaking from long established relations, and setting themselves in array against a mighty empire.

The most of the device composed the seal of Massachusetts, as very recently adopted by the General Court. It presented to the eye the royal armorials, which had so long been a part of its public documents, and which denoted subjection to the crown, deliberately repudiated, and others, exhibiting emblems of freedom, and the sentiment of the patriot, Sydney, adopted in their place.

On each bill the names of three persons, designated to sign it, were to be written — one with red, another with black, and the third with blue ink.

1777. Massachusetts, with the other members of the Union, agrees to the articles of confederation, wherein power is delegated to Congress, to borrow money, issue bills on the responsibility of the States, and regulate the alloy and value of coins.

1784. Massachusetts Bank chartered.

1786. In this year the confederated government entered into a contract for the coinage of a copper coin.—(See "First United States Cent.")

July 8th, the Governor is requested to inquire whether Massachusetts can be supplied with silver and copper coin struck at the United States Mint, when it shall have commenced operations.

October 17th, being much in want of specie, and thinking the National Mint not reliable for it, the Assembly vote that a like establishment should be erected for the coinage of copper, silver, and gold. Of the first sort, they order seventy thousand dollars worth, in cents and half cents, to be coined as soon as practicable.

1787. Joshua Witherel is empowered to have the necessary buildings erected, and suitable machinery provided for the same. July 6th, it was decided that the copper coin bear the following devices — on one face the American eagle having in the right talon a bundle of arrows, and in the left an olive branch — the emblems of defence and peace; also, upon its breast a shield inscribed with the word "Cent," being nearly encircled with the word "Massachusetts," and having at the

---

[1] From the noted line and a half written by Algernon Sydney in the album of the University of Copenhagen.

"————Manus hæc, inimica tyrannos,
Ense petit placidum sub libertate quietam."

bottom the date of its emission, "1787." On the other face, an Indian of full length, with his bow and arrow, a star, denoting this State, near his forehead, and a circumscription of the word "Commonwealth."

September 28th, the Federal Constitution presented to Congress, expressly providing that no State shall coin money, emit bills of credit, or make anything but gold and silver coin a tender in payment of debts.

The cent ordered from the Massachusetts Mint made its appearance. 1788.

November 17th, in conformity with the National Constitution, the Assembly ordered that the copper on hand at the mint be manufactured as soon as possible into cents, and that then the workmen be discharged.

Thus ended the second mint, nearly a century having elapsed since the termination of the first, which long withstood the storms of regal displeasure, while its successor was of short continuance.

PART IV

COLONIAL COINS.

SOMER, SUMMER, OR BERMUDA ISLANDS' COIN.

THOUGH the Bermuda Islands are not a part of our own country—the coins of which I am particularly describing—yet intimately related, as they were, in their early history to the "Old Dominion," I have deemed it of sufficient interest to present it, chronologically, as the first home of American coins.

These islands are a small cluster in the Atlantic ocean, lying in latitude 32° 35' north, and longitude 63° 28' west, in the form of a shepherd's crook, and so formidably surrounded by rocks as to be almost inaccessible. They were discovered by Juan Bermudez, a Spaniard, but were not inhabited till the year 1609, when Sir George Somers was cast away upon them; since which time they have been included in the possessions of Great Britain.

In 1612, efforts were successfully made to colonize them by the Virginia Company, headed for the purpose, by Mr. John More. He was succeeded in authority by Captain Daniel Tucker, under whom the endeavor was made to establish a currency, as we are informed by Captain John Smith, of established Virginian reputation, in the following words: "besides meat, and drink, and clothes, they had for a time a certain kind of brass money, with a hogge on one side, in memory of the abundance of hogges which were found at their first landing."

Though this coin has never been submitted to our eyesight, nor is it to be found in any collection or cabinet of coins in the United States, we have given a fac-simile upon the authority and from the works of Snelling and Ruding—taken by them from the cabinet collection of the celebrated numismatologist, Mr. Hollis, of England, who, in his memoirs, calls it "a coin of the Summer Islands."

Device.—A wild boar, with the Roman numerals XII. over it.
Legend.—SOMER ISLANDS. M. M., a mullet of five points.
Reverse.—A ship under sail, firing a gun.
(Plate VI., Figure 1.)

NEW ENGLAND PATTERN SHILLING.

Device.—A pine-tree in the field, surrounded by a circle of dots.
Legend.—MASSACHVSETS, N. E.
Reverse.—A circle of dots; in the area "1650," and under it the numerals XII.
(Size 8. See Plate VI., Figure 2.)

This piece, as we describe it, is said to be in the possession of a Mr. Brown, of the city of Boston, and has been supposed to be one of the pattern pieces struck off at the Massachusetts Mint. It is unfortunate that the originator or artist should have blundered in the legend, which, upon the genuine, was "MASATHVSETS," for otherwise it might have attained to the credibility of being genuine. As it is, there is no doubt but it is counterfeit — induced by the same spirit which has characterized the manufacturers of "May Flower" furniture.

We feel assured, from the fact of a genuine piece of this kind not yet having made its appearance, that they were all returned to the crucible in 1652; otherwise, they would have been dragged to the light by some enthusiastic virtuoso.

NEW ENGLAND SHILLING.

Obverse.—The letters N. E. near the outer edge of the field, enclosed by a line
irregular in form, the edge forming part of the same.   1652.
Reverse.—The numerals XII. similarly placed, and in the same manner.
(Size 9.)

NEW ENGLAND SIXPENCE.

Differing from the shilling only in size, and the numerals VI.
(Size 5. See Plate VI., Figures 3 and 4.)

These were the pioneer coins of the Massachusetts Mint, and, undoubtedly, of the American portion of the North American continent. In the portion of this work allotted to the "Massachusetts Currency," they have been fully and particularly noticed, and we may add, they are entitled, among American numismatologists, to very marked distinction.

As the fac-similes represent them, they were irregularly circular, but coined of good sterling silver. There was but one type and three varieties of these coins. It is very difficult to find them unmutilated or not clipped.

COLONIAL COINS.

Snelling denominates them plantation shillings and sixpences. They were well planted; as around them clustered the will of the colonists, in regard to a coinage of their own, which they maintained against all opposing authority for upwards of thirty years, and its circulation till the adoption of the Constitution in 1787.

THE TREE COINS.

PINE TREE SHILLING.

1652. *Device.*—The American pine tree in the field, surrounded by a circle of dots.
Legend.—MASATHVSETS IN. Mint-mark, a rose of dots.
Reverse.—A circle of dots; in the area 1652, and under it the numerals XII.
Legend.—NEW ENGLAND AN. DO.
(Size 8.)

PINE TREE SIXPENCE.

Device.—The American pine tree in the field, surrounded by a circle of dots.
Legend.—MASATHVSETS IN.
Reverse.—A circle of dots; in the area 1652, and under it the numerals VI.
Legend.—NEW ENGLAND ANO.
(Size 5.)

PINE TREE THREE-PENCE.

Device.—The American pine tree in the field, surrounded by a circle of dots.
Legend.—MASATHVSETS. Mint-mark, a rose of dots.
Reverse.—A circle of dots; in the area 1652, and under it the numerals III.
(Size 3. See Plate VI., Figures 5, 6, and 7.)

OAK TREE SHILLING.

Device.—The oak tree in the field, surrounded by a circle of dots.
Legend.—MASATHVSETS IN. Mint-mark, a rose of dots.
Reverse.—A circle of dots; in the area 1652, and under it the numerals XII.
Legend.—NEW ENGLAND AN. DOM.
(Size 8.)

OAK TREE SIXPENCE.

Device.—The oak tree in the field, surrounded by a circle of dots.
Legend.—MASATHVSETS IN. Mint-mark, a rose of dots.
Reverse.—A circle of dots; in the area 1652, and under it the numerals VI.
Legend.—NEW ENGLAND ANO.
(Size 5.)

COLONIAL COINS.

OAK TREE THREE-PENCE.

Device.—The oak tree in the field, surrounded by a circle of dots.
Legend.—MASATHVSETS. Mint-mark, a rose of dots.
Reverse.—A circle of dots; in the area 1652, and under it the numerals III.
Legend.—NEW ENGLAND.

OAK TREE TWO-PENCE.

Device.—The oak tree in the field, surrounded by a circle of dots.
Legend.—MASATHVSETS. Mint-mark, a rose of dots.
Reverse.—A circle of dots; in the area 1662, and under it the numerals II.
Legend.—NEW ENGLAND.

(See Plate VI., Figures 8, 9, 10, and 11.)

Of the tree coins, or those bearing upon their face a tree, there were two types and thirty-six varieties in circulation, so far as we have been able, by diligent search, to ascertain.

Those bearing the pine tree, were undoubtedly the first type issued; as the historical incidents, previously given in relation to the currency of Massachusetts, and the testimony derived from the coins themselves, we think, fully warrant the assertion. Of this type, we have examined eighteen distinct varieties—embracing five different kinds or representations of the pine tree; the most remarkable of which bears the representation of a thickly branched oblong tree with an oval top, which occurs on the shillings, sixpences, and three-pences, but in no instance have we been able to find a two-penny coin with either variety of the pine-tree for an emblem.

The oak tree coins we denominate the second type. Of this type, we have examined about the same number of varieties, which embrace six different forms of the oak. In two of the forms, the trees are in clusters of three, their branches intertwining with each other, as we frequently see in the species known as the scrub oak, and of which variety there were coins of all the denominations issued.

The two-penny pieces all bear a representation of the oak tree, and they were only issued in accordance with the following law:—

"The mint-master is enjoined to coin two-penny pieces of silver, of the first bullion that comes into his hands, in the just proportion and alloy of other 1662. monies which are allowed here, to answer the purposes of the country for exchange; that is, £50 the first year for every £100 coined; and, thereafter, £20 of the currency annually for every £100 that may be coined; and the law to continue in force for seven years."[1]

---

[1] Colonial Records.

As this law apparently sought a supply of the lowest denomination of silver coins, proportioned to the other, viz.: 50 per cent. of the whole amount coined the first year, and, subsequently, only 20 per cent. during the existence of the law, it is only generous to infer that that was the full and fair extent of the motive for enacting it. If, however, as some have surmised, none of the oak-tree coins were issued till this enactment, and that they were then coined for the first time, with the peculiar emblem of the oak, from a motive of expediency, calculated, by its reference to an important circumstance in the life of Charles II., to appease him for an invasion of his prerogative, we can see no ground for such a conjecture, except the practicability of such an act under the law — the two-penny pieces bearing date 1662, and all others of the oak-tree emissions being dated in 1652.

That the oak-tree coins were, therefore, first issued under this law, except the two-penny pieces, or that the motive for the law was deception, is very far from being our impression; for, though the colonists were at all times, in view of their position, conciliating in their policy, and often manifested it by special gifts to the king, still we should be very reluctant, from mere inference, to impute the coinage of the oak-tree currency to a collusion between them and the Governor of Nova Scotia, and for such a purpose as mere suspicion supplies — the bold and fearless act of the colonists in establishing a mint, or coining money at all, being ample refutation of any such assumption or charge against them. Their descendants certainly indicated that they had received no such training at the hands of their ancestors, as their open and manly defence of their natural rights against unjust authority clearly proves.

It is clearly established that the oak-tree penny piece is without legal authority for its emission, it being of modern manufacture; for, though a law was enacted for its coinage, it was never carried into execution by the mint. We have seen an entire series of the oak-tree coins, from the penny up to the shilling. They are made of sterling silver, are well calculated to deceive even good judges, and are as eagerly sought for as the genuine, for specimens. The pine-tree coins have, also, been counterfeited, having been cast in silver; the method of their manufacture being easily detected by the application of the lens.

The legend, on the pine-tree shilling, differs in the abbreviation, and, also, in the mint-marks. We illustrate the former, viz.: AN: DO: , AN: DOM: , ANO: DOM: &c. In some specimens of the latter, the rose is composed of four, five, six, eight, and in one instance we have seen nine dots, which, composing the circles, are both round and oval.

COLONIAL COINS.

Good Samaritan Shilling.

Device.—Group of the Good Samaritan; over it, "fac-simile." 1652.
Legend.—MASATHVSETS IN.
Reverse.—Smooth.

  It is stated that there is a variety of this coin, having a reverse thus: in the field, "1652," numerals "XII.," and under it O.

Legend.—"o o o o o o ENGLAND AN."

    (See Plate VI., Figure 12.)

  This shilling, impressed with the group illustrating the "Good Samaritan," which is in the Pembroke collection in England, and engraved in Volume xiv. p. 4, of the Pembroke Museum, is noticed by both Snelling and Ruding, who threw some doubts upon its authenticity, as ever having been issued by any legal authority, in its present form, as a coin or currency.

  From all the information we have been able to collect relative to it, we have concluded that it was a pine-tree shilling, the tree removed by scraping it down to a plain surface, and the "group" then engraved in the circle formerly surrounding the tree. It is not uncommon to find coins thus mutilated or changed, and hence bearing some curious device or legend. The reverse noticed above, taken from a drawing, is, as connected with this piece, inexplicable to us.

  We have given a description of this coin in all its details, because it has been the subject of so much attraction, and, also, because it occupies a place in a very celebrated collection.

MARYLAND CURRENCY.

Lord Baltimore Shilling.

Device.—A profile bust of Lord Baltimore, facing to the left; the head unadorned, and the neck uncovered. Mint-mark, a cross Patee. 1659.
Legend.—CAECILIVS. DNS. TERRÆ-MARIÆ. &CT.
Reverse.—Arms of the Palatinate, surmounted by a crown with XII. on the side of the face of the coin.
Legend.—CRESCITE. ET. MVLTIPLICAMINI.
    (Size 8. See Plate VI., Figure 13.)

Lord Baltimore Sixpence.

Device.—A profile bust of Lord Baltimore, facing to the left; the head unadorned, and the neck uncovered. Mint-mark, a cross Patee.
Legend.—CAECILIVS. DNS. TERRÆ-MARIÆ. &CT.

Reverse.—Arms of the Palatinate, surmounted by a crown, with VI. on one side of the face of the coin.

Legend.—CRESCITE. ET. MVLTIPLICAMINI.

(Size 7. See Plate VI., Figure 14.)

LORD BALTIMORE GROAT.

Device.—A profile bust of Lord Baltimore, facing to the left; the head unadorned, and the neck uncovered. Mint-mark, a cross Patee.

Legend.—CAECILIVS. DNS. TERRÆ-MARIÆ. &CT.

Reverse.—Arms of the Palatinate, surmounted by a crown, with IV. on one side of the face of the coin.

Legend.—CRESCITE. ET. MVLTIPLICAMINI.

(Size 4. See Plate VI., Figure 15.)

CECIL, LORD BALTIMORE PENNY.

Device.—A bust of Lord Baltimore, facing to the left. Mint-mark, the cross Patee on both sides.

Legend.—CAECILIVS. DNS. TERRÆ-MARIÆ. &CT.

Reverse.—Two flags issuing out of a ducal coronet, the crest of Lord Baltimore.

Legend.—DENARVM TERRÆ-MARIÆ.

(Size 5. See Plate VI., Figure 16.)

The silver groat and copper penny we have described, are very rare. Those from which Mr. Ruding was permitted to take drawings, and we have copied them, are now in the cabinet of James Bindley, Esq., of England.

We have herewith compiled, from sources to which we have given credit, some incidents in the history of the Maryland colony, which may prove to be interesting, and, at the same time, aid to fix the attention more particularly upon the main object, its currency.

Among those who became interested in the London or Virginia Company, under its second charter in 1609, was Sir George Calvert, afterwards the founder of Maryland. He was early engaged in the schemes of colonization of those times, and, upon the dissolution of the Virginia Company, of which he had been a member, he was named by the king — James I.— one of the Royal Commissioners to whom the government of that colony was entrusted.[1]

Hitherto, he had been a Protestant,[2] but in 1624 he renounced the Church of England, in which he had been bred, and embraced the faith of the Roman Catholic Church. His conscientious scruples determined him to hold no longer the office of

---

[1] Bozan.   [2] Burnet, Fuller, &c.

PLATE VI.

Secretary of State, which would place him in an unpleasant attitude to those whose faith he had adopted, and he tendered his resignation to the king, informing him at the same time, that he had become a Roman Catholic, and that he felt, in consequence of the discordance between the Established Church and the faith he had adopted, unwilling longer to discharge the duties of the office.[1] The king, pleased with his candor, accepted his resignation, but continued him as a member of his Privy Council for life, and soon after created him Lord Baltimore.

Sectarian animosity at this time ran high, and as Sir George Calvert deprecated this state of things, and had no taste for being an active participant in it, he determined to leave England, and found a new State exempt from this feeling, and where every man could worship God according to his own conscience, and in perfect peace and security.[2]

Accordingly, he embarked for Virginia, with the intention of settling within the limits of that colony, or more probably to explore the uninhabited country 1628. upon its borders, with a view to secure a grant of it from the king. Upon his arrival within the jurisdiction of the colony, the authorities tendered to him the oath of allegiance and supremacy, to which, with his religious views, he could not subscribe. Lord Baltimore framed an oath of allegiance, which he and his followers were willing to accept, but it was rejected. He set sail, and commenced the exploration of the Chesapeake. He was pleased with the beautiful and well-wooded country, which surrounded the noble inlets and indentations of the great bay, and determined there to found his State, being assured that he had found a territory possessing all the elements of future prosperity.

He returned to England to obtain a grant from Charles I., who had succeeded his father upon the throne. Remembering Lord Baltimore's relations to his father, and perhaps aided by the intercessions of Henrietta Maria, his Roman Catholic queen, Charles directed the patent to be issued. It was prepared by Lord Baltimore himself, but before it was finally executed, he died, and the patent was delivered to his son Cecelius, who succeeded to his designs as well as his titles and estates. The charter was issued on the 20th of June, 1632, and the new province was named in honor of the queen, Terra-Mariæ — Maryland. The charter was a solemn grant from the king to Lord Baltimore, his heirs, and assigns, with extensive jurisdiction and powers of government over it. The king reserved to himself one-fifth of the gold and silver which might be found in the province, and the yearly tribute of two Indian arrows.

With a noble territory, the rights and prosperity of his future State seconded by a

---

[1] Fuller.   [2] McMahon.

COLONIAL COINS.

liberal charter, Lord Baltimore prepared to establish his first permanent settlement in Maryland. He fitted out two vessels, which he named the "Ark" and the "Dove," and collected a body of two hundred emigrants, nearly all of them of his own faith, and gentlemen of fortune and respectability, who, like himself and his father, wished to rear up their altars with freedom in the wilderness.[1] The colonists were commanded by Lord Calvert, whom the Lord Proprietary, his brother, had appointed Governor of Maryland — the Lord Proprietary intending to remain in England for a time, to superintend in person the interests of the settlement, and to send out additional emigrants.

November 22d, being St. Cecilia's day, the "Ark" and the "Dove" weighed anchor from Cowles in the Isle of Wight; and on the 24th day of February, 1633. they came in sight of Point Comfort in Virginia, and after spending eight or nine days in the colony of Virginia, again set sail on the 8th of March, steering for the mouth of the Potomac, to which they gave the name of St. Gregory. They had now arrived at the land of their adoption, were delighted with the wide expanse of the noble bay, and the majestic river upon whose shores they were about to rear up a State, and they returned thanks to God for the beautiful land he had given them — for this was Maryland.

An impression prevails that the colony of Maryland had the honor of a mint, and that the coins we have described were its products. The following, from a paper read before the Historical Society of Maryland by S. F. Streeter, Esq., sets the question at rest.

"At a counsell held at Bushwood, Mr. Slye's howse in St. Mary's county, on Saturday, the 3d of March, 1659–60,

"Present: the Gov. Josiah Fendall, Esq., Philip Calvert, Esq., Secretary, Thomas Gerrard, Esq., Coll. John Price, Robert Clarke, Esq., Col. Nathaniell Utye, Baker Brooke, Esq., Doct. Luke Barber.

"Then was read his L'd'p's letter, directed to his Lieutenant and Counsell, dated 12th of October, and directed to the Secretary, touching the Mint, as followeth, viz.:

"After my hearty commendations, &c. Having, with great pains and charge, procured Necessaries for a particular coyne to be currant in Maryland, a sample whereof, in a peece of a shilling, a sixpence, and a groate, I herewith send you. I recommend it to you to promote, all you can, the dispersing it, and by Proclamation to make currant within Maryland, for all payments upon contracts or causes happening or arising after a day to be by you limited in the said Proclamation. And to procure

---

[1] Burnap, Bowman, and McMahon.

an act of Assembly for the punishing of such as shall counterfeit the said coyne, or otherwise offend in that behalfe, according to the form of an act recommended by me last year to my Governour and Secretary; or as neere it as you can procure from the Assembly, and to give me your advice next yeare touching what you think best to be further done in that matter touching coyne; for if encouradgement be given by the good success of it this yeare, there wilbe abundance of adventurers in it the next yeare."

With this communication was also forwarded the following letter to his brother Philip, then Secretary of State.

"To Philip Calvert, Esq., at St. Mary's, in Maryland.

"I sent a sample of the Maryland money, with the directions for procuring it to pass, because I understood, by letters this yeare from the Governour, and you and others, that there was no doubt but the people there would accept of it, which if we find they do, there wilbe meanes found to supply you all there with money enough; but though it would be a very great advantage to the colony that it should pass currant there, and an utter discouradgement for the future supply of any more, if there be not a certain establishment this yeare, and an assurance of its being vented and currant there, yet it must not be imposed upon the people, but by a Law there made by their consents in a General Assembly, which I pray faile not to signify to the Governour and Councell there together from me, by shewing them this letter from

 - Your most affectionate Brother,

C. Baltemore."

London, 12 October, 1659.

"Ten days after the reception of his Lordship's letter, and the discussion in council of the question of the best mode of introducing his new coinage among the people, Governor Fendall, with a part of the council, attempted to revolutionize the province, and, throwing off all dependence upon Lord Baltimore, to concentrate all power in themselves. They were probably incited to this by the unsettled state of affairs in England; but they soon found there was no hope of success, and were glad to give in their submission to the newly restored king, and to Lord Baltimore as the lawful Proprietary of the province.

"The confusion that followed this wild attempt of Fendall and his party, of course rendered it impossible to carry out the proposed plan in reference to a specie currency. According to his Lordship's instructions, the coins were not to be forced upon the people; on the contrary, he would not consent to their introduction until the people, by their representatives, had not only expressed their assent, but had even invited their emission.

"Philip Calvert received his commission to act as Governor in November, 1660, and complied as promptly as possible with the wishes and instructions of his brother. In April following, an Assembly was held at St. John's, and, at his instance, an act was drawn up and passed 'for setting up a mint within the province of Maryland.'

"After a preamble, setting forth the fact that the want of money is a great hindrance to the advancement of the colony in trade and prosperity, the Burgesses agree to the following enactments:

I. "That his lordship be petitioned to set up a mint for the coinage of money within the province.

II. "That the money coined therein be of as good silver as English sterling money.

III. "That every shilling so coined weigh above nine-pence in such silver; and other pieces in proportion.

IV. "That the offences of clipping, scaling, counterfeiting, washing, or in any way diminishing said coin, be punishable with death, and forfeiture of lands, goods, &c., to the Lord Proprietary.

V. "That his lordship receive said coins in payment for rents and all amounts due to him.

"These proceedings were transmitted to the Proprietary in England; upon receipt of which, he prepared to send to the colony a sufficient quantity of coin to supply its wants. The main object was, at once, to throw a considerable amount into circulation, and to this end, the aid of the Assembly was again invoked.

"At the session of April, 1662, an act was passed, requiring every householder and freeman 'to take up ten shillings per poll of the newly issued coin, for every taxable under their charge and custody, and pay for the same in good casked tobacco, at two-pence per pound, to be paid upon tender of the said sums of money, proportionally for each respective family.'

"The effect of this measure was to cause a forced exchange of sixty pounds of tobacco by every tithable for ten shillings of the new coinage; and, as there were at least five thousand tithables then in the province, this act alone, if it were carried fully into effect, must have thrown into circulation coin to the amount of twenty-five hundred pounds sterling.

"It is probable that the new emission proved acceptable to the people, as it must have greatly facilitated exchanges; yet it by no means superseded tobacco as an article of currency. That still continued largely in use, especially in important transactions; and many of the public dues were still collected in tobacco, and not in coin. What was the amount of this new currency at any time after, we have no means of ascertaining; neither do we know when it began to be disused. Nearly ten years after, in 1671, Ogilby states there were in circulation in the colony, beside English and other foreign coins, some of his Lordship's own coins, as groats, sixpences, and shillings.

"From the title of the act of Assembly of 1661, in Bacon's laws of Maryland, some have inferred that a mint was established, and that the coinage was actually done in Maryland; but there can be no doubt that the coins were struck in England, under the supervision of the Lord Proprietary, and transmitted to the Governor, as circumstances made it necessary or convenient."

That the people of this colony, like those of every other of English origin on this continent, were restive under any other authority than their own, is evidenced by the attempt of Governor Fendall and his associates to revolutionize and rid the colony of its dependence upon the Lord Proprietary. We think it not improbable, had Fendall succeeded, the colony would have had a mint of its own, and many other advantages for which they were dependent upon Lord Baltimore.

Lord Baltimore, in all his acts, manifested great kindness, consideration, and justice, toward the colonists; but the atmosphere in this continent — then, as now — appears to have been unsuited to any other relation, between men, than that of entire freedom, which was, and continues to be, apparently uncompromisable upon any conditions, or for any considerations whatever.

TIN PIECE.

Device.—King James II. on horseback, with his name and titles.   1690.
Reverse.—VAL. 24. PART. REAL. HISPAN. around four shields disposed as a cross, bearing the arms of England, Scotland, Ireland, and France.
(See Plate VII., Figure 1.)

This piece was issued by James II. for the American plantations, where the Spanish dollar chiefly circulated, with its parts, reals, and half-reals.

In 1718, under George I., and, subsequently, under George II., a similar issue was made for British purposes in the East Indies. They were termed "Tutanique piec," were of tin and very light. The obverse bore a large crown, above which are the letters G. R., and below, BOMB. The legend, "Auspicio Regis et Senatus Angliæ," with the date, "1718," occupied the whole reverse. There were also half-piec, which have on one side, "1739, ½ P.," and on the other, E. I.

Though we have British authorities to show that this currency was prepared for the American colonies, still it could not have been received with much favor; as we have no knowledge of the existence in this country of a single specimen which has not latterly been imported.

The mines of Cornwall, furnishing, as they did, to the ancient Britons, who used tin as currency, an abundant supply of the raw material, the British government undoubtedly came to the conclusion, not only that the operation would be a profitable one, but that tin money was good enough for such "outside barbarians" as the American colonists and the natives of its East Indian possessions.

CAROLINA HALF-PENNY.

1694. *Device.*—An elephant standing, and facing the left.
Reverse.—God preserve Carolina, and the Lord Proprietors.
Exergue.—1694.
(Size 8. See Plate VII., Figure 2.)

This coin made its appearance according to the date, 1694, during the reign of William and Mary, and has no claim to be of domestic manufacture. It was undoubtedly intended as a currency, which it became for the Carolina colonies, and which, at that time, had made some progress toward stability. It is composed of brass, and from its resemblance to the London half-penny, is presumed to be of the same origin — the latter having been engraved, as Snelling states, by the much celebrated Roetiers. The specimens — four in number — that have come under our observation are in an excellent state of preservation.

The London half-penny, like many other coins, is mysterious in its inception, or the original purposes intended to be subserved by it, except we impute it both to necessity and speculation; the former of which very naturally stimulated the latter with but little regard to either law or prerogative.

The following description and history of the London half-penny may not prove to be uninteresting in this connection.

Device.—An elephant standing, and facing the left.
Reverse.—The shield with the Cross of St. George, and sword of St. Paul in the first quarter, as borne by the arms of the city of London. A star above and below the shield, and the name London divided, and placed on either side of the shield.

This type is very rare, and it appears in a half-penny of Charles II.

The reverse of another type has the same shield — the upper star wanting — the legend being London, God preserve. The elephant on the obverse is the same in all, and it has been suggested that it was the badge of the Royal African colony. Snelling thought they were struck for the West India colonies, but the arms of the city of

London on the reverse would raise a doubt relative to the correctness of any such thought or conclusion. Coins were struck for Bombay in 1678, and as the description of the same is unknown, it may help to solve the mystery of the elephant upon the half-penny, such symbol being peculiarly appropriate in connection with the British East India enterprises of that day.

The Carolina half-penny, as we have described it, is the only light thrown upon a Carolina currency during the colonial administration, except that, on the 14th of July, 1748, Sir Alexander Cuming, Bart., presented a memorial to the Right Hon. Henry Pelham, &c., &c., in which he proposed, "in order to preserve the dependency of the British plantations in North America upon Great Britain, that the coins of Great Britain should be made the lawful current money of the said plantations, and also as the proper measure of value, not only there, but in all countries depending on the British crown and nation; and that £200,000 sterling should be coined at the Tower for that purpose, which sum was to be made the basis of a Provincial Bank for all the British plantations in America, in order that it may have the effect of abolishing the local currency of New England and Carolina, and also the clipped Spanish money in Jamaica and elsewhere."[1] Cuming's memorial failed, being considered visionary, and the author an enthusiast.

This proposition, viewed from this point of time, was far from being visionary, while, at the same time, its author's *national* enthusiasm was not only sagacious, but commendable; for we can now see, that if the colonies had been bound to the mother country by so admirably a constructed money power, their extrication from the political power of the mother country would have been more difficult; as there is no "entangling alliance" so hard to sever, between man and man, as that of a pecuniary character, with the intimately selfish and friendly relations which it begets.

We also find that, in 1753, a proposal was made to the mother country, by Arthur Dobbs, Esq., Governor of North Carolina, to coin copper money for the colony, which was to consist of half-penny, one penny, and two-penny pieces of its currency, which was in the proportion of its value to that of England, as four to three. The quantity to be determined by the Governor and Council, but not to exceed fifty tons. The colony to deliver the copper at the mint, to pay all expenses and fees attending the coinage, and to be permitted to have such a device as should be thought proper.

The mother government, it appears, entertained the proposition, as it was sent by the Treasury to the officers of the mint for their consideration, who suggested that one-half of the amount coined should be in half-pence, of such a size as that sixty-one

---

[1] Lyon's Environs of London, vol. iv. p. 21.

pieces should make one pound avoirdupois; that one-fourth should consist of two-penny pieces, and the other fourth of one penny pieces, of a proportional weight to the half-pence. The remedy to be one-forty-fifth part of a pound avoirdupois, and that, not by design, but accident. The coinage to be performed at the same price as those for Ireland, viz.: five pence per pound to the master of the mint, and twenty shillings per one hundred pounds to the comptroller. The proposition as expressed to be observed, as any increase of half-pence would increase the expense.

One side of the different coins to have the king's effigies, with GEORGIVS II. REX.; on the reverse, the arms of North Carolina inscribed SEPT. CAROLINA, and under it the date of the year.[1] This proposition of the North Carolina Governor, though well matured, was never carried into execution. It was undoubtedly fortunate for the colonies that this, and similar schemes for apparently facilitating the internal industry and commerce of the country, failed to be readily and zealously seconded by the mother country; as it had the effect to throw them more particularly upon their own resources, which gradually induced a spirit of self-dependence; subsequently, brought about a separation from the parent government, and, finally, confirmed them as an independent nation and people.

NEW ENGLAND HALF-PENNY.

1694.   *Device.*—An elephant facing to the left.
         Reverse.—God preserve New England.
         Exergue.—1694.

This coin made its appearance in the early part of the year 1694, in the reign of William and Mary. The object of its emission or the place of its coinage is not positively known; but it is supposed to have been got up in London as a private enterprise, originating — which, cannot be told — either in London or the colonies.

The speculation must have been unsuccessful, as it cannot be found in any of the cabinets in this country, which would not have been the case if it had ever acquired the character of a currency. It was made of brass, and the obverse agreed precisely with the London half-penny. This coin is similar to that struck for Carolina, and which will be found recorded under its proper head.

---

[1] Snelling's views of coins struck in the West India colonies, p. 40.

LOUISIANA COPPER.

Device.—⚜. L. L. crossed diagonally—probably denoting Louis and Louisiana—surmounted by a crown. 1721-22.
Legend.—·SIT · NOMEN · DOMINI · BENEDICTUM.
Reverse.—COLONIES · FRANÇOISES.
Exergue.—1721. H.

(Size 7. See Plate VII., Figure 3.)

Of this coin there were four types and six varieties, three of which were issued in 1721, and one in 1722. This coin was struck in France, under Louis XV., for the colony of Louisiana, and was ordered to be paid to the king's troops, and also to be a legal tender at the "India Company's" stores. Though these and other coins were sent over in comparatively large quantities for the expenses of the colonial government, this means of remittance, from thence to the mother country—the agricultural products being limited—caused it to be either exported or hoarded, nearly as fast as received. The usual embarrassments flowing from such a state of affairs, were imposed upon the colonists, and they found themselves deprived, in a great measure, of a circulating medium.

This state of affairs continued a number of years, when, by an edict of Louis XV., which bears date the 19th day of September, 1735, the depreciated paper money issued by the "India Company," and then in circulation, was called in, and an emission of "card money"—*billet des cartes*—to the amount of two hundred thousand livres, was substituted for it.

This "card money" was ordered to be received at the king's warehouse for ammunition or anything else sold there; or in exchange for drafts on the Treasury of the Marine in France, and it was also a lawful tender. Cards were issued, representing the denominational sums of twenty, fifteen, and five livres; fifty, twenty-five, twelve and a half, and six and a quarter sous, thus assimilating and accommodating the currency to that of the British colonies, viz.: four, three, and two dollars, and one dollar; halves, quarters, and eighths of a dollar.

Any denomination of card money of fifty sous and upwards required the signatures of the Governor and Ordonateur of the province—the others, merely the *paraphe* or flourish of those officials.

Nine years elapsed, and the royal promises to pay became as worthless as their more modest predecessors. The depreciation was so great, that three hundred livres of paper would command but one-third of that amount in coin.

The result of paper money in Louisiana was the same as in all other provinces, colonies, States, or nations, under similar circumstances. A subject State or nation — so by force or voluntary policy — must necessarily sacrifice the fruits of its advantages, labor, and intellect, to the country or government to which it occupies such a relation. Hence, it must become involved in debt; as nothing can prevent it but the entire control over, and diversification of its labor, so that it may be independent in itself for everything which its means will not enable it to buy abroad.

It is, and ever has been, the policy of parent States, towards their colonies, to render them entirely dependent upon them; and hence losing sight of a proper economy or mutual interest, they have driven them, as in the case of the British colonies in America, to a resistance which eventuated in their independence.

All depreciations of paper money are based upon the fact, that the people issuing it have not provided for its redemption by limiting their expenses, whether national or individual, to their income. In such cases, however, they are only proper subjects of sympathy, where their condition, being such, is an involuntary one.

On the 27th of April, the Council of State of the mother country declared that the condition of the finances of the province was prejudicial to the finances of the government; hence, the progress of commerce and the welfare of the colony. It therefore determined to call in the card money at the rate of one hundred livres for every two hundred and fifty of the same issued. This redemption or exchange was not through the medium of specie, but by drafts on the French treasury, subjecting the holder thereby to the loss of a discount upon the same for ready money. It was further provided, that all pasteboard money, not brought in for exchange or redemption within two months, subsequent to the promulgation of the edict, should be deemed to be irredeemable and void. In justification of this high-handed measure, it was urged by the government that it did not feel under obligations to redeem these notes at par, because they had been given in many instances to meet expenses and liquidate claims, which had been increased in proportion to the actual or anticipated depreciation of the currency in which they were paid.

It is related of Charles Lamb, that upon his return to London, from a visit he had been making in Dublin, he was asked how he was pleased with it? His reply was, very much; as it had settled a question which had previously disturbed his mind, and that was, what the beggars of London did with their old clothes.

Where Texas acquired the precedent, and the reasons for refusing to pay her debt in full, is now equally clear; as her statesmen must have been examining the cast off habiliments of the French monarchy, or poring over the dusty volumes of her Louisiana province's history, with the logic of which, and its practical application by Louis XV. to his colonial creditors, they must have been particularly impressed and well pleased.

COLONIAL COINS.

ROSA AMERICANA.

PENNY PIECE.

Device.—A bust of George I.; head laureated, and facing to the right; the neck uncovered. 1722.
Legend.—GEORGIUS · D : G : MAG : BRI : FRA : ET · HIB : REX.
Reverse.—A large full-blown rose in the centre of the field.
Legend.—ROSA · AMERICANA · 1722.
Exergue.—UTILE · DULCI ·
    (Size 9. See Plate VII., Figure 4.)

HALF-PENNY.

Device.—A bust of George I.; head laureated, and facing to the right; the neck uncovered.
Legend.—GEORGIUS · DEI · GRATIA · REX.
Reverse.—A large full-blown rose in the centre of the field.
Legend.—ROSA · AMERICANA ∴ UTILE · DULCI · 1722. ∴
    (Size 7. See Plate VII., Figure 5.)

FARTHING.

Device.—A bust of George I.; head laureated, and facing to the right; the neck uncovered.
Legend.—GEORGIUS · DEI · GRATIA · REX.
Reverse.—A large full-blown rose in the centre of the field.
Legend.—ROSA · AMERICANA · UTILE · DULCI · 1722. ∴
    (Size 6. See Plate VII., Figure 6.)

PENNY PIECE.

Device.—A bust of George I.; head laureated, and facing to the right; neck uncovered. 1723.
Legend.—GEORGIUS · D : G : MAG : BRI : FRA : ET · HIIB : REX.
Reverse.—A large full-blown rose in the centre of the field, surmounted by the crown.
Legend.—ROSA · AMERICANA · 1723.
Exergue.—UTILE · DULCI ·
    (Size 9. See Plate VII., Figure 7.)

HALF-PENNY.

Device.—A bust of George I.; head laureated, and facing to the right; neck uncovered.
Legend.—GEORGIUS · DEI · GRATIA · REX.
Reverse.—A full-blown rose in the centre of the field, surmounted by the crown.
Legend.—ROSA · AMERICANA · 1723.
Exergue.—UTILE · DULCI ·
    (Size 7. See Plate VII., Figure 8.

COLONIAL COINS.

FARTHING.

Device.—A bust of George I.; head laureated, and facing to the right; neck uncovered.
Legend.—GEORGIUS · DEI · GRATIA ·
Reverse.—A large full-blown rose in the centre of the field, surmounted by the crown.
Legend.—ROSA · AMERICANA · 1723.
Exergue.—UTILE · DULCI ·
    (Size 6. See Plate VII., Figure 9.)

We would observe that there is a penny which agrees in every particular with that of 1722, previously described, except that it is without a date. We must conclude, therefore, that it was an unfinished pattern piece or counterfeit, which some speculator has had struck off; as we have heard of a number of such pieces in numismatical collections.

PENNY.

1733. *Device.*—A bust of George II.; head laureated, and facing in a reverse position to
    the others—left; the neck uncovered.
  Legend.—GEORGIUS II · D · G · REX ·
  Reverse.—ROSA · AMERICANA · 1733.
  Exergue.—UTILE · DULCI ·
    (Size 9. See Plate VII., Figure 10.)

ROSA AMERICANA.

LEGEND.

Year	Denomination	Legend	Types.	Varieties.
1722.	Penny.	GEORGIUS · D : G : MAG : BRI : FRA : ET HIB : REX ·	2	6
	Half-penny.	GEORGIUS · DEI · GRATIA · REX.	2	4
	Farthing.	" " " "	3	7
1723.	Penny.	The same as above.	2	4
	Half-penny.	" " "	2	5
	Farthing.	" " "	3	6
1733.	Penny.	GEORGIUS II. D· G REX.	1	1

Owing to the limited number of specimens of these coins which have been preserved in our cabinets, or are known and accessible, we can give only such information as an examination of them discloses.

The above types and varieties, the only attempt at a classification of them we have seen, may or may not be full, as we have no precedent or other means for deciding. We think it probable the number of the same may be increased, and hope that more light may be thrown upon this interesting coin by others.

In one of the varieties of the Rosa Americana half-penny of 1722, in our possession, the letter V is used instead of the modern U, thus: VTILE DVLCI; and the punctuation after ROSA AMERICANA in this piece is a rose of six dots.

The farthing we have described also varies from the ordinary pieces, of that denomination, of 1722; as, upon the latter, it reads on the obverse, GEORGIUS D: G., and on the reverse, ROSA· AMERI., thus making totally distinct types and varieties.

We have lately seen a farthing of the date of 1723, with the full blown rose upon the reverse, without the crown, the legend on the same not being abbreviated as is common on the farthings of that year; also, a half-penny of 1724, whose legend is ROSA· AMERI. These specimens are very rare.

The rose appears to have been a favorite emblem in both ancient and modern times. It was the flower of Venus, and was consecrated by Cupid to Harpocrates, the god of silence, and hence became, mythologically, his symbol.

In English history, in the feuds between the rival houses of York and Lancaster, the white rose was the badge of the former, and the red rose, of the latter.

During the reign of Henry VIII., a rose, surmounted by a crown, appeared upon the golden crown and the silver groat; under the reign of Edward VI., it embellished sixpences and shillings, and in the reigns of Elizabeth and James, it occupied one face of the golden angel — a coin bearing on the other face the figure of an angel,[1] which coin had different values under different princes, but which now is an imaginary sum or money of account, implying ten shillings sterling.

In the reigns of Charles I. and II., the rose was placed upon crowns, half-pence, and rupees — the latter an East Indian denomination of money — and upon the Irish black money; in the reign of George I., the rose, separately, and surmounted by the crown, occupied the reverse upon the "Rosa Americana;" in that of George II., it was continued upon the "Rosa Americana," and also beautified the crown, half-crown, shilling, and sixpence; in that of George IV., it held a place upon the crown and shilling, and it also now graces the beautiful crown piece of the present sovereign of Great Britain — Queen Victoria.

Of the British tokens, issued during the sixteenth and seventeenth centuries, forty of them bear the emblem of the rose; and the jottons or counters, issued at Nuremburgh during the reign of Charles V., have the rose upon the obverse.

The patent for the coining of the "Rosa Americana" was granted to one William Wood in 1722, who, in connection with Kingsnell Eyres, Esq., a Mr. Marsland, a

---

[1] Skinner says, the device was impressed upon it in allusion to an observation of Pope Gregory the Great, who, seeing some beautiful English youths in the market at Rome, asked who they were; being told they were Angli — English — he replied, they might rather be called angeli — angels.

COLONIAL COINS.

hardware dealer in Cornwall, and others, was engaged in the scheme for supplying the American colonies with a copper currency.

Wood also had a patent for Ireland, for what were denominated the "Wood half-pence." An investigation of the patent, growing out of the extreme cupidity of Wood, who, by attempting to defraud the people of Ireland, by making thirteen shillings out of a pound of copper or brass, which caused the total rejection by them of his issues, developed the fact, that the profits arising from this patent were to have been shared with the Duchess of Kendall, one of the frail, but captivating beauties, who reflected their radiance upon the character of George I.

This circumstance was too rich in material not to attract the particular attention of Dean Swift, who used it at the time to give point to some poetical effusions, and, consequently, to indulge in full his proclivity for satire.

The dies for the "Rosa Americana" were engraved in London, and the coin was struck off at the French 'Change in Hog Lane, sign of the "Seven Dials," by an engine that elevated and precipitated a weight upon the metal planchets when in a heated state, thought to be at the time the best method for coining bath metal of which it was composed.

Some of this coin was sent to New York, under the charge of a Mr. Winthrop, and though really very beautiful, it appears, as a speculation, to have been unsuccessful, for whatever may have been the fate of others in connection with it, it ruined Mr. Marsland, in whose cellar were found large quantities of it, which had not for a long time seen the light till thus exhumed.

The letters patent for the "Rosa Americana" specified pennies, half-pennies, and farthings, of the value of the coins of Great Britain. We have only been able to discover five types. The first series were issued in the reign of George I., in 1722; in 1723 the type was altered, as the descriptions and fac-similes show, by surmounting the rose with a crown.

It is stated that, in 1724, a full series of these coins were issued; but we have only been able to discover the farthing, rendering the emissions of the other denominations problematical.

The penny without date, we have noticed, we consider as a pattern piece of 1722; but the penny piece of 1733, which we have described, is a rare specimen of that coin issued in the reign of George II. Of this penny, we have never learned of the existence of but four specimens, which were, until lately, in the cabinets of England. For a fac-simile of it we are indebted to Snelling and Ruding, who derived it from the cabinet of Thomas Hollis, Esq., whose collection was sold at auction in London, on May 18th, 1817, when this piece brought the sum of £6, 6s.; another specimen in the collection of Marmaduke Trattle, Esq., commanded the sum of £3, 1s., in 1832; the third is in the celebrated collection of the British Museum, and the fourth was purchased in England for the sum of £7, or thirty-five dollars, for Charles J. Bushnell, Esq., of New York city, unfortunately placed on board of the steamer Arctic, to be transmitted to him, on her last and fatal voyage, and its pigmy proportions are now added to the vast accumulations that lie imbedded in the sands of the Atlantic ocean.

GRANBY COPPER.

Device.—A deer standing in a circle, and facing to the left. 1737.
Legend.—☞ W¹ALUE . ME . AS . YOU . PLEASE ⚹
Exergue.—III.

Reverse.—Three sledge-hammers, surmounted by a crown.
Legend.—☞ I . AM . GOOD . COPPER. ⁞⁞⋯⋰⋅⋅⁞⁞
Exergue.—1737.

(Size 8.)

Device.—A deer standing in a circle, and facing to the left.
Legend.—☞ CONNECTICUT.
Exergue.—III.

Reverse.—Three sledge-hammers, surmounted by a crown.
Legend.—☞ I . AM . GOOD . COPPER. ⁞⁞⋯⋰⋅⋅⁞⁞
Exergue.—1737.

(Size 8.)

Device.—A deer standing in a circle, and facing to the left.
Legend.—VALUE . ME . AS . YOU . PLEASE ⚹
Exergue.—III.

Reverse.—A broad-axe.
Legend.—☞ J . CUT . MY . WAY . THROUGH.
Exergue.—1737.

(Size 8.)

There is an issue precisely like the preceding, except that it is without a date.

Device.—A deer standing in a circle, and facing to the left. 1739.
Legend.—☞ VALUE . ME . AS . YOU . PLEASE.
Exergue.—III.

---

[1] Spelt in this single type as represented. Subsequent examples show it must have been an oversight; and that Connecticut, the home of Noah Webster, was not so defective in its orthography, as such a spelling would indicate, even before his appearance.

COLONIAL COINS.

Reverse.—Three sledge-hammers, surmounted by a crown.
Legend.—I . AM . GOOD . COPPER. ┊┊∴∴∴∴┊┊
(See Plate VII., Figures 11 and 12.)

Of this copper, there are five types, viz.:

Device.	Legend.	Date.
Three sledge-hammers.	Value me as you please.	1737.
" " "	Connecticut.	"
Broad-axe.	Value me as you please.	"
" "	" " " "	No date.
Three sledge-hammers.	" " " "	1739.

The similarity between these coppers is so great, that we denominate them without varieties. They were stamped upon planchets of the purest copper, and, in consequence, were in demand by goldsmiths for alloy.

The trade of a blacksmith, ever since Vulcan was engaged in forging thunderbolts, has given to the world some very remarkable men; and it affords us great pleasure, at this time, to be able to contribute toward immortalizing one of the craft, who not only devised, but manufactured a currency.

We have seen it stated, that Mr. Highley, the author of these coppers, was an ingenious blacksmith, who resided in the town of Granby, Connecticut—hence the name, "Granby Copper"—and that with all the notions of utility, which he naturally derived from the anvil, he was also ambitious of making a little fame for himself beside.

He has certainly left evidences of having been an artist, as well as a financier; for the creations of his genius and skill were, for the times, well executed, and they also became a currency. Subsequently, we are informed, his cupidity led him into the hazardous experiment of illegally imitating other's issues, which, being discovered, we regret to say, deprived him of a portion of the laurels that had previously encircled his brow.

These coppers bear the symbols of their origin, with a due regard to royalty on some of them—the sledge-hammers being surmounted by crowns—a something very apparent to the minds of the colonists, but which did not always command their sincere reverence.

These coins, at this time, grace but few cabinets, having been so generally impaired by wear—from being stamped upon unalloyed copper—as to be rarely found sufficiently perfect. We were favored by lately finding in New York city an electrotype which was perfect, but we were not so fortunate as to be able to trace it to the original.

PLATE VII.

COLONIAL COINS.

Having given one version of the origin of the Granby copper, we must not omit to state that the "learned professions" have a claim that its honor lies with them. This plain Mr. Highley, blacksmith, as we have denominated him, being, by another authority, transformed into an M. D., who, if he were the originator and manufacturer of these coins, evidenced a much greater proclivity for edge-tools than for Materia Medica.

FLORIDA PIECE.

Device.—The bust of Charles III. of Spain, facing to the right, the hair flowing in ringlets over the neck, and clothed in regal costume.   1760.
Legend.—CARLOS. III. D. G. HISPAN·· REX.
Reverse.—A large full-blown rose with leaf and bud, in a stem.
Legend.—JVAN · ESTEVAN · DE PENA · FLORIDA 1760.
(Size 9. See Plate VIII., Figure 1.)

This very curious, as well as interesting piece, is in silver, and is now in the cabinet of Joseph J. Mickley, Esq., of Philadelphia, who received it in the way of business as a half dollar; that being intrinsically about its value. It has naturally attracted much attention from those numismatologists who have become cognizant of its existence, and they have taken a deep interest in the origin of, and authority for, its emission; but the archives of Spain throw no light upon it.

It may have been designed as a currency for Florida, though the most natural construction we can put upon it is, that it was struck off as a medium between the colonial Governor and the Indians, it being known that titles were conferred, or commissions granted to their chiefs.

We have been informed that one of these commissions is now preserved in Florida, which was found carefully located in the pouch of an Indian chief who was shot. This commission denominated him the chief of the medal; and it indicates pretty clearly that if this piece was not designed as the emblem of an order of distinction among the aborigines, the Spaniards so applied it, after they became acquainted with their natural vanity.

We think a similar piece cannot be found in any other cabinet in our country.

PITT PIECE.

Device.—A bust intended for Pitt, in citizen's plain dress, and facing to the left; the hair in a cue.   1766.
Legend.—THE RESTORER OF COMMERCE.
Exergue.—NO STAMPS. 1766.
Reverse.—A ship under full sail, on the stern of which appears AMERICA.
Legend.—THANKS · TO · THE · FRIENDS · OF · LIBERTY · AND · TRADE.
(Size 8. See Plate VIII., Figure 2.)

The country was indebted to the ubiquitous patriotism of Colonel Paul Revere, of Boston, Massachusetts, for this medalet, who originated and designed it, the artist being, it is said, a Mr. Smithers, of Philadelphia.

The "stamp act" was passed March 22d, 1765, and repealed March 18th, 1766, through the instrumentality of Mr. Pitt, who maintained, with all his great ability and eloquence, that taxation was no part of the governing or legislative power which Parliament had a right to exert over the colonies; and concluded with a motion, "that the stamp act be repealed totally, absolutely, and immediately." The bill received the sanction of the king on the 18th day of March, the stamp act being upon the statute book a few days less than a year.

The admiration felt for Mr. Pitt, for the noble stand he had taken in behalf of the just rights of the colonists, led to the emission of this medalet, which was about the size of a quarter of a dollar, evidently gotten up with much haste, and composed of an inferior quality of brass. As an emblem of gratitude to Mr. Pitt, and a manifestation of popular feeling in the colonies, it possessed all the value that the purest gold could have conferred upon it.

The night after the passage of the "stamp act," Doctor Franklin, then in London, wrote to Charles Thompson: "The sun of liberty is set; you must light up the candles of industry and economy." Mr. Thompson replied: "Be assured we shall light up torches of quite another sort."

Nothing occurred in the history of the colonies that excited such a deep feeling of dissatisfaction, and united and determined opposition to the mother country, as the stamp act; and which continued not only unabatedly, but progressively, till its repeal. Everything was undertaken that genius could devise, or human will accomplish against it, except a resort to arms. Virginia first, and, afterwards, all the rest of the colonies, declared against the right of Great Britain to tax America.

It was this act that imbued Patrick Henry with the patriotic fire which gave rise to that memorable episode in the House of Burgesses of Virginia, in which he asserted that the king, in assenting to the act for taxing the colonies, had acted the part of a tyrant; and alluding to the fate of other tyrants, he exclaimed: "Cæsar had his Brutus, Charles I. his Cromwell, and George III."—he was interrupted by the cry of "treason" —pausing for a moment, he deliberately concluded—"may profit by their example; if this be treason, make the most of it."

Non-importation agreements were entered into; combinations formed against eating lamb, in order to increase the growth of wool, and among the ladies, renouncing every kind of luxury imported from Great Britain. This practical patriotism soon brought the mother country to its senses; and we venture to suggest, though by some it may be denominated "treason," that in the lack of Federal disposition to protect the industry of our country virtually against foreign taxation — similar measures, on the part of the people, would soon consolidate its industry, and restore it to real prosperity.

LOUISIANA COPPER.

Device.—A laurel wreath surmounted by a crown. An oval ring of dots enclosing
  the letters R. F., in the centre of the field.   1767.
Legend.—SIT NOMEN DOMINI BENEDICTUM +
Exergue.—1767.
Reverse.—Two sceptered fleurs crossed.
Legend.—COLONIES. FRANCOISES.
Inscription.—L   XV.
  (Size 8. See Plate VIII., Figure 3.)

This coin was gotten up in France by the Government for a copper currency, to be circulated in its Louisiana colonies, where it appears to have been stamped by the officials with the letters "R. F."— undoubtedly denoting royal favor — and for which the poor colonists were constrainedly thankful; having no means of ameliorating their condition but by apparent gratitude for every aid extended to them, and prompt submission to the royal authority.

Of this coin there is but one type; that is composed of good copper, and well executed. It is a rare piece, and occupies a prominent place among the mementos of the past, in both France and Louisiana.

VIRGINIA HALF-PENNY.

Device.—Bust of George III., neck uncovered, head laureated, facing to the right,
  and the hair in a cue behind.   1773.
Legend.—GEORGIVS III. REX.
Reverse.—Arms in an ornamented shield, surmounted by a crown: First, impaling
  Scotland; second, France; third, Ireland; fourth, the Electoral Dominions.
Legend.—VIRGINIA — divided by the shield.
Exergue.—1773 — divided by the crown.
  (Size 7. See Plate VIII., Figure 4.)

SILVER HALF-PENNY.   1774.

The design the same.   (Size 7. See Plate VIII., Figure 5.)

Of the former, our information extends to six types, and of the latter, two. They are as follows:

1773. VIRGINIA COPPER HALF-PENNY.

1. *Legend.*—{ Georgius III Rex
{ Georgius III Rex—large planchet.
2. " Georgius III. Rex.
3. " Georgius III· Rex.
4. " Georgius. III. Rex.
5. " Georgius· III· Rex·
6. " Georgius · III · Rex .

1774. SILVER HALF-PENNY.

1. *Legend.*—Georgius III Rex
2. " Georgius · III · Rex ·

These types are determined by the punctuation. That which has heretofore been denominated the Virginia penny, is nothing more than the type No. 1, struck upon a somewhat larger and thicker planchet, which occurs in no other type we have seen. The reverse being the same in all, there is no basis for varieties.

These beautifully designed coins of copper and silver made their appearance according to date, were struck off in England, and designed for circulation in the Virginia colony. We can find no authority for their being of Governmental origin, and therefore incline to the opinion that, by the tacit consent of the authorities, they were the result of individual enterprise.

The obverse is an exact copy of the gold coins of that period of time. The silver coins are very rare, but the copper are frequently met with among those now-in circulation; their generally imperfect preservation, however, rendering them undesirable for cabinet collections. They were gotten up with an imperfect edge, and thicker in the centre, and hence have been the victims of serious abrasion.

Some few years since, a quantity of these copper coins was dug up from the summit of the hill, on which the college now stands at Knoxville, Tennessee; and quite a number were exhumed from a locality near Easton, Pennsylvania, showing that they must have been extensively circulated, and have amply rewarded the projectors.

From a paper read before the Historical Society of Maryland by S. F. Streeter, Esq., we learn, "that in November, 1645, the Governor, Council, and Burgesses, having maturely weighed and considered how advantageous a quoine current would be for the colony, and the great wants and miseries that do happen unto it by the sole dependency upon tobacco, resolved to take Spanish pieces of eight at six shillings, and other

Spanish coins in proportion; and to introduce coins of copper from a colonial mint into circulation.

"The people were, therefore, forbidden to use tobacco any longer as a circulating medium, and it was determined to coin pieces of the value of two, three, six, and nine-pence, for general use, to be redeemed by the public, in case it should become, from any cause, not current. On each coin there were to be two rings, one for a motto, and the other to receive an impression, which was to be changed every year. The appointment of a mint-master general, to superintend this formidable emission of copper, completed the grand financial measure of the day.

"Whether it was ever carried into effect we are not informed; but if it was, the conflicting legislation, the various expedients, and the depressed condition of the colony in after years, show that the new issue neither supplied the place of tobacco, nor met the wants of the community for purposes of convenience or traffic."

This is not the only instance in the history of the colonies, in which necessity prompted a project for a currency which proved to be impracticable.

WASHINGTON PIECE.

Device.—Thirteen oval dotted rings, in each of which is impressed one of the thirteen United States; and in the centre of the field are the initials "G. W." 1776.
Legend.—LONG LIVE THE PRESIDENT, in circular form around the "G. W."
Reverse.—Smooth.

(Size 10. See Plate VIII., Figure 6.)

This "piece" has been carefully preserved in a number of cabinets, and has been deemed rare. I have therefore described it, in order to dissipate the illusion that has heretofore existed in relation to it. It is simply a button manufactured in England, thus ornamented to flatter the pride of the Americans, and thereby assure large sales and a profitable speculation.

On June 12th, 1855, a piece was sold in this city, denominated the Franklin penny, at a large price. On the obverse, it bore the bust of Franklin, cap on the head, and below the bust, "BALE," with a dog stamped in front of the bust.

An old Revolutionary soldier lately informed us, that in his youth, large brass and copper buttons, bearing on their exterior surface the bust and name of distinguished men, were worn upon overcoats. The "Washington piece" was quite commonly in use, but was then what it was designed to be, a button. We regret exceedingly that we are compelled to deal thus summarily with what otherwise might have contributed much pleasure to those who are the possessors of what, at this time, may be deemed at least a very remarkable button.

COLONIAL COINS.

It is thus established, that the love of gain overrides in many breasts every other sentiment; for foreign manufacturers and designers have not hesitated, at all times, to reflect upon themselves and their country, by placing upon their wares and merchandise any patriotic emblem or motto which they supposed would contribute to our pride or gratification, and, at the same time, fill their pockets.

CONTINENTAL CURRENCY.

1776. *Device.*—The rising sun reflecting its rays upon a dial, with the word FUGIO at the left side.
Legend.—MIND YOUR BUSINESS.
Exergue.—CONTINENTAL CURRENCY, 1776, with a circle or ring around the edge.
Reverse.—Thirteen small circles, connected like the links of a chain, in each of which is inscribed the name of one of the thirteen original States of the Union.
Legend.—AMERICAN CONGRESS — in a ring — central to the thirteen — and in the centre of the same — WE ARE ONE.
(Size 12. See Plate VIII., Figure 7.)

There were two distinct types of this "continental currency," and five varieties. In one variety the letter R is added in the inner circle; on the reverse, AMER^N CONGRESS instead of AMERICAN CONGRESS.

By whomever designed, this coin or medal unburdened the patriotic genius of some one, and it was eminently worthy of the glorious period whose date it bears. It was in itself a treatise, in the then condition of our country, in behalf of liberty; and contrasted now with the more artistic, but much less vigorous, designs upon the present coinage of our national mint, is worthy of imitation.

Our forefathers neglected no opportunity which offered for stimulating the patriotism of the people; for their coins and paper money bore emblems and mottoes calculated to inspire love of country and love of liberty in the every day relations of both business and pleasure, of which money was, as now, the medium.

With all our admiration for this coin or medal, we have not been able to determine that it was designed for, or that it became to any great extent, a currency. As it made its appearance only in white metal, the idea is strengthened thereby that it was in reality a medal, struck off to commemorate the bold, fearless, and patriotic acts of the Congress that declared our country a free and independent nation.

COLONIAL COINS.

JANUS COPPER.

Device.—A head with inverted faces. 1776.
Legend.—STATE OF MASSA: ½ D.
Reverse.—The Goddess of Liberty seated on the globe, holding in her right hand the liberty pole, and in the left the scales, emblematic of justice.
Exergue.—1776.
(Size 6. See Plate VIII., Figure 8.)

Janus, the son of Apollo, went to Italy, where he planted a colony and founded a town, which he named Janiculum. He is represented, as is well known, with two faces, because, by the ancients, he was believed to be capable of relating all things of the past, and revealing everything in regard to the future. Hence, with the endowment of supernatural power, he was accepted by the Romans for a god, worshipped as such, and had a temple erected in his name, which was never closed except in a time of universal peace. History informs us, that it was closed but three times in a period of upwards of seven hundred years, during which time the Romans were engaged almost incessantly in war.

This coin is in the collection of M. A. Stickney, Esq., of Salem, Massachusetts, to whom we are indebted for a fac-simile, and who informs us, that the die was gotten up and cut by the distinguished mechanic, patriot, and gentleman, Colonel Paul Revere, of Boston; that he thinks it was designed for a currency, the value, half-pence, being impressed upon it, and that the head on the obverse was supposed to refer to the Whig and Tory parties of 1776. This is probably the only specimen of this coin to be found in our country, and it is consequently very rare and valuable.

Janus upon an American coin invites speculation. As representing the Whig and Tory parties, it was truthful, for they looked different ways.

Could the idea have been suggested, however, from the planting a colony and founding a town? The principles of liberty at this time — 1776 — were planted, which resulted in the founding of an independent nation. That may have induced the idea, though we are inclined to think that its application was exclusively to the Tories; as they looked one way, and thus attempted to disguise the fact that they were operating in a contrary direction; so that with fair protestations in behalf of the liberty of the colonies, that sterling patriot, Colonel Revere, saw that Janus was their prototype, and hence his effigy was a fit emblem for a device illustrative of the fact, and the Goddess of Liberty on the reverse, as the antidote or true symbol of devotion.

COLONIAL COINS.

MASSACHUSETTS COPPERS.

1776. *Device.*—The pine tree.
Legend.—AMERICAN : LIBERTY :
Reverse.—A harp.
(Size 8. See Plate VIII., Figure 9.)

Device.—The American eagle, standing with extended wings — as if about to leave it — upon a crown. Around the margin thirteen stars.
Reverse.—A large shield, surrounded by thirteen stars.
(Size 7. See Plate VIII., Figure 10.)

We are indebted to M. A. Stickney, Esq., previously referred to, for fac-similes of the above described coins, who ventures the opinion, that they were also designed and executed by Colonel Revere, of Boston. They are certainly novel to us, and aid much in developing the character and variety of the currency in circulation among, and the patriotic impulses that governed, the people of Massachusetts at that time.

They were substantial indexes to the mother country of the determination of the colonists to set up for themselves — pine trees, eagles, &c., being no part of the insignia of royalty.

PINE TREE COPPER.

1776. *Device.*—A pine tree in the centre of the field.
Legend.—MASSACHUSETTS STATE.
Reverse.—A female seated on a globe, holding in her right hand an olive leaf, in her left, a staff.
Legend.—LIBERTY AND VIRTUE.
Exergue.—1776.
(Size 9. See Plate VIII., Figure 11.)

By some, for want of particular history, such coins as this have been denominated medals. We think, however, in the absence of the needful currency, they were originated and prepared as a speculation — the captivating legends often rendering them acceptable for preservation ; and, in the matter of a copper, not much discrimination or querulousness being manifested in regard to their reception as change.

This coin, a description of which appeared in the tenth number of the "Historical Magazine and Notes and Queries," over the initials J. G., in whose collection it has a place, is otherwise unknown, so far as we have been able to learn, to numismatologists; and, therefore, may be properly esteemed as both rare and valuable. It is of course made of copper, as its title indicates, and is nearly of the size of a half dollar.

PLATE. VIII.

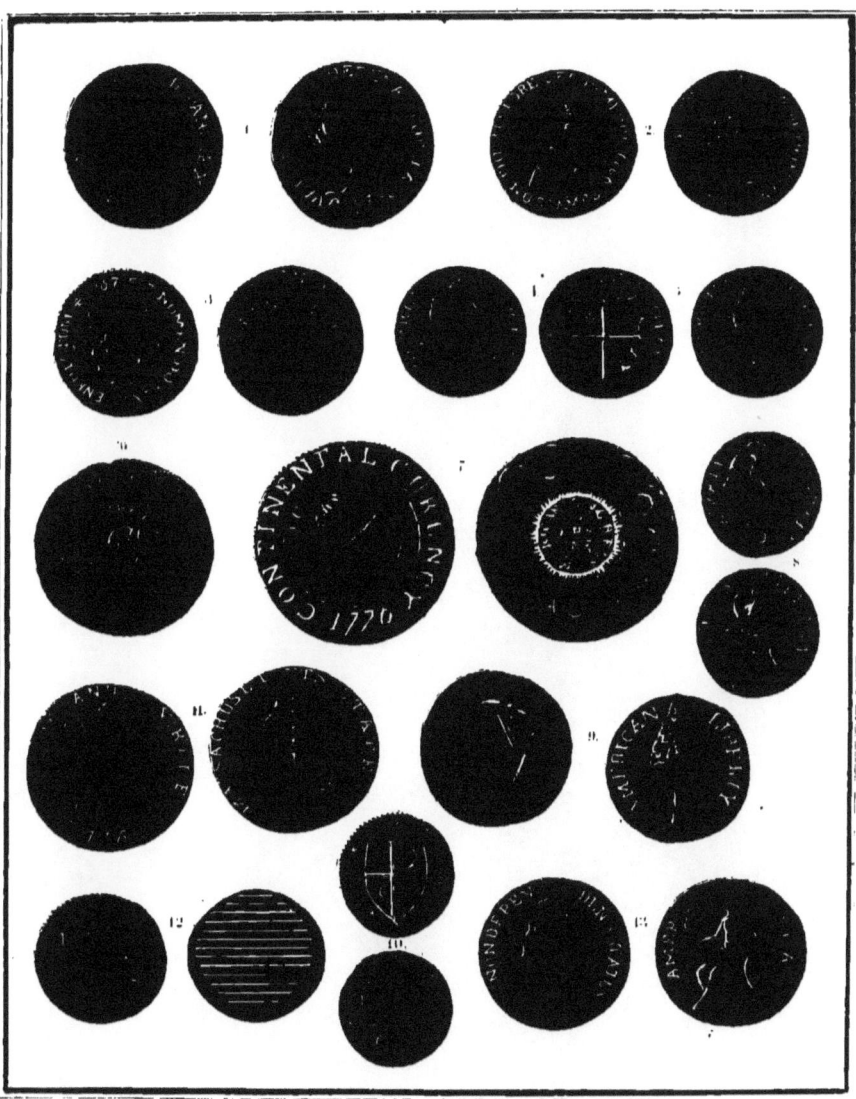

COLONIAL COINS.

U. S. A. COPPER.

Device.—Thirteen bars which run parallel to, and equidistant from, each other—typical of the thirteen United colonies or States.
Reverse.—The letters U. S. A.
(Size 7. See Plate VIII., Figure 12.)

One other emission, precisely the same. (Size 6.)

Of the above coppers, there is but a single type and two varieties. They bear no date. It is asserted by some, they were issued in 1776—favoring the idea, that the issue of a coinage at this time was intended as an endorsement of the Declaration of American Independence; by others, that they made their appearance in 1783—the year of its recognition by Great Britain.

They were, at any rate, merely a private enterprise, and we have learned, satisfactorily to ourselves, that they were really gotten up and struck off in Cherry street, in Philadelphia.

As this location is the birthplace of the "Washington cent of 1791," it looks a little as if the Mr. Harper, therewith so prominently connected, might possibly have paid some attention to the art of coining, before the period when he became so famous.

NON. DEPEN-DENS. STATUS.

Device.—A bust, facing to the right, hair plain and flowing, resembling an Indian chief. On the shoulder, in a small circle, is a flag and sword crossed, and 1778. in the angle, thus formed, are four fleur-de-lis—arms of France. On the breast is a small head with wings extending half-way up toward the shoulder.
Legend.—NON · DEPEN-DENS · STATUS ·
Reverse.—Full length figure of an Indian seated on a globe, around his loins an apron of feathers; in his right hand he holds a bunch of tobacco leaves, in the left a shield, on which is the American flag and a sword crossed, and in each angle, formed thereby, a fleur-de-lis, same as on the shoulder-knot on the obverse.
Legend.—AMERICA.
Exergue.—1778.
(Size 8. See Plate VIII., Figure 13.)

An engraved piece, so elaborately designed as was this, we are sorry to say, is without a history. It certainly must have thoroughly taxed the powers of design of some one, to combine so many emblems, and, at the same time too, so suggestive of facts and ideas, upon a single copper.

In the absence, however, of authoritative emissions of a currency, nothing more natural than that the field of speculation for supplying it should have been occupied with every variety of an article which could meet the public taste, and thus open the way for a more important result, which, for many of these copper emissions, was fully realized.

We found this specimen in the cabinet of Mr. Howard, of the city of New York, and it is the only one of the kind we have seen.

NOVA CONSTELLATIO.

1788. *Device.*—An eye, symbolical of Supreme power, reflecting its rays upon thirteen six-pointed stars, emblematic of the States of the confederacy; and a single four-pointed star out of their circular line — the punctuation.
Legend.—NOVA · CONSTELATIO ✤
Reverse.—A laurel wreath, enclosing the letters U · S
Legend.—·LIBERTAS ⚭ JUSTITIA ·
Exergue.—1783.
(Size 8.—Copper. See Plate IX., Figure 5.)

Of the pieces issued in this year, we have found three types and five varieties; the former of which may be distinguished by the punctuation of the legend on the obverse, as follows:

Type 1.— ✤ NOVA · CONSTELATIO
" 2.— ★ NOVA · CONSTELLATIO
" 3.— ✱ NOVA · CONSTELLATIO

In Type 1, the points of the rays terminate bluntly.

1788. *Device.*—An eye, symbolical of Supreme power, reflecting its rays upon thirteen six-pointed stars, emblematic of the States of the confederacy.
Legend.—NOVA CONSTELLATIO ∴
Reverse.—A wreath, enclosing the letters U. S and 1000.
Legend.—·LIBERTAS · JUSTITIA.
Exergue.—1783.
(Size 8½.—Silver. See Plate IX., Figure 2.)

Another, same as the preceding, except that the mint-mark is a flower with three leaves, and 500 is enclosed in the wreath instead.

Exergue.—1783.
(Size 7.—Silver. See Plate IX., Figure 3.)

Device.—An eye, symbolical of Supreme power, reflecting its rays upon thirteen six-pointed stars, emblematic of the States of the confederacy.   1785.
Legend.—NOVA CONSTELLATIO
Reverse.—The figure of Justice seated, supporting with her right hand a flag-staff, surmounted by the liberty cap — the flag drooping over the arm — and holding the scales in her left.
Legend.—IMMUNE COLUMBIA ·
Exergue.—1785.
    (Size 7.—Silver. See Plate IX., Figure 4.)

Device.—An eye, symbolical of Supreme power, reflecting its rays upon thirteen six-pointed stars, emblematic of the States of the confederacy.   1785.
Legend.—NOVA CONSTELLATIO
Reverse.—The figure of Justice seated, supporting with her right hand a flag-staff, surmounted by the liberty cap — the flag drooping over the arm — and holding the scales in the left.
Legend.—IMMUNE COLUMBIA.
Exergue.—1785.
    (Size 7.—Gold. See Plate IX., Figure 1.)

The first of the pieces we have described, and represented by figure 5, in plate 9, is of copper; those by the figures 2 and 3, same plate, were of silver, and formerly belonged to Charles Thomson[1] — a contemporary and particular friend of Benjamin Franklin — who was a very decided advocate of the just rights of the colonies, and distinguished himself greatly by his uniform patriotism.

They were discovered, after the death of his son, which occurred, we are informed, some fifteen years ago, near Newark, Delaware, in the secret drawer of an old desk that formerly belonged to the father.

They are now in the possession of a gentleman of this city, who values them very highly, not only as memorials of the past, but for their direct association with one of those noble men, whose visions were never obscured by anything that was, or could be, interposed between them and their country.

---

[1] Mr. Thomson was born in Ireland, in 1729, and came to America when eleven years of age. He was chosen Secretary of the first Congress, assembled in Philadelphia, the duties of which he continued to discharge with great reputation to himself, and advantage to his country, until the close of the war. He assisted in the organization of the new government after the adoption of the Constitution, and was the person deputed to inform Washington of his nomination to the Presidency. Washington wished to retain him in the service of his country, but in his own words, "the suitable hour for his retirement had come." It is asserted, that he began the opposition to the "stamp act" in Pennsylvania. His death occurred in 1824.— *Encyclopædia Americana*, vol. xii.

COLONIAL COINS.

That represented by figure 4, plate 9, is also of silver; it is in the cabinet of Joseph J. Mickley, Esq., of this city, and is very rare.

The last described — to be found in Plate IX., figure 1 — is of gold, and is in the United States Mint of Philadelphia.

These coins were also struck off in brass. Of the silver, there are specimens in different collections of coins in New York and Boston; those of copper are common. They were undoubtedly gotten up in England, with special reference to being circulated in this country, and we have no doubt, relative to their being an American enterprise. The U. S., prominent upon the reverse, does not give them a claim to have been of home manufacture.

They were a success, being extensively circulated throughout the country at that time; but by whom issued, has ever remained a mystery. Mr. Felt, who possessed unusual facilities, and improved them, for investigating the currency of Massachusetts, where they first made their appearance, says: "I am unable to find any authority for their issue, though they are connected with the earliest remembrances and enjoyments of many now alive." This was about twenty years ago.

We have examined several hundred specimens of the copper coins, but have found but three types and five varieties for this year. The types can be determined by the number of lines making a point in the rays of the meridian sun. In that, which we designate as the first type, there are seven lines, and in the second, but five. There does not appear to have been any issue of these coins in 1784. The gold and silver coinage presents but a single type and two varieties.

NOVA CONSTELATIO.

1785. *Device.*—An eye, symbolical of Supreme power, reflecting its rays upon thirteen six-pointed stars, emblematic of the States of the confederacy.
Legend.—NOVA CONSTELATIO
Reverse.—A laurel wreath, enclosing the letters U. S.
Legend.—·LIBERTAS ET JUSTITIA·
Exergue.—1785.
(Size 8. See Plate IX., Figure 6.)

Of the copper coin issued in 1785, I have found three types and seven varieties. The types may be distinguished by the non-punctuation or punctuation of the legend on the obverse, thus:

Type 1.—NOVA CONSTELATIO
" 2.—NOVA. CONSTELLATIO ✦
" 3.—NOVA ✦ CONSTELLATIO.

Type 2 also differs from the others by the outer ends of the points or rays of the meridian sun terminating bluntly, while those that tend to the centre are pointed, thus changing the aspect of the blaze. Between each of the large points there are two smaller ones, making in all, thirty-nine points.

The dates of these coins can be determined, when obliterated, by observing that the legend on the obverse of those of 1783, reads, LIBERTAS JUSTITIA, and on those of 1785, ·LIBERTAS ET JUSTITIA· — the legend having but one L, thus: in CONSTELATIO.

GEORGIUS TRIUMPHO.

Device.—A bust, the head laureated, and facing to the right.   1783.
Legend.—GEORGIVS TRIUMPHO .
Reverse.—The Goddess of Liberty erect, facing to the left — holding a laurel branch in the right hand, and supporting the liberty pole with the left. In front of the figure, a frame, with fleur-de-lis at each corner, and on the field of the same, thirteen stripes, emblematic of the thirteen United States.
Legend.—VOCE POPOLI
Exergue.—1783.
                 (Size 8. See Plate IX., Figure 7.)

Of this copper, known as the "Tory penny." we have found only one type and three varieties.

It has a history. From the head of the bust, being an effigy of George III., and the legend, GEORGIVS TRIUMPHO, much hostility was manifested toward it at the time of its appearance; the lingering evidences of which still prevail among those who possess or see it, the legend being supposed to refer to the triumph of George, the king, instead of George, the patriot.

There being, at the time of its issue, no victory for his British majesty, but, on the contrary, the greatest triumph that has ever been achieved by man for his race, the acknowledgement of our national independence, no basis exists for prejudice against this harmless copper, not purely constructive.

Gotten up in England, it is said to have made its first appearance in this country in Georgia, though we have found no evidence to show that it was designed for exclusive circulation in that State; which we are informed, unfortunately contained an undue proportion of the partizans of the British monarchy and its king — a circumstance calculated to excite and strengthen the impression that it was designed at least to reflect upon the triumph of the Revolutionary cause.

We are informed, the feeling ran so high in Virginia and elsewhere against it, that many of them were mutilated and destroyed. We must, however, relieve the Tories of Georgia, of that day, of any connection or complicity with either its origin or circulation.

It is related of this unhappy class, that, about this time, it emigrated in a body to the Island of Jamaica, since which, those composing it have incurred by their sins — moral and physical — a condition of degeneracy which must ultimately result in their total extinction. A portion, perhaps the entire remnant of them, finally found a home at Key West, where they are known by the name of "conchs"—mere wreckers and fishermen, picking up a precarious living, and who, by isolation and close intermarriage, are as distinguished for very moderate physical power and mental ability, as the lowest of the human species anywhere.

In regard to the effigy upon this coin, it is not the only instance in the colonial currency, as this work discloses, where either carelessness, ignorance, or the want of something more appropriate, has given us a fac-simile of the head of George III., as represented upon British coins; but, in our opinion, not designed to have any intended connection with the then living original, the numerals being left out, and thereby rendering the head as applicable in intention to George Washington as George De Este or Guelph.

Further, the Goddess of Liberty with the pole, and the thirteen stripes — emblematic, clearly, at that date, of the States of the Union — were too distinctive of a fact that could not be ignored, to suppose that royalty or Toryism would adopt as emblems such distasteful evidences of their own humiliation. We trust then we have established the claim of the GEORGIUS TRIUMPHO to equal favor with its associate colonial coins.

MARYLAND.

ANAPOLIS SHILLING.

1783. *Device.*—A wreath enclosing two hands clasped.
Legend.—J. CHALMERS . ANAPOLIS.
Reverse.—In the field the figures of two birds, with a bough in their beaks.
Legend.—ONE SHILLING.
Exergue.—1783.
(Size 5. See Plate IX., Figure 8.)

ANAPOLIS SIXPENCE.

Device.—A wreath enclosing two hands clasped.
Legend.—J CHALMERS ANAPOLIS.
Reverse.—In the field the figures of two birds, with a bough in their beaks.
Legend.—SIX PENCE.
Exergue.—1783.
(Size 4. See Plate IX., Figure 9.)

COLONIAL COINS.

ANAPOLIS THREE-PENCE.

Device.—A wreath enclosing two hands clasped.
Legend.—J CHALMERS ANAPOLIS.
Reverse.—In the field the figures of two birds, with a bough in their beaks.
Legend.—THREE-PENCE.
Exergue.—1783.
(Size 2. See Plate IX., Figure 10.)

The above described coins were very well executed in sterling silver, and were issued by J. Chalmers, Annapolis, Maryland, as an individual speculation. From being seldom met with in cabinet collections, it is inferred their circulation was not very extensive. They, however, show to what difficulties the people were driven for a currency, and the creditable enterprise that sought to relieve them.

WASHINGTON CENT.

Device.—The bust of Washington in military costume, a star upon the epaulet, head laureated, and facing to the left, and the hair formed into a cue behind. 1783.
Legend.—WASHINGTON AND INDIPENDENCE.
Exergue.—1783. The edge grained.
Reverse.—The Goddess of Liberty seated, holding in the right hand the olive branch, and in the left the liberty pole, surmounted by the cap.
Exergue.—" T. W. I." in small capitals on the left, and K. S. on the right hand side.
(Size 8. See Plate XII., Figure 2.)

Device.—The bust of Washington in military costume, plain epaulet and buttons on the coat, head laureated, and facing to the left, and the hair formed into a cue behind.
Legend.—WASHINGTON.
Exergue.—An oblong star of eight points.
Reverse.—Same as the obverse — bust of Washington, &c.
Legend.—ONE CENT.
Exergue.—An oblong star of eight points.
(Size 7. See Plate XIII., Figure 2.)

Of these coins we have found but the single types as described, and no varieties. The latter is without date, but as it appeared at the same time with the former, it is assumed to have been issued in the same year. The former, from the letters "T. W. I." and K. S. upon it, not only indicates a private enterprise, but a copartnership, so that the latter conforms in appearance more to a design for a regular currency.

Their origin is undoubtedly distinct, and though we have presented them under one head, "Washington cents," which name collectors and others seem disposed to give them, their claim to the same rests exclusively upon the adoption of the bust of Washington as a device.

The fair inference is, that these cents or tokens were gotten up by American speculators in England, who, aware of the want of a currency, looked to the successful introduction of this at a large profit. This was undoubtedly realized, for there was such a scarcity of small change, that everything of that character was available. This state of affairs continued; as three years later, 1786, we find Massachusetts establishing her second mint, because she finds she cannot rely upon Congress for an adequate coinage.

It appears that previous to 1783, there had been a lull both in the importation and manufacture of money, owing to some of the States having resorted to legislation for its suppression, in consequence of quantities of base coins making their appearance in circulation among the people, upon whom the loss must ultimately fall, they being issued without any known or avowed responsibility. The following action in Pennsylvania upon this subject will illustrate it:

"Whereas divers ill-disposed persons have manufactured or imported into the States, quantities of base metals, in the semblance of British half-pence and other coins, but much inferior in value and weight to the genuine, to the great depreciation of those coin, thereby oppressing the community in general and the poor in particular — such practices having a natural tendency to raise the necessaries of life, and introduce new confusions into the currency of the country,

"We have, therefore, thought proper to prohibit, and do, hereby, strictly enjoin on all officers, employed in the receipt of taxes or other public dues, not to receive such base coins in any payment whatsoever, and to earnestly recommend to all faithful inhabitants of this State, to refuse it in payment, and by all other lawful means and ways discourage the currency thereof; and we do, in a special manner, direct any, and all Magistrates, Sheriffs and other officers within this State, to make enquiry after offenders in the premises, that they may be brought to a speedy and condign punishment.

"Given by order of the Counsil, under my hand, and the less seal of the State of Pennsylvania, the 14th day of July in the year of our Lord 1781.

JOSEPH REED, President.　　　　　　　　　　ALBERT Y. MATLACK, Scct.

COLONIAL COINS.

WASHINGTON TOKEN.

Device.—The bust of Washington, with the head laureated, and facing to the left. 1783.
Legend.—WASHINGTON AND INDEPENDENCE.
Exergue.—1783.
Reverse.—A wreath of laurel enclosing the words "ONE CENT."
Legend.—UNITY STATES OF AMERICA.
Exergue.—₁⁰⁰⁰
     (Size 8. See Plate XII., Figure 1.)

This coin is known among some by the name of the "Unity cent"—called so for the purpose of distinguishing it from others, bearing the bust of Washington, of the same date.

Like all others whose origin is unknown, it has been the subject of much speculation, it being the pleasure of numismatologists to have a coin accompanied with a *truthful* history. Relative to this piece then, we can offer nothing not purely conjectural, or of a very uncertain tradition.

By some it is thought to have been designed and gotten up by Benjamin Franklin while in France, for circulation in America. It is stated too, with more probability, that it was gotten up and struck off by one John Kean, a dealer in coins, in Philadelphia, and that some, if not the whole of them, were moulded in fine sand, instead of being stamped. We incline decidedly to the latter opinion, because Philadelphia was at one time the parent of much unauthorized coin. We have never seen this coin in anything but brass.

Device.—The bust of Washington in the Roman toga, head laureated, and facing
   to the left. 1783.
Legend.—WASHINGTON & INDIPENDENCE.
Exergue.—1783.
Reverse.—The Goddess of Liberty seated, holding in her right hand the olive branch, and
   supporting by her left the liberty pole, surmounted by the cap.
Legend.—UNITED STATES
     (Size 8. See Plate XIII., Figure 1.)

This coin occurs frequently in copper, and in the cabinet of Joseph J. Mickley, Esq., of Philadelphia, we have found it in silver.

COLONIAL COINS.

CONFEDERATIO COPPER.

1785. *Device.*—Thirteen radiating points, in the centre of which there are thirteen small stars.
Legend.—CONFEDERATIO.
Reverse.—An Indian chief, holding in his left hand a bow, in the right an arrow, and from the back depends a quiver. Standing at the right hand is an altar.
Legend.—AMERICANA INIMICA TYRANS.
Exergue.—1785.
(Size 8. See Plate IX., Figure 11.)

This copper is not only interesting in itself, but because it is very rare; the specimen of which, in the cabinet of Charles J. Bushnell, Esq., of New York city, is probably the only one in America.

It is well executed; and its peculiar rarity has induced us to conclude that it was a pattern piece, gotten up at the same time with the "Nova Constellatio" in England. This, however, is mere conjecture, as it may possibly have been as extensively circulated as some others, but not as highly favored in regard to its general preservation. Our opinion is, that all these coins subserved a very useful purpose in their day, and though not a legally established, were still a tolerated currency.

VERMONT.

VERMONTS. RES. PUBLICA.

1785. *Device.*—An eye, symbolical of Supreme power, reflecting its rays upon thirteen six-pointed stars, emblematic of the States of the confederacy.
Legend.—QUARTA · DECIMA · STELLA ·
Reverse.—The sun rising from behind the mountains; in the foreground a plow.
Legend.—VERMONTS · RES · PUBLICA ·
Exergue.—1785.
(Size 8. See Plate IX., Figure 12.)

VERMONTENSIUM. RES. PUBLICA.

1786. *Device.*—An eye, symbolical of Supreme power, reflecting its rays upon thirteen six-pointed stars, emblematic of the States of the confederacy.
Legend.—QUARTA · DECIMA · STELLA ·
Reverse.—The sun rising from behind the mountains; in the foreground a plow.
Legend.—VERMONTENSIUM · RES · PUBLICA ·
Exergue.—1786.
(Size 8. See Plate IX., Figure 13.)

Nothing could be more beautifully expressive than the device upon these coins. A supreme overruling power had truly cast the rays of approval upon the thirteen infant States of the American confederacy, in their contest for liberty and the just rights of humanity, against the then, as now, leading power of the world. The rays of Omnipotence protected them, and finally led them from vassalage to victory.

The reverse upon these coins is equally appropriate; the sun, emblematic of rising liberty, even beyond the distant mountains, and that implement of husbandry and emblem of peace — the plow — in the field beneath.

Of the "Vermonts. Res. Publica," 1785, there were two types and six varieties, the reflected rays on the obverse being in one pointed, and in the other obtuse; the device the same. The "Vermontensium. Res. Publica," but one type and no variety. This currency bears the unmistakable impress of an American mind: it was well executed upon good copper, and also in an inferior metal. They are now quite valuable, because it is difficult to procure perfect specimens.

In 1785, the legislature of Vermont granted to Reuben Harmon, Jr., the right to coin the copper money, we have been describing, for the period of two years. The mint for this operation was established in the town of Rupert.

In 1786, the legislature extended Harmon's right to coin these coppers for eight years, from July, 1787. Harmon's association under the original grant, consisting of three others beside himself, added to it, under the extension, some half a dozen others. Thus organized, they agreed upon two mints or places for the manufacture of their coins; one at Rupert, above named, in Bennington county, and the other, near "the great pond" in the county of Ulster.

The subsequent emission of 1788 undoubtedly wound up the coining operations of this association.

VERMON. AUCTORI.

Device.—A bust in a coat of mail, head laureated. 1787.
Legend.—VERMON AUCTORI.
Reverse.—The Goddess of Liberty seated, holding in her right hand the liberty pole, and in her left, the olive branch.
Legend.—INDE ET LIB.
Exergue.—1787.
(Size 7 and 8. See Plate IX., Figure 15.)

Of the emission of this coin, we have only been able to discover three types and five varieties, which indicate that they made their appearance so late in this year, as to be superseded in a measure by the large coinage of 1788. In this way we account for their scarcity. The types and varieties were as follows:

COLONIAL COINS.

Types.	Position.	Decoration.	Varieties.
1. VERMON AUCTORI	Left	Laureated	3
2. VERMON. AUCTORI	Right	"	1
3. VERMON AUCTORI ·	"	"	1

TORY COPPER.

1785. *Device.*—The bust of George III., head laureated, and facing to the right.
Legend.—GEORGIVS III. REX.
Reverse.—The Goddess of Liberty seated, holding in her right hand the liberty pole, surmounted by the cap, from which droops over the right shoulder the flag, and in the left the scales of justice.
Legend.—IMMUNE . COLUMBIA·
Exergue.—1785.
(Size 8. See Plate X., Figure 1.)

Two years after the acknowledgment of our independence by Great Britain, this coin — from the date — was thrust in some way upon republican America. It is peculiar that there should have been such persistence in doing what, at that time, could not have been agreeable to the mass of the people; and, then, in the designs — assuming a connection between George III. and the Goddess of Liberty — is an act difficult to be either comprehended or accommodated.

There may have been, as undoubtedly there were, partizans of the British monarchy then living — in fact, we have heard of such specimens of mankind — with whom it was a difficult task to appreciate the blessings of self-government; but the feelings or designs of such would hardly have exhibited themselves by the effigy of George III., on the obverse of a coin, and the Goddess of Liberty, with the liberty pole, cap, and scales of justice, on the reverse. Certain it is, that, at that day, there was much less connection between the British monarchy and liberty than now, when such emblems as the latter would not be tolerated. Hence, we are at a loss to comprehend the origin or motive for the coinage or issue of this piece. There, in the plate, however, is the fac-simile, speaking for itself, awakening associations and inviting speculations of the past.

When we contemplate our condition as a nation and a people now, with what it was at the date of this coin — 1785 — and previously, under the old confederated government — involved in debt; with the discontent that preceded the disbanding of the army, when it became necessary for Washington to preface his answer to its clamors by — after first wiping his spectacles — uttering the talismanic words: "My eyes have grown dim in the service of my country, but I never doubted her justice;" and the great dissatisfaction for want of immediate or undeveloped resources of every kind, which begat, and subsequently, openly showed itself in portions of New England — we

PLATE IX.

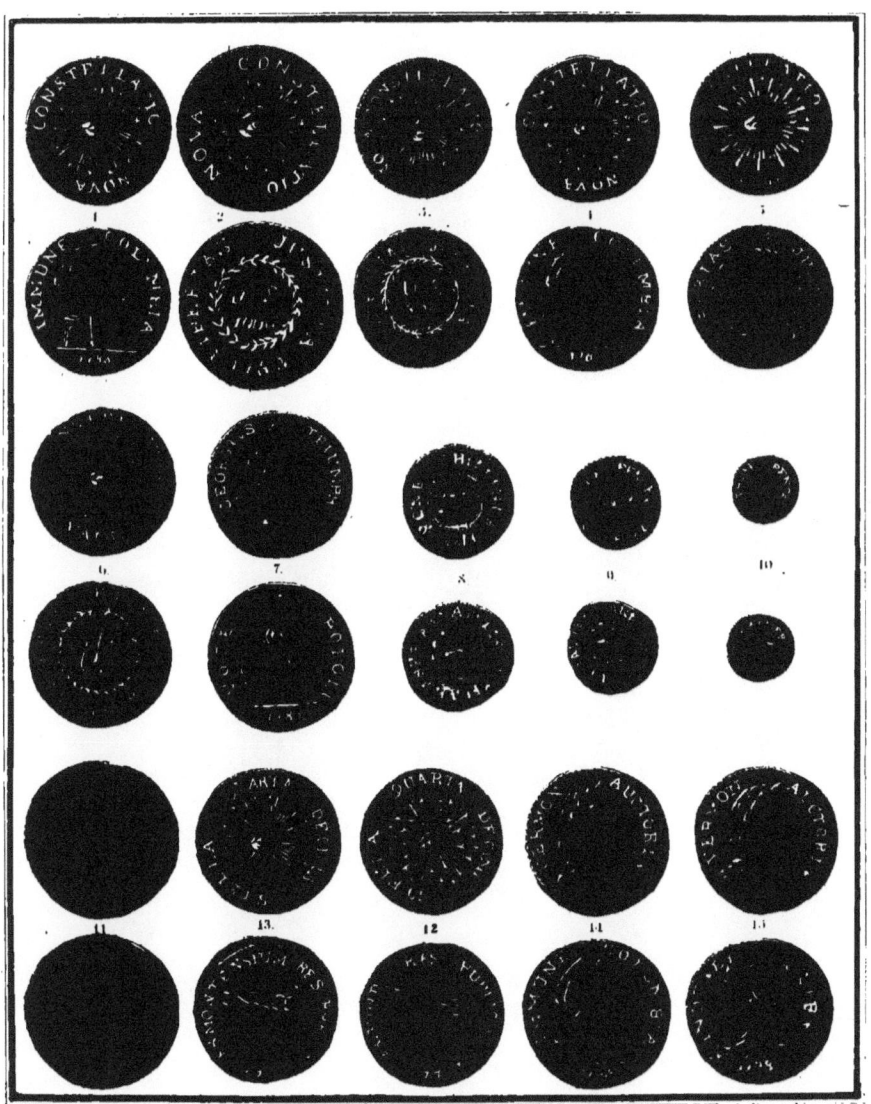

COLONIAL COINS.

have much to be thankful for; and also, that instead of a currency — symbolical of monarchal power on one side, and the liberty and justice on the other, which is weighed in such scales, we have our free native eagle and other insignia of true liberty and independence.

VERMON AUCTORI.

1788. *Device.*—A bust in a coat of mail, head laureated.
Legend.—VERMON AUCTORI
Reverse.—The Goddess of Liberty seated, holding in her right hand the liberty pole, and in her left, the olive branch.
Legend.—INDE * ET LIB *
Exergue.—1788.
(Size 7 and 8. See Plate IX., Figure 15.)

From the following described types and varieties, it is evident that the coining association, we have previously referred to, was equally emulous, with similar organizations in other States, in supplying the people with a copper currency; as this emission, though limited to the single year it bears date, consisted of two sizes, thirteen types, and twenty-six varieties.

1788.	TYPES.		VARIETIES.	DEGREES OF RARITY.	DECORATION.
1	VERMON	AUCTORI	3		Laureated.
2	VERMON	AUCTORI	2	• •[1]	Fillet-Festooned.
3	VERMON .	AUCTORI	2	• • •	" "
4	VERMON .	AUCTORI	3	• • •	Laureated.
5	VERMON .	AUCTORI .	1	• •	"
6	VERMON .	AUCTORI .	2	• •	Fillet-Festooned.
7	.VERMON .	AUCTORI .	4	• • •	" "
8	.VERMON .	AUCTORI .	1	• •	Laureated.
9	VERMON :	AUCTORI	2	• • •	"
10	VERMON .	AUCTORI *	2	•	Fillet-Festooned.
11	VERMON *	AUCTORI *	1	• • •	Laureated.
12	VERMON +	AUCTORI +	2	•	"
13	+ VERMON +	AUCTORI +	1	• •	"
	VERMON	AUCTORI		• • •	Bust of George III. Legend. — Georgius III. Reverse.— A figure of Brittannia.

¹ * Scarce.   * * Rare.   * * * Very rare.

The last noted, not formally included in the types, is said to have been issued at the time when leading men in Vermont were tampered with by partizans of the British crown. We think it furnished a bust for the domestic article.

The varieties of the types are determined by the punctuation of the legend, facing of the bust, or decking of the head. In some of the varieties there are peculiarities, viz: in Type 2, one variety has no legend on the reverse; in Type 4, one variety has INDE ET placed on the left hand side of the field; and in Type 7, the legend reads, LIB ET INDE.

Five years after this famous issue of copper, New York relinquished its claims to jurisdiction over Vermont, which was admitted into the Union in 1793.

CONNECTICUT.

AUCTORI CONNEC.

Device.—A bust in coat of mail, head laureated. and facing to the right. 1785.
Legend.—AUCTORI CONNEC
Reverse.—The Goddess of Liberty seated on the globe, facing to the left, the liberty pole, surmounted by the cap, in the left hand, and the olive branch in the right.
Legend.—INDE : ET LIB.
Exergue.—1785.

(Size 8. See Plate X., Figures 4 to 10.)

Connecticut in 1785 granted exclusive permission to Samuel Bishop, Joseph Hopkins, James Hillhouse, and John Goodrich, to establish a mint, and coin money for the State.

The grantees subsequently formed a copartnership with Pierpont Edwards, Jonathan Ingersoll, Abel Buel, and Elias Shipman, for coining coppers. Six pennyweights was the required amount of copper in each of the pieces as defined by statute, which also designated a device.

A Board for the inspection and approval of these coppers was appointed by the General Assembly, composed of Roger Sherman, James Wadsworth, David Austin, Ebenezer Chittendon, and Isaac Beers. The amount inspected, during the three years the mint was in operation, was twenty-eight thousand, nine hundred and forty-four pounds, of coined copper.

In 1786, Edwards, Shipman, and Ingersoll, sold their interest to James Jarvis, who took their places in the company. In the same year, the mint-works were leased to Mark Leavenworth for six weeks, at the expiration of which, Leavenworth became a purchaser and stockholder in the company. With frequent changes made in the division of shares up to this period, the company continued to coin coppers till June, 1787, when operations were brought to a close.

In 1788, Major Eli Leavensworth prepared blank coppers, which were stamped in New York, with various impressions.

The affairs of this company were investigated by James Wadsworth and Daniel Holbrook, by authority of an act of Assembly in 1789. The report was honorable to the parties concerned.

The date, 1785, determines the first appearance of these coins, and our investigations have resulted in establishing for them seven distinct types, consisting of twenty-eight varieties. In five of these varieties, the bust faces to the right, and in the other two, to the left. The head is unusually large, the face full and round, and the features manly—the anatomical lineaments being better proportioned in fact than the generality of effigies of that period; the bust in most specimens, represented in armor, and the workmanship decidedly better than the issues of similar coins in succeeding years. They are very irregular, however, in size and weight, varying in the latter, by tests made at the United States Mint, from 94 to 144 grains.

These coins must have been a necessity, and a great convenience to the people of Connecticut at that time. There may be a few, still living in the commonwealth of their origin, whose memories are cognizant of much that would be interesting in relation to them, beside the statutes that gave them existence. Certain it is, that they are the representatives and memorials of an epoch in American State coinage, when subjective relations had been succeeded by those of entire independence, and the Goddess of Liberty, adopted on the reverse of the coins, could be symbolized and worshipped without reproach or fear.

The prominent genius and actor in this coinage appears to have been Mr. Abel Buel, who was also the master-spirit in the construction of the machinery, which was so efficient as to turn out one hundred and twenty pieces of the coin in a minute.

With us this coinage had, without any authority for it, become associated with Simsbury mines. We have not, however, been able to learn that any of the copper used in it came from that locality. All we can learn is, "that the mines were first wrought in 1707, and at that time, and subsequently, up to the breaking out of the Revolutionary War, and that at some period the ore must have been smelted, as appears from tradition and the remains of old furnaces." [1]

From about the period of the adoption of the Constitution, till 1827, they were famous as the penal locality of Connecticut, furnishing an industrial home for a class who will not appreciate honest labor, nor be contented with the moral restrictions of true freedom.

The types of this coin are as follows:

---

[1] Jeffrey O. Phelps, Simsbury, Connecticut.

1785.	TYPES.		VARIETIES.	DEGREES OF RARITY.	POSITION.		DECORATION.
1	AUCTORI	CONNEC	1	•••	Facing right.		Laureated.
2	AUCTORI.	CONNEC	3	•••	"	"	"
3	. AUCTORI.	CONNEC.	4	••	"	left.	"
4	AUCTORI.	CONNEC:	3	•	"	right.	"
5	. AUCTORI:	CONNEC.	6	•	"	"	"
6	AUCTORI:	CONNEC:	8	•	"	left.	"
7	AUCTORI:	CONNEC:	3	••	"	right.	"
8	AUCTORI:	CONNEC:	1	••	"	"	Fillet-Festooned.

This classification furnishes, by the punctuation and the direction of the face, an index by which the type can be determined. Either the figure, legend, punctuation, or the olive branch, in the left hand of the Goddess of Liberty, on the reverse, determines the variety. In some of the types there are peculiarities, which may not at first attract the attention of the numismatic student. In No. 1, the head of the bust is entirely different from the others, the neck being unusually short and thick, giving it a peculiar appearance; No. 2, the neck long; No. 3, the head large, neck short and thick, and the bust robed in a Roman tunic, looped upon the shoulder; No. 4, head singular, and the face so distorted as to be anything but handsome.

Our attention has also been directed to what I believe to be an imperfect specimen of Type No. 1, which appears to have been impressed upon another copper, and the letters of the two coming in contact in such a manner as to cause the legend to read ACTI, instead of AUCTORI.

AUCTORI CONNEC.

The coinage in this year was increased in the number of the types, and more care was observed in milling the copper into the required thickness, before 1786. subjecting it to the dies; thereby avoiding injury to the edge of the coins, which is so perceptible in the emissions of the preceding year. Of the issues of this year, we have found eleven types, consisting of twenty-seven varieties — four of the types facing to the right, and the other seven to the left. But two of the types fillet-festooned, all the others laureated; in some, the edges of the leaves are serrated.

The types are as follows:

COLONIAL COINS.

1786.	TYPES.	VARIETIES.	DEGREES OF RARITY.	POSITION.		DECORATION.
1	AUCTORI CONNEC	2	• •	Facing right.		Laureated.
2	AUCTORI CONNEC	1	•	"	left.	"
3	AUCTORI. CONNEC	1	• •	"	"	"
4	AUCTORI. CONNEC.	1	• • •	"	right.	"
5	AUCTORI: CONNEC	1	• •	"	"	"
6	AUCTORI. CONNEC:	3	• • •	"	"	"
7	AUCTORI. CONNEC:	1	•	"	left.	Fillet.
8	AUCTORI: CONNEC.	7	•	"	"	Laureated.
9	AUCTORI.. CONNEC.	1	•	"	"	"
10	AUCTORI: CONNEC:	4	• • •	"	"	Fillet.
11	AUCTORI: CONNEC:	5	•	"	"	Laureated.

In Type 1, the head of the bust differs from the others in the arrangement about the neck, which is much shorter; No. 2, the face is not prepossessing; No. 3, the neck is unusually long, the bust in a coat of mail; No. 5, the head very large, the neck very short and thick.

AUCTORI CONNEC.

1787.   *Device.*—A bust in coat of mail, head laureated, and facing to the left.
   Legend.—AUCTORI CONNEC
   Reverse.—The Goddess of Liberty seated on the globe, facing to the left, the liberty pole, surmounted by the cap, in the left hand, and the olive branch in the right.
   Legend.—IND ET LIB
   Exergue.—1787.
            (Size 8. See Plate X., Figures 4 to 10.)

The issue this year must have been very large, and have circulated in our country very extensively; for, at this time, they can be occasionally found in circulation in every State of the Union, where a copper currency is tolerated. The number of types and varieties struck off is uncertain; but, from an extensive examination, we have been enabled to distinguish seventy-four distinct types, consisting of one hundred and sixty-four varieties — sufficient changes to ring upon a copper coin, even if it does not embrace a description of every such coin issued.

The blanks upon which these coppers were struck were generally very rough, but of excellent material, and many of the dies were very poorly executed. The apparent haste with which these pieces were gotten up, and the large number coined, and put in circulation, evinced an energy of purpose allied closely, undoubtedly, to gain, which, taking into consideration the varying weight of from 94 to 144 grains — the latter being required by the statute authorizing their coinage—must have been amply gratified.

It is believed and expressed by some, that the bust upon these coins was originally intended to represent George III. As we would not question the patriotism of those interested in this coinage, we must conclude that the art of design was at so low a standard at that time, as to compel the copying of some bust of their late sovereign, which was probably the case, as we have heard of a type of these coins absolutely bearing the name of George III. We must suppose, however, for the honor of the State of Connecticut and its enterprising merchant coiners, that the artist of this type had not heard of the recognition of our national independence.

The great variety of punctuation found upon the preceding and succeeding emissions of the Connecticut coinage, suggests the idea that mere fancy would hardly have been indulged in to such an extent without some purpose of utility in connection with it.

Our conclusion, therefore, is, that it may have been adopted to designate the various interests of the parties concerned — who may have been sub-lessees under the original grantees — or to distinguish the issues made to purchasers; which would, if either of our positions is correct, account satisfactorily for the very numerous distinctive designs and marks which the tables disclose.

These humble coppers were the heralds of that genius for invention which has since so strongly marked the people of Connecticut; and its results have been distributed in all sorts of manufactures all over our country — a particular article of which has even been sent abroad, to enable our trans-atlantic friends to measure time by republican pendulums.

Whatever has emanated from this State, we may say, without designing to make any invidious comparison with her sister States, has, partaking of the character of her people, been of utility; whether it has been the small currency we have described in these pages, or the cotton-gin — an invention for which the world was waiting, and absolutely essential to its advancement—inaugurating, as it did, an industrial movement which is still onward, and to be onward, beyond the ken of human prescience or calculation.

CONNECTICUT
TYPES AND VARIETIES.

1787.	LEGENDS.		DEGREES OF RARITY.	POSITION.	DECORATION.	VARIETIES.
1	AUCTORI	CONNEC	• • •	Left	Laureated.	1
2	AUCTORI	CONNEC	• • •	Right	"	2
3	AUCTORI	CONNEC.	• •	Left	Fillet-Festooned.	2
4	AUCTORI	CONNEC.	• •	Right	Laureated.	3
5	AUCTORI.	CONNEC.	• • •	Left	Fillet-Festooned.	3
6	AUCTORI.	CONNEC.	• • •	Right	"	1
7	. AUCTORI .	CONNEC .	•	Left	Laureated.	1
8	. AUCTORI .	CONNEC .		Right	Fillet-Festooned.	1
9	AUCTORI	CONNEC:	• •	Left	Laureated.	1
10	. AUCTORI ∴	CONNEC.	• •	"	"	2
11	. AUCTORI ..	CONNEC .	• •	Right	"	1
12	AUCTORI .	CONNEC:	• •	Left	"	2
13	AUCTORI .	CONNEC:	• • •	Right	Fillet-Festooned.	1
14	AUCTORI ..	CONNEC	•	Left	Laureated.	2
15	AUCTORI ..	CONNEC	• • •	Right	Fillet-Festooned.	1
16	AUCTORI:	CONNEC	• •	Left	Laureated.	2
17	AUCTORI:	CONNEC	• • •	Right	Fillet-Festooned.	1
18	AUCTORI:	CONNEC:	•	Left	Laureated.	3
19	AUCTORI:	CONNEC:	• • •	Right	Fillet-Festooned.	1
20	AUCIORI: +	CONNEC:	• • •	Left	Laureated.	2
21	AUCTORI: + −	CONNEC:		"	"	2
22	AUCTORI: +·	CONNEC: +	• • •	"	"	2
23	+ AUCTORI: +	CONNEC:	• • •	"	"	3
24	+ AUCTORI: +	CONNEC: +	• • •	"	"	1
25	AUCTORI: + +	CONNEC	• • •	"	"	1
26	AUCTORI: + +	CONNEC:	•	"	"	1
27	+ AUCTORI: + +	CONNEC:	•	"	"	3
28	AUCTORI: + +	CONNEC: +	• •	"	"	1
29	+ AUCTORI: + +	CONNEC: +	• • •	"	"	1
30	+ AUCTORI + +	CONNEC +	•	"	"	1
31	+ AUCTORI + +	CONNEC +	• • •	Right	Fillet-Festooned.	2
32	+ AUCTORI: + +	CONNEC:	• •	Left	Laureated.	3
33	+ AUCTORI: + +	CONNEC:	• • •	Right	Fillet-Festooned.	2
34	+ AUCTORI + + +	CONNEC +	• •	Left	"	2

TYPES AND VARIETIES—Continued.

1787.	LEGENDS.		DEGREES OF RARITY.	POSITION.	DECORATION.	VARIETIES.
35	+ AUCTORI + + +	CONNEC + .	...	Left	Fillet-Festooned.	3
36	AUCTORI ★	CONNEC	...	"	"	2
37	AUCTORI: ★	CONNEC	..	"	"	2
38	AUCTOPI: ★	CONNEC.	...	"	"	1
39	AUCTORI: ★	CONNEC:		"	"	3
40	AUCTORI ★	CONNEC ★	...	Right	"	2
41	AUCTORI: ★★	CONNEC:	...	Left	Laureated.	1
42	AUCTORI: ★★	CONNEC: ★	•	"	"	2
43	★ AUCTORI: ★	CONNEC: ★	..	"	"	1
44	★ AUCTORI: ★	CONNEC: ★	•	Right	Fillet-Festooned.	1
45	★ AUCTORI ★★	CONNEC ★	...	Left	Laureated.	4
46	★ AUCTORI ★★	CONNEC ★	..	Right	Fillet-Festooned.	3
47	★ AUCTORI ★★	CONNEC. ★	...	Left	Laureated.	1
48	★ AUCTOBI ★★	CONNEC. ★	...	"	"	1
49	★ AUCTORI. ★★	CONNEC. ★		"	"	6
50	★ AUCTORI: ★★	CONNEC:		"	"	3
51	★ AUCTORI: ★★	CONNEC: ★		"	"	36
52	★ AUCTORI: ★★	CONNEC: ★	...	"	"	1
53	★ AUCTORI ★★★	CONNEC ★	...	"	"	1
54	★ AUCTORI ★★★	CONNEC ★★	...	"	"	2
55	★ AUCTORI ★★★	CONNEC ★★	...	Right	Fillet-Festooned.	1
56	★ AUCTORI ★★★★	CONNECT ★★	...	Left	"	1
57	AUCTURI ★★★★	CONNEC ★★	...	"	"	1
58	AUCTORI ✶	CONNEC	...	Right	"	1
59	AUCTORI ✶ .	CONNEC	..	Left	Laureated.	2
60	AUCTORI ✶ ✶	CONNEC ✶	..	Right	Fillet-Festooned.	2
61	AUCTORI ✶ ✶	CONNEC ✶	...	Left	"	2
62	★ AUCTORI ✶ ✶	CONNEC ✶		"	Laureated	1
63	★ AUCTORI ✶ ✶	CONNEC ✶	...	Right	Fillet-Festooned.	1
64	★ AUCTORI ✶ ✶ ✶	CONNEC	..	"	"	1
65	★ AUCTORI ✶ ✶ ✶	CONNEC.	..	"	"	1
66	AUCTORI ↔	CONNEC	...	Left	Laureated.	2
67	AUCTORI. ↔	CONNEC	..	"	"	1
68	AUCTORI: ↔	CONNEC	...	"	"	2
69	AUCTOBI: ↔	CONNEC	...	"	"	1
70	AUCTORI: ↔	CONNEC: ←	..	"	"	4
71	→ AUCTORI: ↔	CONNEC: ←	•	"	"	3
72	→ AUCTORI ↔←	CONNEC. ←	..	Right	Fillet-Festooned.	2
73	→ AUCTORI ↔←	CONNEC: ←	...	"	"	1

Auctori Connec.

Types.—Though the preceding table clearly designates each and every type 1787. it has been our good fortune to discover, by the different punctuations of the legends, we have deemed it relevant to notice more particularly a few of the specimens of this coin which are peculiar, or considered to be extremely rare.

No. 1. The head is large, and the fillet extends down to the legend, which, on the left hand side of the goddess, on the reverse, reads, "INDE ET," and on the right hand, LIB.

No. 2. The head is unusually small, faces to the right, and the ends of the fillet are quite short. The legend on the reverse, on the left hand side of the goddess, reads, "LIB ET," and on the right hand, "INDE." This type is considered extremely rare, and is found but in few cabinets.

No. 5. Not peculiar, but extremely rare. We have, in all our researches, seen but two specimens of this type.

No. 6. The head small and nearly round, and the neck and bust short. Reverse legend reads, "ET LIB INDE." Extremely rare; but one specimen has come under our notice.

No. 8. The head small and round, facing to the left, and the hair a series of continuous small lines. The fillet terminates in a bow, in the centre of which there is a circular ring. This type is quite thin, the lightest, we believe, coined in this year. It is known as the "laughing effigy piece;" the legend thus, "INDE : * * * ET · LIB :"

Nos. 9 and 10. Both of these types are extremely rare, the latter the most so, being familiarly known as the "Africanus, or negro head."

Nos. 11, 13, 15, 17, and 19, we notice on account of the variation in the punctuation, and their extreme rarity.

No. 20. This type is peculiar on account of an error in the legend—I occupying the place of T, thus: "AUCIORI," instead of "AUCTORI." It is considered to be extremely rare.

No. 22. This type is much more rare than any of those punctuated with the cross, that precede it.

Nos. 23, 24, 25, 29, 31, and 35, are rarely met with, and are found but in few cabinets.

No. 39. The legend on the obverse reads, "AUCTOPI," and the letters are unusually large. We have seen it in two specimens, and it is extremly rare.

Nos. 41, 42, 44, 46, and 48. All extremely rare.

No. 49. The legend, on the obverse of this type, reads, "AUCTOBE." We have seen two specimens of the same."

No 53. This type is in our cabinet. We have neither seen nor heard of a similar piece, and it is considered by all who have seen it, as unique.

Nos. 54, 55, and 56, are seldom met with, and extremely rare.

No. 57. The legend in this type ends with the letter T, thus: "AUCTORI CONNECT," and, from the number of stars with which it is punctuated, it has been denominated one of the "seven sleepers," from having slept so long undiscovered. There is a peculiar coincidence in the design or arrangement of this coin: there are seven letters in each of the words which form the legend, which is punctuated with seven stars; the fillet is ornamented with seven balls; there are seven divisions of the coat of mail on the shoulder; and the goddess, on the reverse, holds a branch with seven divisions or leaves. We have seen but four specimens of this type, two of which are in our cabinet.

Nos. 58, 59, and 60. The legends upon these types are punctuated with six-pointed stars; considered extremely rare.

No. 62. Small head and bust, and the punctuation commences with a small cross or quatre-foil, and terminates with six-pointed stars. On the reverse, the punctuation is reversed. This type is exceedingly rare.

Nos. 65 and 67. Fleur-de-lis punctuation; seldom found in any cabinet.

No. 68. This is the most extraordinary combination of errors in lettering that we have met with in any type. The legend, on the obverse, reads, "AUCTOBI," and on the reverse, "INDE ET LIR." We have seen but a single specimen, which is in our cabinet.

Nos. 72 and 73. Types which are extremely rare.

AUCTORI CONNEC.

According to our researches and classification which follow, there were, of 1788. the issue of this year, twenty-five types and thirty-four varieties; and if the number of the latter is an index of the amount of circulation, the business of the year could not have been large. The inference that the circulation of this year was limited, is sustained by the fact, that specimens of this emission are scarce, and consequently, rare. We may certainly conclude that this was the final emission of these coins, the Federal Constitution — adopted the previous year — having assumed entire control over the coinage of the country.

It will be found, previously stated — derived from the records of the State of Connecticut — that the company, to whom the coining of these coppers was granted, closed its operations in June, 1787; that Major Leavenworth prepared blank coppers, which were struck off in New York; also, that the Board for inspection and approval of these coppers, exercised that authority for three years. A few blanks may have been impressed in New York, but the question arises, was the emission of this year struck off in New York or Connecticut? The former would have involved the removal of dies and machinery, or the constructing and putting up of new; and we are, therefore, inclined to think that it was struck off in Connecticut, as the affairs of the company were not finally investigated till 1789.

AUCTORI CONNEC.

1788.	TYPES.		VARIETIES.	DEGREES OF RARITY.	POSITION.		DECORATION.	
1	AUCTORI	CONNEC	2	•••	Facing left.		Fillet-Festooned.	
2	AUCTORI.	CONNEC	1	•••	"	"	"	"
3	AUCTORI.	CONNEC.	2	••	"	"	"	"
4	.AUCTORI.	CONNEC.	1	•••	"	"	"	"
5	AUCTORI.	CONNEC: •;•	1	•••	"	"	Laureated.	
6	AUCTORI: +	CONNEC: +	1	•••	"	right.	"	
7	AUCTORI	CONNEC ✷	2	••	"	"	"	
8	AUCTORI.	CONNEC ✷	2	••	"	left.	"	
9	AUCTORI:✷	CONNEC	1	••	"	"	"	
10	★AUCTORI	CONNEC ✷	1	•••	"	"	"	
11	AUCTORI ✷✷	CONNEC.	1	••	"	right.	Fillet-Festooned.	
12	AUCTORI ✷✷	CONNEC ✷	3	••	"	"	"	"
13	★AUCTORI ✷✷	CONNEC	2	••	"	left.	Laureated.	
14	AUCTORI.✷	CONNEC ○✷	2	•••	"	right.	"	
15	★AUCTORI ✷✷	CONNEC ✷	1	•••	"	left.	"	
16	★AUCTORI.★★	CONNEC ✷	2	••	"	"	"	
17	★AUCTORI.★★	CONNEC. ✷	1	•••	"	"	"	
18	★AUCTORI ★★★	CONNEC ✷	1	•••	"	"	"	
19	★AUCTORI ★★★★	CONNECT ✷✷	2	•••	"	"	Fillet-Festooned.	
20	AUCTORI.★	CONNEC	1	••	"	right.	Laureated.	
21	AUCTORI ★★	CONNEC ✷	1	•••	"	left.	Fillet-Festooned.	
22	★AUCTORI ⚜	CONNEC ⚜	1	•••	"	right.	Laureated.	
23	AUCTORI ✷✷	CONNEC ✷	1	••	"	left.	"	
24	★AUCTORI ✷	CONNEC ✷	1	•••	"	"	Fillet-Festooned.	
25	★AUCTORI ✷✷	CONNEC ✷	1	•••	"	"	"	"

In addition to the preceding, our attention has been arrested by a specimen, which, by some, is supposed to be another distinct type—the device being struck, as we think, crosswise of a "Franklin copper," and the two thus so blended together as to render neither intelligible. The head on this piece is unusually small, and faces to the right, the features of the face very regular, the hair folds under, a band crosses to the back part of the head, and the ends of the same protrude behind. The legend is not decipherable; and if it is a type, which we are inclined to doubt, it is entirely new to us.

Of the types. No. 8, an unusually small head, very regular features, and considered to be very rare. No. 10, head and neck immoderately large, and quite rare. No. 14, the punctuation of which terminates with the amulet and a five-pointed star, is extremely rare, and perhaps unique, as we have never seen but one specimen. No. 19, like No. 57, in the issues of 1787, reads as in that specimen, AUCTORI CONNECT, and like that, is punctuated by seven five-pointed stars.

AUCTORI PLEBIS.

1787. *Device.*—An unusually large bust, the head laureated, and facing to the left.
Legend.—✥ AUCTORI : ✥ PLEBIS.
Reverse.—The Goddess of Liberty seated on a bale, the right hand resting on the globe. On her left a large anchor, on which she is reclining, while her foot rests upon a lion.
Legend.—INDE ET LIBER., with amulets.
Exergue.—1787.
(Size 8. See Plate X., Figure 2.)

Some authors have stated that this coin was struck off in England, and sent to Connecticut for circulation. We have been unable to find any authority to sustain this statement. On the contrary, its resemblance to the "Auctori Connec," indicates that it was coined in Connecticut, though for reasons which are not apparent, the emission must have been very limited.

Of this coin, we have met with but one type, consisting of three varieties. They are in an unusually fine state of preservation, having been manufactured of good copper, properly tempered and milled.

It is considered to be particularly rare, and can be found in but few cabinets.

NEW JERSEY.

NEW JERSEY COPPERS.

Device.—A shield, in the shape of a heart, with stripes thereon, running longitudinally.   1786.
Legend.—E . PLURIBUS . UNUM.
Reverse.—A plough, surmounted by a horse's head.
Legend.—NOVA CÆSAREA.
Exergue.—1786.
(Size 8. See Plate X., Figures 11 to 21.)

COLONIAL COINS.

The earliest record, relative to a copper circulation in the State of New Jersey, was in the year 1682, which State was then called Nova Cæsarea. It appears that the Assembly of that year passed a resolution, "that for the more convenient payment of small sums of money, Mark Newby's coppers — called 'Patrick half-pence'— should pass as half-pence, current pay; provided he give security to the Speaker of the Assembly that he, his executors, and administrators will redeem them on demand; it being further provided, that no one should be obliged to take more than five shillings of them in any one payment."

These Newby coppers, or Patrick half-pence, were really Irish half-pence, which Mark Newby had purchased and brought over with him from England, and which, with other coins of a similar character subsequently introduced, constituted the copper circulation of what is now New Jersey for upwards of a century.

"During the year 1786, a proposal was made to the Legislature of the State of New Jersey, then in session, by Walter Mould, Thomas Goadsby, and Albion Cox, for authority to coin a certain sum in copper. The proposal was referred to a committee, of whom Abraham Clark was chairman, who, after having had a conference with the petitioners upon the subject, made a report favorable to the object of the petition. Accordingly, on the first day of June following, an act was passed by the Legislature, authorizing the parties to strike copper coins to the amount in value of £10,000, at the rate of fifteen coppers to the shilling, each coin to be of the weight of six pennyweight and six grains, to be manufactured in the State, and to have such marks and inscriptions as shall be directed by the Justice of the Supreme Court, or any one of them.

"The contractors, before proceeding upon the business of coining, were, moreover, to enter into bonds to the Governor, to the use of the State, in the sum of £10,000, with at least two sufficient securities, that they would, within two years from the publication of the act, coin the full sum of £10,000 in copper, and faithfully and honestly perform their contract. They were also to deliver to the Treasurer of the State, for the use of the State, one-tenth part of the full sum so struck by them, which amount was to be paid quarterly, and they were likewise required to account to the Legislature for the faithful execution of the trust reposed in them.

"On the 22d day of November in the same year, a supplemental act was passed, in the preamble to which, after setting forth that the good intentions of the people of the State were likely to be defeated by the circumstance of the parties being jointly bound to execute the contract, Thomas Goadsby and Albion Cox were authorized to coin two-thirds of the amount of £10,000, and Walter Mould the remainder, and in case of any neglect or refusal on the part of Mr. Mould to comply with the conditions, and

COLONIAL COINS.

enter upon the performance of his part of the coining, within two months from the date of the passage of the act, then the whole amount of the coinage was to be carried on by the other parties; any neglect on the part of either party to give the required bond, rendering him liable to forfeit and pay the sum, to be recovered in the same manner that other persons were made liable to pay, for striking or coining copper by the previous act.

"The Legislature desirous to protect the contractors in their operations as far as possible, it was still further enacted on the 4th day of June, 1789, that a penalty of ten times the nominal value of the sum or sums so offered in payment, should be imposed on any person or persons who offered to pass in payment or exchange any coppers others than those coined under and by the authority of the acts subsequently passed by the Legislature of the State, or any which might be issued under the authority of the government of the United States.

"Albion Cox and Walter Mould, two of the before named contractors, were merchants of standing and responsibility in the city of New York — the former carrying on business at No. 240 Queen st., and the latter at No. 23 William st."[1]

Thus we have the origin of, and authority for, the "Nova Cæsarea," numerous varieties of which were issued in 1786, '87, and '88. Of one hundred specimens, taken indiscriminately, we find that they vary in size from 7 to 9, and in weight, from 123 to 156 grains — showing that but little system existed in their coinage.

In the following description of the coins, we have been compelled to depart from the generally established rule of numismatologists, of giving the obverse, because it would be impossible to type them in that way, for the reason that the punctuation is nearly the same, and the shields, except in a few cases, without sufficient variation to establish a proper distinction. On the reverse, however, there is ample material, in the form of the plow and its appendages, the horse's head and the legend, to designate satisfactorily and clearly each and every type of these coins, that diligent and extensive research has brought to our notice.

---

[1] Bushnell.

COLONIAL COINS.

TYPES AND VARIETIES OF THE NOVA CÆSAREA.

1786.	LEGENDS.	FACING RIGHT.	DEGREES OF RARITY.	HANDLES TERMINATING SQUARE.	HANDLES TERMINATING ROUND.	HANDLES TERMINATING IN IRREGULAR LENGTHS.	HANDLES TERMINATING LONG.	HANDLES TERMINATING SHORT.	BEAM STRAIGHT.	BEAM STRAIGHT—WITH CURVED END.	BEAM CURVED AT EACH END.	WITH COULTER.	WITHOUT COULTER.	WITH SINGLETREE.	VARIETIES.
1	NOVA CÆSAREA	+	..	+			+		+			+		+	3
2	NOVA CÆSAREA	+	.	+			+		+			+		+	4
3	NOVA CÆSAREA	+	..	+	+		+	+				+		+	4
4	NOVA CÆSAREA	+	..		+	+		+	+			+		+	3
5	NOVA CÆSAREA	+	...	+		+	+			+		+		+	2
6	NOVA CÆSAREA	+	...	+		+	+			+		+		+	2
7	NOVA CÆSAREA	+	...	+			+			+		+		+	1
8	NOVA CÆSAREA	+	...	+			+				+	+		+	2
9	NOVA CÆSAREA	+	...	+			+				+		+	+	2
10	NOVA CÆSAREA	+	..	+	+	+					+	+		+	3
11	NOVA CÆSAREA	+	..	+			+				+	+		+	2
12	NOVA CÆSAREA	+	...	+		+	+				+	÷		+	2

Nova Cæsarea.

The types and varieties of this coin, issued in this year, were of the former, twelve, and of the latter, thirty. We have deemed it assisting to the student to particularize some of the types, and describe the most prominent features of the same, in order to facilitate the use of the table. 1786.

Types.—No. 1 may be determined by the long, straight beam in the plow, which is nearly on a line with the upper part of the handles. The shield is of the medium size. We have met with but three varieties of this type, and consider it rare.

No. 2. This differs from the preceding in the size of the horse's head, which is much smaller; the single-tree is placed further back from the end of the beam; the space between the handles is somewhat wider, and the beginning of the legend is double the distance from the handles.

No. 3. The handles in this type are much shorter, and converge toward the ends till they meet; the legend, in both its beginning and ending, closely approaches the plow. This type is getting to be scarce.

No. 4. The handles of the plow in this type terminate with round ends, and being the only one of the kind we have found, this feature of itself will be sufficient to distinguish it. The shield is small in all the varieties of this type, which is rare.

No. 5. In this type, the handles of the plow are very long, and the beam is straight, with a short curve at the end; the shield is badly proportioned. It is found but in few cabinets, and is quite rare.

No. 6. The horse's head is small, and placed up high above the plow, the mane is thin, and the die was slightly broken near the figure six. The shield is among the largest; and this type is very rare, we having never seen but one variety of it.

No. 7. In this type, the handles of the plow are closed, the beam curves very much upwards; the mould-board is twice the ordinary length; the lettering of the legend is very roughly executed, and irregularly arranged, and the shield is long and narrow. As a whole, it is a very rude effort at die-sinking.

No. 8. The handles of the plow are unusually long and slight, with the legend very near to them; the beam is placed much lower than any of the others, and the shield is among the largest. We have found but one variety of this type, which is quite rare.

No. 10 may be distinguished by the figure six in the exergue, not extending beyond the termination of the curve of the handles of the plow. This peculiarity, we believe, does not occur in any other type. The shield is narrow and long.

No. 11. The handles are widely apart in the centre; the beam is very thick; the horse's head placed up high above the plow, and the shield is small and long. There are but two varieties of this type, which is extremely rare.

No. 12. In this type, the handles of the plow are much wider apart than any previously described; the beam is quite short, and curved at both ends, and the single-tree touches the coulter and runs parallel with it. The shield is one of the largest. This type affords but two varieties, and though it is considered the most common among those having the large shield, yet it is by no means numerous.

TYPES AND VARIETIES OF THE NOVA CÆSAREA.

1767.	LEGENDS.	FACING RIGHT.	DEGREES OF RARITY.	HANDLES TERMINATING SQUARE.	HANDLES TERMINATING ROUND.	HANDLES TERMINATING IRREGULARLY IN LENGTH.	HANDLES UNUSUALLY LONG.	HANDLES LONG.	HANDLES SHORT.	BEAM STRAIGHT.	BEAM CURVED AT EACH END.	WITH COULTER.	WITH SINGLE-TREE.	BEAM WITH CURVED END.	WITH LEAF BELOW THE HEAD.	VARIETIES.
1	NOVA CÆSAREA	+	..	+		+		+		+		+	+			4
2	NOVA CÆSAREA	+	...	+				+		+		+	+			2
3	NOVA CÆSAREA	+	.	+				+		+		+	+			5
4	NOVA CÆSAREA	+	..	+			+			+		+	+			2
5	NOVA CÆSAREA	+	..	+			+			+		+	+			1
6	NOVA CÆSAREA	+	...	+	+	+		+		+		+	+			1
7	NOVA CÆSAREA	+	...		+	+		+		+		+	+			2
8	NOVA CÆSAREA	+	...		+	+	+			+		+	+			2
9	NOVA CÆSAREA	+	.	+			+					+	+	+		2
10	NOVA CÆSAREA	+		+		+	+				+	+	+			3
11	NOVA CÆSAREA	+	.	+			+				+	+	+			4
12	NOVA CÆSAREA	+	.	+			+					+	+	+		2
13	NOVA CÆSAREA	+	..	+					+			+	+	+		1
14	NOVA CÆSAREA	+	...	+					+			+	+	+		5
15	NOVA CÆSAREA	+		+					+			+	+	+		5
16	NOVA CÆSAREA	+	.	+			+					+	+	+		3
17	NOVA CÆSAREA	+	...	+					+	+		+	+			1
18	NOVA CÆSAREA	+		+					+	+		+	+			3
19	NOVA CÆSAREA	+	.	+					+			+	+			2
20	NOVA CÆSAREA	+	..	+					+			+	+	+		1
21	NOVA CÆSAREA	+	...	+			+					+	+	+		1
22	NOVA CÆSAREA	+	...	+			+					+	+	+		1
23	NOVA CÆSAREA	+			+	+	+					+	+	+	+	4
24	NOVA CÆSAREA	+	..		+	+						+	+	+	+	3
25	NOVA CÆSAREA	+	.	+		+	+					+	+	+		2
26	NOVA CÆSAREA	+	..		+	+						+	+	+		2
27	NOVA CÆSAREA	+	..	+			+					+	+		+	3
28	NOVA CÆSAREA	+	...	+			+					+	+		+	1
29	NOVA CÆSAREA	+	...		+	+						+	+	+		1
30	NOVA CÆSAREA	+	...	+			+					+	+	+		1

COLONIAL COINS.

1787. The number of types and varieties of this year's issue, as far as we have been able to determine from the examination of several thousand specimens, is thirty of the former, and seventy of the latter.

Types. — No. 1. This type may be determined by the lower handle of the plow being much shorter than the upper; the upper one being almost on a parallel line with the beam; the space between the handles, very narrow, and they nearer to the legend than the beam, by one half. The letter C in the legend is between the horse's ears; the centre of the shield, which is the medium size, points between the letters B and U in the legend on the reverse.

No. 2. The handles of the plow of nearly equal length, close together, and nearly in a line with the beam; both being the same distance below the legend. The single-tree in this type is double the distance from the end of the beam of that in No. 1.

No. 3. The handles and beam in this type, nearer a level than in either of the types named in this year, the legend nearly touching them; the left ear of the horse points midway to the C in the legend. The shield, of the medium size, points from its centre to the first line of the U in the legend. Two of the varieties in this type were struck off on large planchets.

No. 4. The handles of the plow in this type are thick and heavy, with a decided curve, the beam straight; it touches the lower part of the thick line of the A in the legend, and the handles are about their own thickness below the N in the same. The coulter is thick and terminates squarely; the letter C between the horse's ears, and the shield, the medium size, points from its centre to the hair line in the U in the legend.

No. 5. The handles and beam of the plow are low, and about their thickness, at each end, below the legend. The right ear of the horse's head touches the letter C in the same, midway; the shield is of the medium size, and points from the centre to the outer form of the letter S in the legend.

No. 6. May be determined by the handles being wrought down small at the ends, and terminating in balls. The horse's ears are to the left of the letter C in the legend; the shield, of the medium size, points from its centre, between the letters B and U, in the legend on the reverse.

No. 7. The handles of the plow, the same as in the preceding type, but the C in the legend is between the horse's ears, and the beginning of the same much higher. A medium shield, the centre of which points midway to the letter B in the legend, on the reverse; the R in the same shows that the die must have been broken.

No. 8. The balls on the handles of the plow in this type, are double the size of those previously described. The shield of the medium size, and points from its centre between the B and U in the legend on the reverse, and in many of this type there is a line, from a defective die, which strikes diagonally the U in "PLURIBUS."

No. 9. In this type the handles reach above the N in the legend, and the beam curves up to the A in its termination. The letter C not exactly between the horse's ears; the shield of the medium size, and its centre points to the first line of the letter B in the legend on the reverse.

No. 10. The plow large and heavy, the beam slightly curved at each end, the lower handle the longest, the coulter rests on the mould-board, and the single-tree is close to the end of the beam. The letter C, in the legend, nearly between the ears of the horse; the shield slightly below the medium size, and its centre points slightly to the right of the first line of the letter U in the legend on the reverse.

No. 11. The planchets of this type are unusually small, and the devices accordingly. The horse's ears point between the letters C and A; the beam of the plow has a gradual curve toward the letter A in the legend. The shield on the reverse points from the centre to the first line of the letter U in the legend.

No. 12. In this type the beam has as decided a curve as a sleigh-runner,— a name by which it is known among collectors.

No. 13. The plow in this type is very short but high; the curve of the beam regular but short; the coulter extends beyond the mould-board, and the horse's head is small. The shield is small, and the centre elevation points to the after portion of the U in the legend.

No. 14. May be distinguished by the plow being unusually small, and the letter A in NOVA solid in the centre, the letter being imperfect in the die.

No. 15. Differs from all the other types in the diminutive size of the horse's head, it being less than in any other type. The ears of the horse point to the A in Caesarea.

No. 16. The head of the horse is small in this type, but long and narrow; the ears point between C and A, the first letters in CÆSAREA. The coulter does not pass through the beam of the plow, which is an exception to all the other types.

No. 17. In this type there is a very marked curve in the horse's neck and mane; the plow is thick, heavy and awkward, and the beam curves downward, which occurs in no other type. The figure seven in the date is placed at the edge of the curve of the handles of the plow.

No. 18. Resembles type No. 15, except that the horse's head is larger, and the ears point between C and A as in type No. 16. Just above the beam in the plow, where it connects with the handles, there is a circular piece or stay which occurs in no other type.

No. 19. The legend on the obverse, in this type, at its termination, is punctuated with an oval dot; the shield is long, and at its centre-point, sunk.

No. 20. The beam in this type is like a "sleigh-runner," but it differs from that of type No. 12, being much longer, and extending out to the inner circle of the legend, while No. 12 curves inside of the circle; the single-tree is, also, much nearer the coulter.

No. 21. The beam of the plow with an angular curve, the handles nearly on a level with it, which is long. The single-tree is in almost a continuous line with the coulter; this occurs in no other type.

No. 22. The beam similar to type 20, but not so long; though it extends beyond the inner circle of the legend. This is an extremely rare type.

No. 23. A large planchet, and a corresponding plow; one of the varieties of this type is broken at the inner corner of the shield. The horse's neck is long and slight, and beneath it are three leaves; the beam of the plow curves very much; the shield is long, and a small wreath crosses the lower points of the upper portion of the same.

No. 24. The same as the preceding type, except that the legend, in the obverse, is punctuated at its termination.

No. 25. The plow in this type is large, though the planchet is small; the coulter starts from the *bead* beneath the horse's head, and continues down to the mould-board; the line holding the single-tree is quite faint, which gives the impression of another coulter, and which has given it the name of "double-coulter."

No. 26. May be designated by the extreme thickness of the beam of the plow, at its base, and the gradual narrowing of the same, to the end. The leaves appear, in this type, under the horse's head.

No. 27. The legend on the reverse of this type is "E. PLURIBS."

No. 28. In this type the legend on the obverse is punctuated with the five-pointed star, and the leaves appear under the horse's head. This is the only specimen of the kind we have seen, and hence we think it particularly rare.

No. 29. The legend on the obverse is punctuated with a large round dot at its termination—occurring in no other type.

No. 30. The beam of the plow curved abruptly at the end; the coulter shorter than in any other type in this year; the single-tree starts from the end of the coulter, at the same angle with it, and follows the edge of the mould-board to its point. We have seen no other specimen of this kind.

The great number of types, in this year, embrace peculiarities enough, we would suppose, to have actively employed the constructive powers of a number of the human family. Whatever the purpose to be subserved by this multiplicity of variations of the devices upon a copper, is beyond all our sources of information or even conjecture. They at least exhibit a devotion to the subject-matter, which indicates that the occupation was in complete harmony with the mind that directed, and the hands that executed it.

PLATE X.

COLONIAL COINS.

IMMUNIS COLUMBIA.

Device.—A shield in the shape of a heart, with stripes thereon, running lengthwise
of the same. 1787.

Legend.—E . PLURIBUS · UNUM ·

Reverse.—The figure representing Justice, seated upon the globe, holding in the right hand a flag-staff surmounted by the liberty-cap, the flag drooping over the arm, and in the left hand the scales.

Legend.—IMMUNIS COLUMBIA.

Exergue.—1787.

(Size 8. See Plate X., Figure 21.)

The design of this piece is very beautiful and forcible; it is particularly rare, and is found but in few cabinets.

It has the reputation of being merely a pattern piece; but we are inclined to believe that it was gotten up, and designed, like other coins of the same character, for a currency in New Jersey. The late day of its appearance, however, following by a year the emission of the "Nova Cæsarea," gave to the latter the pre-occupancy of the field.

TYPES AND VARIETIES OF THE NOVA CÆSAREA.

1788.	LEGENDS.	FACING RIGHT.	DEGREES OF RARITY.	FACING LEFT.	HANDLES TERMINATING SQUARE.	HANDLES LONG.	HANDLES SHORT.	BEAM STRAIGHT.	BEAM WITH CURVED END.	BEAM CURVED AT EACH END.	WITH COULTER.	WITH SINGLETREE.	WITHOUT SINGLETREE.	VARIETIES.
1	✧ NOVA ✧ CÆSAREA ✧	+	•••		+			+	+			+	+		2
2	✶ NOVA ✶ CÆSAREA ✶	+	•		+	+				+	+	+			2
3	NOVA CÆSAREA		•••	+	+	+			+			+		+	4
4	NOVA CÆSAREA		•••	+	+	+			+			+		+	1
5	NOVA CÆSAREA	+	•••		+	+			+			+	+		1

In this year we have discovered but five types and ten varieties.

Types.—No. 1. The legend on the obverse of this type is punctuated with 1788. a small cross at the beginning, middle and end.

No. 2. The legend on the obverse is punctuated with three six-pointed stars, in this type.

16

COLONIAL COINS.

No. 3. The plow in this type is differently constructed, and it may be determined by the horse's head facing to the left.

No. 4. The same as the preceding, except the size of the bend, and the pointing of the horse's ears.

No. 5. The legend has no punctuation in this type.

NEW YORK.

NEO EBORACENSIS.

1786. *Device.*—A bust, facing to the right, intended for that of Washington, in the costume of the Continental army, the hair in a cue.
Legend.—NON VIVIRTUTE VICE.
Reverse.—The Goddess of Liberty, seated on a pedestal, holding in her right hand a staff surmounted by the Liberty cap, and in her left the scales of justice.
Legend.—NEO EBORACENSIS.
Exergue.—1786.
(Size 8. See Plate XI., Figure 1.)

This piece has been denominated, and is known as the "New York Washington penny." The bust, so far as we have been able to discover, constitutes its only claim to the addition of the name of Washington. Of this emission, there were two types and four varieties; and, partaking of the general history of much of the copper currency then in use, it had its origin in England, which was, and ever has been conspicuous in the protecting care she has exercised toward our interests and convenience; but always in proportion to the profit which was to inure to herself.

NEW YORK GOLD COIN.

1787. *Device.*—A range of hills, in front of which the sea is represented, and the sun emerging from behind them.
Legend.—NOVA EBORACA . COLUMBIA . EXCELSIOR .
Reverse.—A spread eagle, surrounded by a wreath.
Legend.—UNUM E PLURIBUS. Outside of the wreath.
Exergue.—1787.
(Size 8. See Plate XI., Figure 2.)

This coin is in the cabinet of the U. S. Mint, in Philadelphia, beside which we have seen three others, and is remarkably well executed. It was coined in the city of New

York, in the year of its issue, by a Mr. Blasher, a goldsmith, whose name it bears. It is said to have been duplicated in silver. We have met with but one type.

As the Federal Constitution was adopted this year, and it involved entire authority over the coinage, it is inferable that this coin was gotten up as a pattern piece — perhaps, also, in the same manner in silver; as the artists in gold and silver would naturally have been attracted to the subject of the coinage, and as the General Government might be expected to make some provision for a national currency. The device was undoubtedly derived from the beautiful bay of New York, the surrounding country furnishing the elevations denominated hills.

NEW YORK COPPERS.

IMMUNIS COLUMBIA.

Device.—The figure of Justice seated upon the Globe, holding in her right hand a flag-staff, surmounted by the Liberty-cap — the flag drooping over the arm — and in her left the scales.   1787.
Legend.—IMMUNIS COLUMBIA.
Exergue.—1787.
Reverse.—A large Eagle with wings expanded, and covering nearly the whole of the field; grasping a bundle of arrows in the right talon, and a laurel branch in the left.
Legend.— ✳ E ✳ PLURIBUS ✳ UNUM ✳
(Size 7. See Plate XI., Figure 3.)

All we know of the "Immunis Columbia" is, that it had an existence, and perhaps as important a one, in relation to the events of its day, as any of its copper competitors. Its design and appearance would certainly have recommended it to public favor — covered all over as it was, and as we now see it, with national emblems — and at a time, too, when the intensity of our nationality acquired form and substance by the adoption of the Federal Constitution.

NOVA EBORAC.

Device.—A bust, facing to the right, in Roman armor, with a fillet of laurel.   1787.
Legend.— ✣ NOVA ✣ EBORAC ✣
Reverse.—The Goddess of Liberty seated, and facing to the right; holding a sprig of laurel in her right, and a pole surmounted by the Liberty-cap in her left hand; at her side a shield bearing the arms of the State. The figure, which was intended for the Goddess of Liberty, resembles very much that used as the emblem of Brittania on the old English coins.
Legend.— ✣ VIRT ET·LIB ✣
Exergue.—1787.
(Size 8. See Plate XI., Figure 4.)

This is of British origin—the emblem of Brittania, on the reverse, for want of something more original — though intended for republican use — playing the part of the Goddess of Liberty for the occasion. There were of this copper, two types and six varieties. The types can be determined thus:

    No. 1. Nova Eborac, facing right, three varieties.
    No. 2. " " " left, " "

The varieties are disclosed by the Goddess of Liberty, on the reverse, facing either to the right or the left, the arrangement of the legend on each side of the effigy, and the differences of punctuation of the legend VIR ET LIB ·

Large quantities of this coin were sent to America, and it is stated that a single shipment of eight tons, instead of safely arriving to delight the New Yorkers, went to the bottom of the ocean within a few days' sail of its destination; and it is as true that they were the subject of a quarrel among the mermaids for counters and head ornaments, as it is that that species of half woman and half fish have a veritable existence. The coins were composed of good copper, but poorly struck off; proper care not having been taken to place the planchet truly upon the face of the die. We have seen specimens of this coin in brass, but they are very rare.

      LIBER NATUS LIBERTATEM DEFENDO.

1787. *Device.*—An Indian chief standing, with a raised tomahawk in his right hand, in the left a bow, and from his back depend the quiver and arrows.
   Legend.—LIBER NATUS LIBERTATEM DEFENDO ✻
   Reverse.—Crest of the State Arms; an Eagle, proper—standing upon a half globe with wings expanded.
   Legend.—NEO EBORACUS EXCELSIOR.
   Exergue.—1787.
      (Size 8. See Plate XI., Figure 5.)

This was, also, of English manufacture, and it possesses no history apart from its competitors. It had four types, was composed of the best of copper, and somewhat less than a cent in weight.

LIBER NATUS LIBERTATEM DEFENDO.

Device.—An Indian chief standing, a raised tomahawk in the right hand, a bow in the left, from his back depend the quiver and arrows, and the head is surmounted by the feathers. 1787.

Legend.—LIBER NATUS LIBERTATEM DEFENDO *

Reverse.—The arms of the State—the figures representing Justice and Liberty on each side of a shield, standing—surmounted by an Eagle.

Legend.—EXCELSIOR.

Exergue.—1787.

(Size 8. See Plate XI., Figure 6.)

The obverse of this coin is the same as that immediately preceding; it differs on the reverse, and is, therefore, a distinct variety. This bears the arms of the State complete; the other only the crest of the arms. There are three other types, making in all five varieties, so far as we have been able to discover. There may be more types and varieties, but if so they have not found their way into the best cabinet collections.

We have thoroughly examined the Colonial records, the laws of the State of New York, and the works of its historians, but could find no other authority for these coppers than is disclosed by themselves. M. Vatimar, while sojourning in this country, endeavored to form a cabinet of our Colonial coins, and obtain a history of their mintage. He failed, however, to obtain anything authentic relative to the coinage of the "New York coppers." They possess the merit, at least, of being quite rare, and, as relics of the past, are held in high estimation by those whose cabinets they adorn. We are satisfied that no gold, silver, or copper coins were minted by the authority of the province or State of New York. Though Massachusets previously, and some of the other States subsequently to the Revolution, established mint-houses and coined money, no demonstration of the kind was made by New York.

We may attribute this to her superior regard to law, during Colonial servitude, and, after the Revolution, to the anticipation of the establishment of some general authority over the whole subject. It is clear to us that these coppers were a currency, and, subserving as they did a useful purpose, they encountered no opposition from the local authorities.

COLONIAL COINS.

First United States Cent.

1787. *Device.*—A dial with the hours expressed upon the face, with "Fugio" on the left, and 1787 on the right; a meridian sun above the dial, and below it the —
Legend.—MIND YOUR BUSINESS.
Reverse.—Thirteen circles linked together, forming a large circle; in the centre of the same, a small circle with "UNITED STATES" around it, and in the centre," "WE ARE ONE."
(Size 8. See Plate XI., Figure 7.)

An ordinance for establishing a Mint of the United States, and for regulating the value and alloy of the coin thereof, was passed by Congress, October 16th, 1786. On July 6th, 1787, the government ordered that its copper coin—for the minting of which it had already entered into a contract—should bear the device, &c., as above described.

This cent being the first legally authorized coin of the government of "THE UNITED STATES OF AMERICA," possesses, we think, more than ordinary interest; it is a very creditable relic of the Confederated government, and the devices, to our view, were very appropriate. As a work of taste and interest it throws into the shade the very uninteresting emissions of the same denomination which succeeded it, and which constitute, in part, our present currency.

This cent has borne the name, with some, of the "FRANKLIN PENNY," an appellation to which it has no claim, it being but a fanciful application, because the legend was one of those sententious utterances imputed to Franklin, and for which he was so justly distinguished.

There are two types and four varieties of this cent, viz. :

No. 1. Thirteen circles with a plain field,   4 varieties.
No. 2.   "   "   each containing the name of one of the States, 1

The latter type has, also, a blaze radiating from the circles.

"Kentucky Copper."

1791. *Device.*—A hand holding a scroll, on which is inscribed OUR CAUSE IS JUST.
Legend.—UNANIMITY IS STRENGTH OF SOCIETY.
Reverse—Fifteen stars in the form of a triangle; each star bearing the initial of one of the States of the Union—Kentucky leading. Around the edge, "Payable in Lancaster, London, or Bristol."
(Size 8. See Plate XI., Figure 8.)

This coin, it is said, was struck off in Lancaster, England, in 1791, evidently as a speculation for circulation in America. Because Kentucky leads in the triangle on the reverse, it has been denominated the "Kentucky Cent."

PLATE XI.

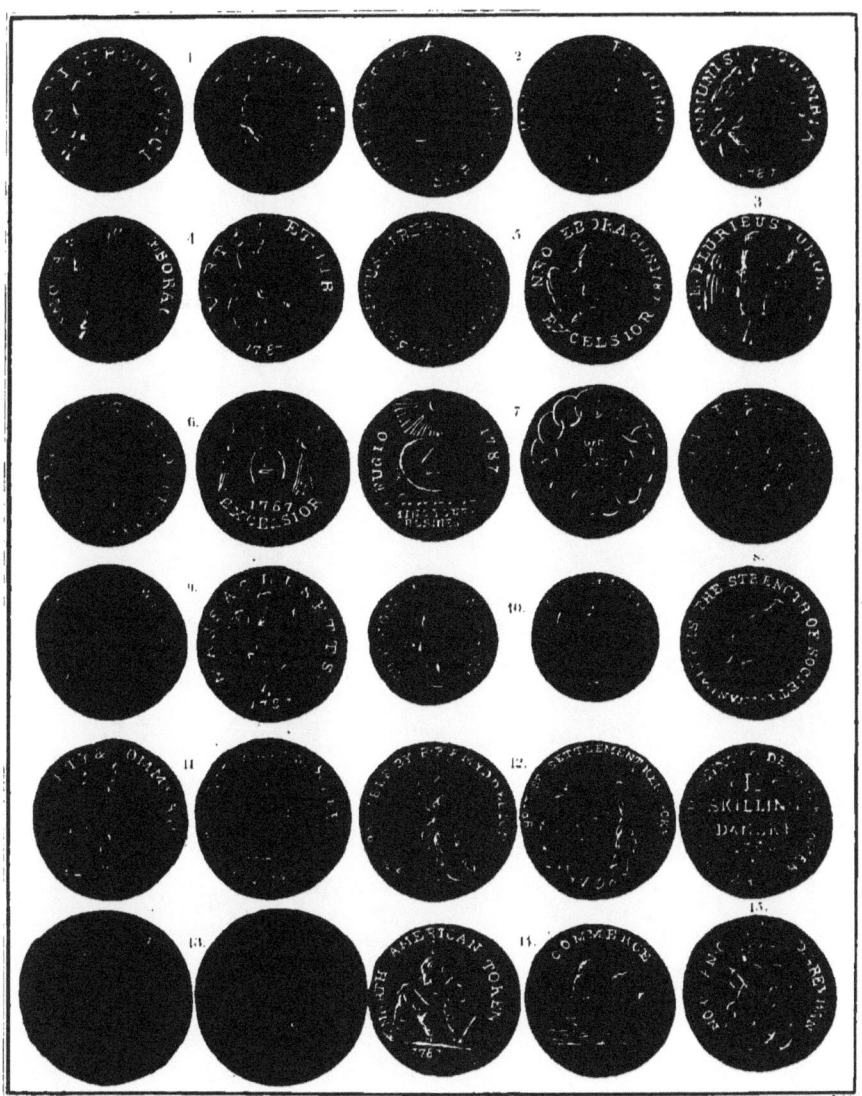

As a speculation, however, whether for English or American account, it could not have been very successful, as it made its appearance at a time when the General and State governments had commenced a war of repudiation upon all foreign or Colonial wares of this kind.

They are yet quite plenty among coin dealers in England, and are known among her collectors as the "Kentucky Token." We have seen but two types.

MASSACHUSETTS CENT.

Device.—An Indian chief with his bow and arrow, and a star on the left side near his forehead. 1787
Legend.—COMMONWEALTH.
Reverse.—The American eagle holding in its right talon a bundle of arrows, and in the left an olive branch; on its breast a shield, in which is the word CENT.
Legend.—MASSACHUSETTS.
Exergue.—1787.

(Size 8. See Plate XI., Figure 9.)

MASSACHUSETTS HALF-CENT.

Device.—An Indian chief with his bow and arrow, and a star on the left side near the forehead. 1787.
Legend.—COMMONWEALTH
Reverse.—The American Eagle holding in its right talon a bundle of arrows, and in the left an olive branch; on its breast a shield, in which is the words HALF-CENT.
Legend.—MASSACHUSETTS.
Exergue.—1787.

Size 6. See Plate XI., Figure 10.)

A precisely similar cent and half-cent were issued in 1788.

The act authorizing this currency, and the proceedings under it, are noticed in the "Massachusetts Currency." It was passed October 17th, 1786, immediately subsequent to the act for establishing the second Massachusetts Mint. The coinage under it did not take place until 1787, and, from the date of the second issue of these cents, 1788, it must have ceased in view of the Federal authority over this subject, early in the latter year.

The device upon these coins was that which was upon the first seal of the colony, though at the period of its adoption it had a new seal; for we find in February, 1781, the authorities of Massachusetts paid Col. Paul Revere, of Boston, £8 in silver, £15 of the new emission of State paper money, and £600 of the old emission, for engraving the same.

Of the first emission of these cents in 1787, there was but one type, consisting of thirteen varieties, and of the second, in 1788, there was also but one type and nineteen varieties; that is, so far as we have been able to learn from the examination of numerous specimens. The obverse of these coins differs in the length and curve of the bow, and in the length of the arrow; but the slight difference in the die, we do not deem sufficient to form or constitute a different type. Any change, however, in the varieties would be important, as the slightest difference of arrangement on the reverse becomes noticeable. We are unable to determine anything in relation to either the number of types or varieties of the half-cents, in consequence of their great scarcity.

No. 1.

WASHINGTON CENT.

1791. *Device.*—The bust of Washington, facing to the left, with the hair in a cue, and in continental uniform.
Legend.—WASHINGTON PRESIDENT.
Exergue.—1791.
Edge.—UNITED STATES OF AMERICA.
Reverse.—The American Eagle with wings expanded, bearing on the breast a heart-shaped shield with six parallel stripes. In the right talon a laurel branch, in the left a number of arrows, and a scroll held in the centre of the beak, upon which is inscribed, "UNUM E PLURIBUS."
Legend.—ONE CENT.
(Size 8. See Plate XII., Figure 4.)

No. 2.

Device.—The bust of Washington, facing to the left, with the hair in a cue, and in continental uniform.
Legend.—WASHINGTON PRESIDENT.
Reverse.—The Eagle with upraised wings; eight stars below a circle of clouds; in the right talon of the Eagle a branch of olive, in the left a number of arrows.
Legend.—ONE CENT.
Exergue.—1791.
Edge.—UNITED STATES OF AMERICA.
(Size 8. See Plate XII., Figure 3.)

COLONIAL COINS.

No. 3.

Device.—The bust of Washington, facing to the left, with a cue, and in continental uniform. 1791.
Legend.—WASHINGTON PRESIDENT.
Reverse.—The Eagle with upraised wings, six stars below a circle of clouds; in the right talon of the Eagle a branch of olive, in the left a number of arrows.
Legend.—ONE CENT.
Exergue.—1791.
Edge.—UNITED STATES OF AMERICA.
(Size 8. See Plate XII., Figure 5.)

These Washington cents of 1791, as described, are the real "Simon Pures," which were gotten up as pattern pieces by authority of the General Government, and which, we think, we can establish to be such, beyond controversy. The two last differ only in the number of stars on the reverse.

October 16th, 1786, the Congress of the confederated United States passed a resolution establishing a Mint, and the "first United States cent"—noticed fully under that head—was authorized to be coined by contract, and made its appearance in 1787. This, then, appears to have been the only legal coinage of copper coins until 1793, except of the pattern pieces at the head of this article—the present Mint having been established by a law of Congress, in 1791.

Thus the act of coinage by our general government, except as experimental, remained in abeyance from 1786 to 1792, when Washington in his message, refers to the coining of half-*dismes*.

To sustain this reasoning Washington says, in his third annual message to the House of Representatives, October 25th, 1791. "The disorders in the existing currency, and especially small change, a scarcity so peculiarly distressing to the poorer classes, strongly recommend the carrying into immediate effect the resolution already entered into concerning the establishment of a Mint. Measures have been taken pursuant to the resolution for procuring some of the necessary artists, together with the requisite apparatus."

From this statement of the President it is clear that the subject of the coinage had been considered, and that the incipient measures had been taken by the Committee of Congress and the Secretary of the Treasury, for carrying into execution the resolution in relation thereto, by inviting designs, procuring dies, and getting up pattern pieces to be submitted to Congress.

This preparation embraced the services of both foreign and American artists.

In confirmation of this we find in Washington's fourth annual message to the House of Representatives, November 6th, 1792, the following—" In execution of the authority given by the legislature, measures have been taken for engaging some artists from abroad, to aid in the establishment of our Mint. Others have been employed at home, provisions have been made for the requisite buildings, and they are now being put in proper condition for the purposes of the establishment. There has been a small beginning in the coinage of half-dismes, the want of small coins in circulation calling the first attention to them."

Among the American artists referred to by Washington, in 1791, a Mr. John Harper, a manufacturer of saws, corner of Sixth and Cherry streets, Philadelphia, bore a conspicuous part: the cents at the head of this article having been designed and struck off by him, and upon his premises.

The device upon these coins—the effigy of Washington, then President, in imitation of royal emissions, which bear the bust of the sovereign, under whom they are minted, and which are emblematic of royal authority—met with Washington's decided disapprobation; and though it could not, in his case, if it had been adopted, have conflicted with the popular confidence in, and regard for, that confirmed patriot, yet, at Washington's suggestion, the device was rejected, and the dies were subsequently broken.

We must think that though the effigy of a living President of the United States upon our coins would partake too much of the character of royalty, or man-worship—of the daily evidences of which, in the social and political relations of our country, there is abundant cause for mortification and humility with that portion of our countrymen, imbued with a due sense of the natural dignity of freemen, and a conscientious and intelligent regard for our social and national welfare and safety—still we can see no objection to transferring the portraits of Washington or his successors to our coins, seeing that all doubts of his or their patriotism have been removed by a thoroughly tried and accepted devotion, while living, to not only the political equality and liberty of their own countrymen, but to mankind everywhere.

The Rev. Dr. Boardman contended before the Historical Society of Pennsylvania—the subject inducing it being the device for the " new cent"—very eloquently for the effigy of Christopher Columbus on one of our national coins.

In pursuance of the Doctor's retrospective and prospective ideas on this subject, we regret much that we are unable to describe some piece of either our Colonial or National coin bearing the portrait of Christopher Columbus, who, in proportion to the services which he rendered to discovery and hence the world, met with more ingratitude while living, and less honor dead, than any man that ever lived.

COLONIAL COINS.

"WASHINGTON CENT."

Device.—A bust of Washington in continental uniform, facing to the left, and the hair in a cue.   1792.
Legend.—G . WASHINGTON PRESIDENT I.
Exergue.—1792.
Reverse.—An Eagle with the wings partially expanded and turned upward; between the tips of the same are fifteen six-pointed stars; on the breast is a heart-shaped shield, containing seven bars of three stripes each; in the right talon an olive-branch, and in the left a number of barbed arrows.
Legend.—UNITED STATES OF AMERICA.
(Size 10. See Plate XII., Figure 6.)

This is a pattern-piece, known to collectors of coins, and designated by every authority we have seen, as the "Washington Cent of 1792."

The die for this piece was designed and cut by Peter Getz, of Lancaster, Pa., for a pattern-piece, at the invitation of the General Government, for designs for coins; brought by him to Philadelphia, and, in the presence of several gentlemen, among whom was Adam Eckfeldt, Esq., subsequently chief coiner of the Mint, struck off upon copper planchets; the number of which could not have been large, as they are now very rare, and even then, must have been novel and valuable enough to have commanded careful preservation.

The scene of this coining operation was in an old coach shop in Sixth street, above Chestnut, upon a press erected by John Harper, under the superintendence of Adam Eckfeldt. Subsequently a number of half-crown pieces were prepared, and struck off on this die, some of which are still treasured up by collectors of coins, and are known as the "Washington Half-Dollar."

From this circumstance we think we are excusable in conjecturing that in getting up this die, Mr. Getz may have had a more exalted idea for it than that of a cent, as its merit was subsequently acknowledged by the close resemblance of the reverse on the half-dollar of 1806, and others; the bust of the Goddess of Liberty being substituted on the obverse for the effigy of Washington.

Burdened as this piece was with the bust of Washington, and the legend, "WASHINGTON PRESIDENT I."—though the numeral upon it could not have been tortured into a reference to anything but a popular succession in the office of President of the United States—it was calculated to arouse prejudices against it, which were summarily deprived of their basis by Washington's own action, which repudiated its adoption—an evidence among the many that preceded and succeeded it, of his personal disinterestedness relative to everything connected with the administration or welfare of the infant republic.

We have been favored with the following leading facts in the life of Mr. Peter Getz, by J. Franklin Reigart, of Lancaster, Pa. They illustrate the force of native talent and energy which unassisted are often assisted most.

"Mr. Adam Getz was born in Lancaster, Pa.; his occupation was that of a silver-smith; but he was, otherwise, a very skilful mechanic and remarkable for his ingenuity. He excelled as a seal-engraver, and an engraver on steel, and was the inventor of a very ingenious hand-vice. He built the three first fire-engines for his native town, the 'Active,' 'Sun,' and another, which is still in existence in the county, and invented an improved printing press—noticed in the 'Lancaster Journal,' January 8th, 1810—worked by rollers instead of the screw, which, by printers, was considered a great improvement.

"In 1792 he was a candidate for the position of chief coiner or engraver of the Mint, and at that time sustained his peculiar superiority as a self-taught mechanic, by exhibiting to Dr. Rittenhouse, the director, a small pair of scales—such as are called gold scales—which were of exquisite workmanship and great exactness. The Doctor, in those days of conscientious economy, could not think of taxing the government with anything so elaborate and costly. This decision induced Mr. Getz to solicit the Doctor's acceptance of them, which he courteously declined; subsequently receiving them, however, upon the condition of being permitted to pay twenty dollars for them, which was accepted—thus harmonizing the admiration of the Doctor with the skill of the artist. Soon after, Mr. Getz made very complete scales for the Bank of the United States.

"Compelled as he was to manufacture his own tools—no other facilities than his own brain and hands existing at that time—his triumphs rank him among the most ingenious of his countrymen.

"Mr. Getz died, December 29th, 1809, at 47 years of age, leaving a large family, a number of the descendants of which are living to cherish his memory.

"Mr. Getz was personally complimented by Washington for his artistic skill in producing the die for what is called the 'Washington Cent,' and it was also officially recognized by the Government. This letter was often exhibited by Major John Getz, a son of the artist, during his lifetime. Memory must, however, supply the place of this documentary proof, as it cannot now be found."

COLONIAL COINS.

WASHINGTON CENT.

Device.—A bust of Washington, facing to the right— across the head a band, and in front of the same, a continuation of small curls.   •   1792.
Legend.—WASHINGTON PRESIDENT.
Exergue.—1792.
Reverse.—The American eagle with its wings partially expanded, and turning upward, and on each side of the neck three stars — six in all. The breast bears a heart-shaped shield with six parallel stripes; in the right talon is grasped a bundle of arrows, and in the left, a branch of laurel.
Legend.—CENT.
Edge.—UNITED STATES OF AMERICA · × · × · × · × ·
(Size 8. See Plate XII., Figure 7.)

We do not think this coin has been previously described, as we have never met with but two specimens. The artist, in the features, had evidently made the harsh expression of the emperors upon Roman coins a study; for it really bears more resemblance to a North American Indian than to the father of his country. It has been supposed that this coin was gotten up in our own country; but it is now conceded that it was struck off in England, among the artizans of which, as illustrated by their designs, theoretic patriotism admits of no superiors.

The date, the circumstances then existing, and the piece itself, are all in favor of its having been gotten up for a currency. In regard to that, however, conjecture can supply only what history has failed to preserve or perpetuate. It may, therefore, have been gotten up as a pattern piece, to be submitted to a committee of Congress having the subject in charge. It is now quite valuable and rare.

WASHINGTON HALF-DOLLAR.

Device.—The bust of Washington in continental uniform, facing to the left, with the hair in a cue.   1792.
Legend.—G. WASHINGTON PRESIDENT I.
Exergue.—1792.
Reverse.—An eagle with the wings partially expanded; on the breast, a harp-shaped shield; in the right talon an olive branch, and in the left, a number of arrows.
Legend.—UNITED STATES OF AMERICA.
(Size 10. See Plate XII., Figure 8.)

This piece bears a very close resemblance to the Washington cent of 1792," and our theory relative to it is, that Mr. Getz, in getting up the latter, did not arrive at a satisfactory experiment by a single effort; and that hence the former was struck off upon one of his rejected dies, upon which he had expressed the seal of his condemnation, by putting a mark upon it, as if cut across by a mallet and chisel.

It is a very rare and valuable piece notwithstanding its mutilation, and descended, in good company, from a period of time of which it is a memorial; and, though of doubtful paternity, it is held in much esteem by those who look to it for instruction, without reference to its origin or popularity.

WASHINGTON CENT.

1792. *Device.*—A bust of Washington in military costume, facing to the left, and the hair in a cue.
Legend.—WASHINGTON PRESIDENT.
Exergue.—1792.
Reverse.—An eagle with the wings partially expanded, holding in its beak a scroll, upon which is E. PLURIBUS UNUM; over the head of the same, a star, and above that, twelve others in circular form; in the right talon the olive branch, and in the left, a bundle of arrows.
(Size 8. See Plate XII., Figure 9.)

This is a well executed piece, of which we have seen one type and three varieties.

Like the cents of 1791, previously described, it was undoubtedly gotten up for the same purpose; that is, under the invitation to foreign and native artists, as a pattern piece or specimen for a currency to be submitted to Congress. It may, therefore, be esteemed equally as valuable and rare, and entitled to the same history and importance.

NEW YORK CENT.

1794. *Device.*—A ship under full sail.
Legend.—TALBOT, ALLUM & LEE, NEW YORK.
Exergue.—ONE CENT.
Reverse.—A full length figure of Liberty, a bale of merchandise at her feet, holding in her right hand a pole, surmounted by the liberty cap, while she supports a rudder in her left.
Legend.—LIBERTY & COMMERCE.
Exergue.—1794.
Edge.—PAYABLE AT THE STORE OF +
(Size 8. See Plate XI., Figure 11.)

The die for this piece was gotten up in England in 1794. It is simply a card or token of the firm whose name it bears, and which, it is said, was largely engaged in the shipping business in the city of New York. Similar emissions have been made of late years, but much less elaborate in design.

This, at the time, seemed to take the public fancy, and hence it obtained an active circulation, which was succeeded by another issue in 1795. We have met with two distinct types and seven varieties of the emission of 1794, and one type of that of 1795, all well executed as to workmanship, but composed of very brittle, and consequently, inferior metal.

KENTUCKY COPPER.

Device.—The Goddess of Liberty standing, and facing to the left; the right hand is extended toward two naked children, who are urged toward the Goddess 1796. by a female figure at their backs; with the left arm the Goddess supports the liberty pole, surmounted by the cap. On one side of her is a cornucopia, on the other a fruit tree, and in the back-ground of the figure, on the left, is an anchor.

Legend.—BRITISH SETTLEMENT, KENTUCKY.

Exergue.—1796.

Reverse.—Britannia seated, the left arm resting upon a broken shield, bearing the British cross; in her right rests a spear, point downward; her head drooping, as if surveying the broken sword, scales, &c., which lie at her feet.

Legend.—PAYABLE BY P. P. P. MYDDELTON.

(Size 8. See Plate XI., Figure 12.)

The above devices are rich in the budding sentiments that began to find a place wherever the mind had become enlightened in regard to the principles that had been planted, and taken root on this western continent.

A figure on the obverse, which we may denominate the hand-maid of the Goddess of Liberty, is urging forward, to the goddess' protection, the poor and down-trodden children of despotism; exhibiting to view, as does the goddess by her extended hand, the protecting ægis in the liberty pole and cap, with the emblems of plenty in the cornucopia and fruit tree on either side; and also in the back-ground, the anchor—the emblem of security and hope.

On the reverse, Britannia rests upon a broken shield, bearing the British cross, illustrative of defeat, with the reversed spear, indicative of fallen power, and gazing at the broken sword, scales, &c., at her feet—the paraphernalia of departed authority.

This piece was, as the legend—"Payable by P. P. P. Myddelton"—proves, a private enterprise, undoubtedly gotten up by a leader in a "British settlement," designed for, if it did not actually take place in, Kentucky. It is valuable as an exponent of the feelings of many of our early settlers, full as they were of the spirit of liberty, and which their descendants still enthusiastically cherish.

CASTORLAND HALF-DOLLAR.

1796.   *Device.*—A bust with a laurel wreath, surmounted by a mural crown, and facing to the left.
Legend.—FRANCO-AMERICANA COLONIA.
Exergue.—CASTOR-LAND. 1796.
Reverse.—A figure of Ceres standing, facing to the right, holding in her right hand a cornucopia, and in her left, a carpenter's brace; at her feet a sheaf of wheat; near her is a maple tree, from which the sap is running into a tub.
Legend.—SALVE MAGNA PARENS FRUGUM.
Exergue.—A beaver lying down.
(Size 9. See Plate XI., Figure 13.)

The design of this piece embraces such emblems as would naturally cluster around the thoughts of an agricultural community, seeking a home in the New World; and they are peculiarly appropriate. It was said to have been struck off in Paris by Duvivier, as a pattern piece for a currency for the French settlement, whose history follows.

Composed, as that settlement appears to have been, of persons of wealth and intelligence, and probably but little acquainted with our mint laws and consequent facilities, we are not surprised that it made some provision for a currency.

We gather from Hough's history of Jefferson county, New York, that, "on the 31st of August, 1792, William Constable, one of the three owners of Macomb's great purchase, sold to Peter Chassanis, of Paris, a large tract of land in the present counties of Lewis and Jefferson, east and north of Black river, and intended to contain 640,000 acres, but which, upon subsequent survey, was found to fall short several hundred thousand acres. Chassanis organized a company, which he sent over under the direction of Rudolp Tillier as agent, about the year 1794. These settlers made the first road north from Steuben to the Black river, and began a settlement in the present town of Greig, adjacent to the High Falls.

"A small beginning was made at the head of navigation on Beaver river, named Castorville, and at the present village of Carthage in Jefferson county.

"The French Revolution drove into exile many families of rank and wealth, some of whom settled on this tract, but most of them after a few years returned to France, and the settlements were ultimately abandoned."

PLATE XII.

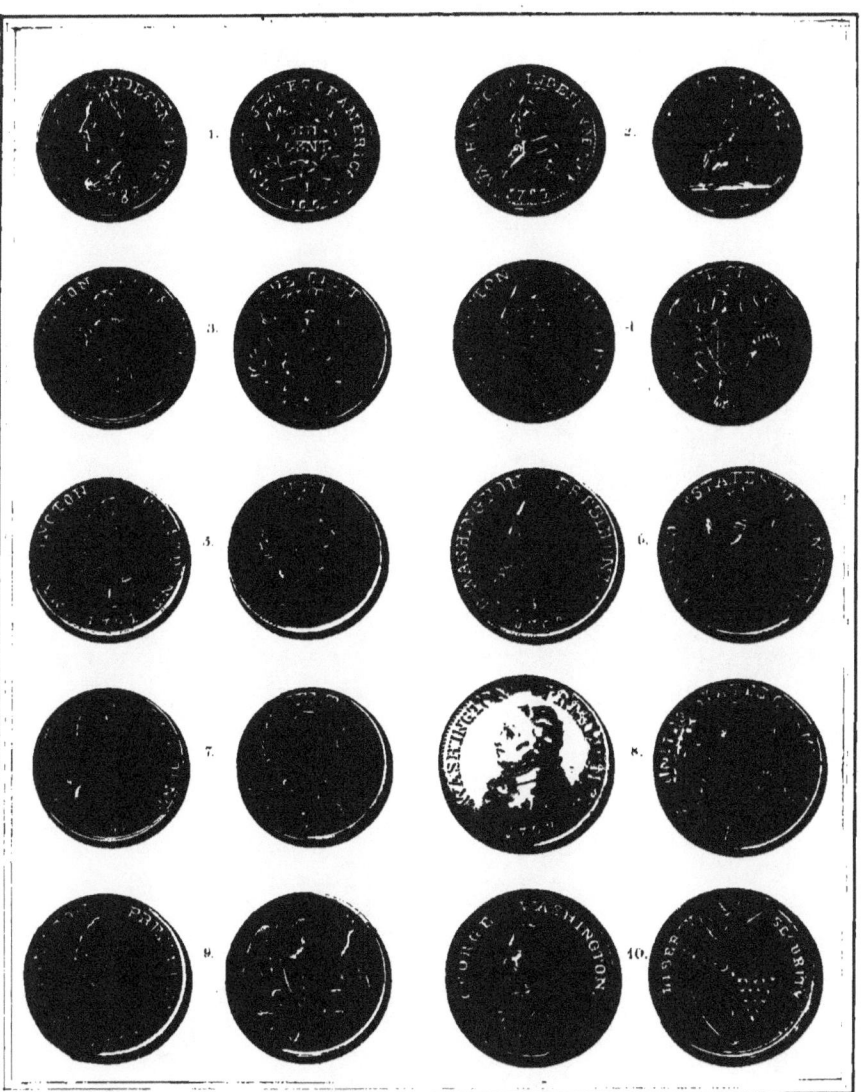

COLONIAL COINS. 137

WASHINGTON TOKENS, COPPERS, AND MEDALETS.

Under this head the following are described. They are part and parcel of collections held in much regard by those who possess them, and in a work designed, as far as practicable, to embrace everything of the kind, whether possessing any particular history or not, we have judged they might, as indexes of the past, prove to be interesting.

No. 1.

"WASHINGTON COPPERS."

Device.—A bust of Washington, facing to the left, in military costume; the hair in a cue.
Legend.—GEORGE WASHINGTON.
Reverse.—A harp surmounted by a crown.
Legend.—NORTH WALES.
(Size 6. See Plate XIII., Figure 8.)

No. 2.

Device.—A finely executed bust of Washington, facing to the left, in continental uniform; the hair in a cue.
Legend.—GEORGE WASHINGTON.
Reverse.—The American Eagle, with wings expanded, holding in the right talon the olive branch, and in the left barbed arrows — over a heart-shaped shield, fifteen stars and stripes.
Legend.—LIBERTY AND SECURITY.
Edge.—AN ASYLUM FOR THE OPPRESSED OF ALL NATIONS.
(Size 10. See Plate XII., Figure 10.)

WASHINGTON MEDALET.

Device.—The bust of Washington in military uniform, and the hair in a cue, facing to the left. 1790.
Legend.—GEO. WASHINGTON BORN VIRGINIA.
Exergue.—Feb. 11, 1732.
Reverse. — GENERAL OF THE AMERICAN ARMIES 1775. RESIGNED 1783. PRESIDENT OF THE UNITED STATES, 1789.
Exergue.—J. MANLY &c. 1790.
(Size 14.)

COLONIAL COINS.

WASHINGTON HALF-PENNY.

1791.   *Device.*—The bust of Washington, facing to the left, in military costume, and the hair in a cue.
Legend.—WASHINGTON PRESIDENT.
Exergue.—1791.
Reverse.—A ship under full sail.
Legend.—HALF PENNY.
Edge.—PAYABLE IN ANGLESY, LONDON OR LIVERPOOL.
(Size 8. See Plate XIII., Figure 4.)

The same as the above, bearing date 1793; and also an issue varying thus—under the ship are two laurel branches crossed.

"LIVERPOOL HALF-PENNY."

1791.   *Device.*—The bust of Washington.
Legend.—WASHINGTON PRESIDENT.
Exergue.—1791.
Reverse.—A ship under full sail.
Legend.—LIVERPOOL HALF PENNY.
(Size 8. See Plate XII., Figure 6.)

WASHINGTON TOKEN.

1795.   *Device.*—The bust of Washington.
Legend.—GEORGE WASHINGTON.
Reverse.—A spread Eagle over the American shield, on which is emblazoned the stars and stripes.
Legend.—LIBERTY AND SECURITY.
Exergue.—1795.
(Size 8.)

"WASHINGTON COPPERS."

1795.   *Device.*—The bust of Washington, facing to the left, in military uniform, and the hair in a cue.
Legend.—GEORGE WASHINGTON
Reverse.—A harp-shaped shield, surmounted by an Eagle with expanded wings, grasping in the right talon three arrows, and in the left, a laurel branch. The shield equally divided—the left portion containing fifteen stars, and the right, the same.
Legend.—LIBERTY AND SECURITY.
Exergue.—1795.
(Size 10. Similar to Figure 10., Plate XII.)

Another precisely the same except size, which is 8.

COLONIAL COINS.

Device.—The bust of Washington, facing to the right, in continental uniform, and
hair in a cue. 1795.
Legend.—G. WASHINGTON THE FIRM FRIEND OF PEACE & HUMANITY ✦
Reverse.—A coal-grate elaborately ornamented in front.
Legend.—PAYABLE BY CLARK & HARRIS 13 WORMWOOD S? BISHOPS-GATE.
Exergue.—LONDON 1795.
(Size 9. Edge grained.)

Of this, there were four varieties—determined by the arrangement and ornamentation of the grate, by a variation in the pillars—ornamented or plain, and the grate without ornament. These pieces evidently found their way into the hands of coin-dealers, instead of subserving the purpose for which they were gotten up—that of a card—and have been deemed worthy of preservation by the curious. They were made of good copper, and the workmanship is superior.

WASHINGTON MEDALET.

Device.—A bust of Washington. 1796.
Legend.—GEORGE WASHINGTON.
Exergue.—1796.
Reverse.—Military trophies, on a banner of which is inscribed REPUB : AMER :
Legend.—GEN'L OF THE AMERICAN ARMIES, 1775. RESIGN'D THE COMM'D,
1783. ELEC'D PRESIDENT OF THE UNITED STATES, 1789. RE-
SIGNED THE PRESIDENCY, 1796.
(Size 12.)

WASHINGTON MEDALET.

Device.—The bust of Washington, in citizen's dress, hair in a cue, and facing right. 1799.
Legend.—GEORGE WASHINGTON ESQ^R LATE PRESIDENT OF THE
UNITED STATES OF AMERICA.
Reverse.—A festooned wreath, divided by thirteen five-pointed stars, surmounted by thirteen
barbed arrows bound together in the centre.
Inscription.—WITH COURAGE AND FIDELITY HE DEFENDED THE RIGHTS
OF A FREE PEOPLE. DIED DEC? 14. 1799. AGED 69.
Legend.—MADE COMMANDER OF THE AMERICAN FORCES THE 15 JUNE 1775.
(Size 12.)

WASHINGTON MEDALETS.

Device.—The bust of Washington, facing to the right.
Legend.—G^E WASHINGTON E^R GENERAL OF THE CONTIN^L ARMY IN AMERICA.
Reverse.—A group of warlike implements—viz., a cannon, mortar, balls, and drum in the foreground, and in the background flags, trumpets, &c.
Legend.—REUNIT PAR UN RARE ASSEMBLAGE LES TALENS DU GUERRIER ET LES VERTUS DE SAGE.
(Size 12.)

Device.—In the foreground, the bust of Washington in a medallion of oval form, suspended from the beak of an Eagle, who is in the act of flying; in the background a blaze festooned with drapery, in the centre of which is the
Legend.—PATRIA PATER.
Reverse.—STRUCK & DISTRIBUTED IN CIVIC PROCESSION FEB^{RY} 22ND 1832., THE CENTENNIAL ANNIVERSARY OF THE BIRTH-DAY OF WASHINGTON BY THE GOLD & SILVER ARTIFICERS OF PHILAD.
(Size 9.)

This collection, with similar single specimens we have described, shows that, at the periods of time they were issued, the name and fame of Washington were inseparable from the daily thoughts of mankind in a state of civilization, inscribed as is his name or bust upon every piece.

Perhaps no man that ever lived has been the subject of so much honest adulation—that flowing directly from the heart—as Washington; and it is universally admitted that no one more justly merited it.

The feeling, manifested by inscriptions upon gold, silver, brass, and copper coins, tokens, medalets, &c., &c., still exists; for, since the times when they were issued, monuments have arisen, and are still rising to his memory; his name has been given to cities, towns, counties, lakes, mountains, &c., &c., and an embryo commonwealth will soon be added to the galaxy of sovereign States of the Union, still further attesting the love and admiration with which his name is remembered.

Potentates, by the authority of force or their own laws, have impressed their names and effigies upon coins; and superstition, bigotry, love of splendor, courtier adulation, and demagoguism have originated medals, statues, monuments, &c., to living and departed greatness. But all these, unlike the voluntary tributes of freemen to Washington, have no connection with the great humanitarian work by which he sought to enlighten and elevate mankind, and which has immortalized him.

Whatever, then, relates to Washington in the past, is not only an index of the by-gone, but an earnest of the future for his memory, which will be as imperishable as the planet upon which we live.

Though our present form of government may ultimately fail, and the people of this now glorious Union sink into subjective degradation — the consequence only of the neglect of the principles he left them as a legacy for their guidance — his name will survive for the just and humane part which he personated in the great drama of universal human rights.

WASHINGTON MEDALET.

Device.—A bust of Washington, in military uniform, the hair in a cue, and facing 1799. to the left, surrounded by a wreath of laurel.
Legend.—HE IS IN GLORY , THE WORLD IN TEARS.
Reverse.—A large Urn with the initials G. W. in the side.
Legend.—B. F. 11, 1732. G. A. ARM. '75. , R. '83, P. U. S. A. '89, R. '96. G. ARM. U. S. '98. , OB. D. 14, 1799.
(Size 8. See Plate XIII., Figure 5.)

Deeming them interesting, we have described a number of these medalets in our pages. This one made its appearance at the time of the death of Washington, in type-metal, copper, silver, and gold. The dates, though not so noted, are O. S. which prevailed at the time of the birth of Washington. The artist, so far as we have been able to discover, is unknown.

Like other medalets of Washington, it undoubtedly had its basis in the love and esteem in which he was held by his countrymen ; and also to commemorate the birth, public employment and death of that distinguished civilian and soldier.

It can excite no surprise that every species of emblem that ingenuity could devise and art execute, should have been produced to enliven and perpetuate his memory ; seeing as we do, that they are now treasured up with a regard and an affection as fresh and as durable as they were half a century ago. Time can make no mutations upon Washington's peerless escutcheon, nor can it diminish the admiration with which his memory will ever be held by the civilized world.

142   COLONIAL COINS.

WASHINGTON MEDALETS.

Device.—A bust of Washington, face front, and in citizen's dress.
Legend.—GENERAL WASHINGTON.
Reverse.—The American eagle, facing front, with expanded wings, on the breast our national shield with stripes, and holding in its talons the arrows and olive branch.
Legend.—IN UNITATE FORTITUDO.
Exergue.—SPIEL-MUNZE.
(Size 5.)

Device.—The bust of Washington, face front, and in citizen's dress.
Legend.—GENERAL WASHINGTON.
Reverse.—The bust of the Goddess of Liberty, facing to the left, around the head the word LIBERTY, and under the bust ten six-pointed stars.
Legend.—COMPOS . SPEIL MUNZE.
(Size 7.)

These pieces were gotten up in Germany, but from what motive or for what purpose we are unable positively to state. Probably, however, for counters—the civilized world, at the time of their manufacture, being so full of the name and fame of Washington, that it was quite natural that his effigy, in the absence of the original, should be made a household god in some form.

They were of two sizes, and the portrait of Washington upon them is so good, that it not only confers credit upon the artist, but would render it a fitting adornment for any similar production.

Of the former, we have seen seven varieties. Though like some others we have introduced into this work, not important in themselves, we have described them, in order that their proper relation and value may be established in our general purpose. These medalets are composed of brass, and the largest of the two we have seen heavily gilded with gold, making it a very pretty cabinet ornament

WASHINGTON MEDALET.

Device.—The bust of Washington, facing to the right, in military costume, a military cloak thrown negligently over the shoulders, and the hair in a cue.
Exergue.—Conradt No. 170. N. Fourth street.
Reverse.—A wreath, composed of the oak and laurel, with acorns and laurel blossoms, connected at each end by a five-pointed star.
Legend.—THE FATHER OF HIS COUNTRY.
Exergue.—Feb. 22, 1832. Philadelphia.
(Size 9.)

This medalet is of modern origin, and was gotten up by Mr. Conradt, an ingenious mechanic of Philadelphia. Its execution shows that he possessed very considerable natural ability as a die-sinker — the bust of Washington on the same being excellent, and falling but little below the standard of the best we have seen.

The motive for getting it up may have been a test of skill, laudable admiration for the character of the "Father of his Country," that fills every heart, and is fain to exhibit itself in every form and upon every practicable occasion, or, united with this, perhaps as a card.

COLUMBIA COPPER.

Device.—A head in the field.
Legend.—COLUMBIA.
Reverse.—A female figure seated, holding a balance.

This coin is about the size of our dime, is without a date, and is familiarly known among collectors as the Columbia token. We notice it because it has had the reputation, from various public sources, of being a North American coin. This coin and its history is well known in Birmingham, England, where it was struck off in 1830, and designed for circulation in Columbia, South America. There are four types; we have seen them in both copper and mixed metals, but most generally in brass.

DE DANSK. AMERIC.

Device.—A figure formed of inverted C's and 6's, surmounted by a crown.   1740.
Legend.—NORY · VAN · G · D · G · REX · DAN.
Reverse.— · II · SKILLING · DANSKE · 1740 · · C · W ·
Legend.—EYLAND · KABB · MYNT · DE · DANSK · AMERIC ·
(Size 8. See Plate XL, Figure 15.)

This coin was issued for the Danish West India Islands, as the date shows, in 1740, during the reign of Christian VI., king of Norway and Denmark, and duke of Holstein.

It is known among collectors as we have designated it; and though it has no connection with the Anglo-American colonies, we have given it a place in this work on account of its antiquity; but chiefly, because it is found in many cabinets, and is highly esteemed by its possessors.

This is the only piece of the kind we have seen, that occupies so early a relation to the history of money in this hemisphere. Looking back to the period of its emission— one hundred and eighteen years ago — we are reminded of the feeble condition and undeveloped power of a continent, which, in its rapid advancement, threatens soon to become the seat of empire for the world—at least for the dissemination of the principles of self-government, without which no nation can avail itself fully of either its intellectual or physical resources — as man thought for is a mere machine, falsifying the great purposes of his creation and destiny.

NORTH AMERICAN TOKEN.

1781. *Device.*—A female figure seated, and supporting with her left hand a harp.
Legend.—NORTH AMERICAN TOKEN.
Exergue.—1781.
Reverse.—A brig under full sail.
Legend.—COMMERCE.
(Size 7½. See Plate XI., Figure 14.)

This piece, among the numerous experiments of the kind, was undoubtedly originally intended for a currency. It had the recommendation of a figure of a female, who, from the accompaniment of a harp, must have been somewhat musical; and for a legend, commerce, exemplified by the figure of a brig, the design and proportions of which would carry one back to an early period in naval architecture. Of this piece there were two types.

PLATE XIII.

PART V.

UNITED STATES.

COINS OF THE UNITED STATES MINT.

These have been so fully and ably described, and treated of, by Messrs. Eckfeldt and Du Bois, the very able Assayers of the Mint, in their "Manual" of 1842, and Supplement to the same, of 1851, that, to the latter date, we find the field of knowledge not only harvested, but gleaned. The extracts from their works will be credited by the usual quotation marks.

"On the 22d of April, 1792, a code of laws was enacted for the regulation of the Mint, under which, with slight changes, the coinage was executed for forty-two years.

"The denominations of coins, with their rates, were as follows, viz:

"Gold.—The eagle or ten dollars, to weigh 270 grains; the half and quarter eagle in proportion; all of the fineness of 22 carats or 917-1000ths.

"Silver.—The dollar, of one hundred cents, to weigh 416 grains; the half, quarter, dime (one-tenth), and half-dime (one-twentieth), in proportion.

"Copper.—The cent, by the act of 1792, to weigh 264 grains, the half-cent in proportion. Since that act, the following alterations of the standard have been made. On the 14th of January, 1793, the weight of the cent was reduced to 208 grains, and the half-cent in proportion. January 26th, 1796, President Washington issued a proclamation, as he had been empowered to do by law, that 'on account of the increase of the price of copper and the expense of coinage, the cent would be reduced to 7 dwts. or 168 grains, and the half-cent in proportion.' The copper coins have since remained at this standard.

"June 28th, 1834, an act was passed changing the weight and fineness of the gold coins, and the relative value of gold to silver. It was found that the estimate of gold, upon the original basis of being worth fifteen times as much as silver, was too low for the market value, which, though always fluctuating, was nearer sixteen to one upon a general average. The effect of our legal proportions was to reduce the coinage of gold, and to restrain its circulation. Being always at a premium, the coin was immediately exported to Europe in the course of trade, and then quickly wrought into other shapes.

"To provide a remedy for this evil, engaged the attention of some of our most eminent statesmen for a term of fifteen years.[1] At length, in June, 1834, the weight of the eagle was reduced by law to 258 grains — the parts in proportion — of which 232 grains must be of fine gold, making the fineness 21 carats $2\frac{13}{16}$ car. grains, or $899\frac{225}{1000}$. This was an increase of $6\frac{66}{100}$ per cent. on the former value of gold. The silver coinage was unchanged.

"The disadvantage of the complex standards of fineness, both in gold and silver, which were difficult to be expressed or remembered, and very inconvenient in regard to the frequent calculations which were based upon them, early determined the Director to endeavor to effect an improvement. The standard of nine-tenths fine, as adopted in France and some other countries, was obviously the most simple, and, upon any consideration, the most suitable.

"To bring our silver coins to that proportion, without changing the amount of fine silver in them, it was only necessary to put less copper by three and a half grains in the dollar, reducing its weight to $412\frac{1}{2}$ grains. The weight of the gold was not to be changed, but the fineness increased about three-fourths of one-thousandth, a difference much within the scope of the legal allowance, and of course hardly appreciable. These proportions were incorporated in a carefully digested and consolidated code of mint laws, which was enacted by Congress in January, 1837. By that act, the eagle is to be 900 thousandths fine, and to weigh 258 grains, the half and quarter in proportion; and the dollar, at the same fineness, to weigh $412\frac{1}{2}$ grains, the parts in proportion: the relative value, therefore, of silver to gold is 15.9884 to 1. The

---

[1] Eminent statesmen engaged for a term of fifteen years, to provide a remedy for the exportation of gold! An expressive commentary upon the economical perceptions and practical reasoning of American statesmen! Surely, the theoretical knowledge acquired at college or in a law office, relative to political economy, is of but little practical use. Could not that little matter of a balance of trade against the country, and which unceasingly drained it of its gold, have been obviated by the necessary protection to American labor; thereby making the exports, independent of gold, equal to the imports? If that had been done — practicable at any moment — urged as it was by the most patriotic statesmen ever devoted to any country's service and welfare, experience shows that it would have been unnecessary to have legislated up the value of gold to have prevented its exportation. Subsequently, our trans-atlantic friends sought our silver, which was the subject of active export.

allowed deviations in fineness for gold, is from 898 to 902, for silver, 897 to 903 — the practical limits here are, for gold, 899 to 901, silver, 898 to 902.

"Until the year 1835 there was but one mint, which was located in Philadelphia. In that year three branches were created by act of Congress: two of these were for the coinage of gold only, and were to be situated at the towns of Charlotte, in North Carolina, and Dahlonega, Georgia — central points in the gold mining region. The third branch was for both gold and silver, and located at New Orleans."

By act of Congress of July 3, 1852, the Branch Mint at San Francisco, California, was established. By act of March 4, 1853, an assay office was established in New York, for the melting, refining, parting, and assaying of gold and silver bullion and foreign coins, and for casting the same into bars, ingots or disks, either of pure metal or standard fineness, as the owner might prefer — provided that no ingot, bar, or disk, shall be cast of less weight than five ounces, unless the same be of standard fineness, and of either one, two, or three ounces in weight. And all gold or silver bullion, and foreign coin, intended by the depositor to be converted into the coins of the United States, shall, as soon as assayed and its net value is certified, be transferred to the Mint of the United States, under such directions as shall be made by the Secretary of the Treasury, and at the expense of the contingent fund of the Mint, and shall there be coined.

"These institutions are respectively managed by superintendents, who are under the control of the director of the parent Mint.

"The whole Mint establishment is thus constituted, in itself, a bureau or branch of the Treasury Department of the General Government, and is under the supervision of the Secretary of the Treasury. Its operations are annually reported through the President to Congress, and are laid open to the public through that body.

"By the act of March 3d, 1849, two new gold coins, the double-eagle and the dollar, were added to the list, the former weighing 516 grains. or 21½ pennyweights, the latter 25$\frac{8}{10}$ grains.

"The new Postage law of March 3d, 1851, provided for the coinage of a three-cent piece, composed of three-fourths silver and one-fourth copper, and weighing 12⅜ grains;" and by the act of Congress of March 3d, 1853, this three-cent coin was altered from 12⅜ grains, to weigh the three-fiftieths of the weight of the half-dollar—reduced under the same law from 206¼ grains to 192—or 11$\frac{28}{50}$ grains. Of this coin, "pattern-pieces" were gotten up, which we have described under that head, the very diminutive size of which, on their first appearance, suggested, outside of the Mint, the form of a flat ring on the score of safety—a pattern for a gold dollar, subsequently, having been gotten up in that form. As issued, however, it is a very useful coin, and custom has rendered it not only very convenient, but a safe size. By the act of March 3d, 1853, it was also enacted that the weight of the half-dollar or piece of fifty cents should be 192 grains, and the quarter, dime, and half-dime respectively, one-half, one-fifth, and one-tenth the weight of said half-dollar. Thus it appears that the dollar was reduced in weight, by the act of January 18th, 1837, from 416 to 412½ grains, and the parts in proportion; which reduced the half-dollar 1¾ grains in weight, and by the act of March 3d, 1853, the half-dollar was reduced from 206¼ grains to 192—14¼ grains—and the quarter, dime, and half-dime in proportion — the silver dollar under this act being untouched, and remaining as under the act of January 18th, 1837, at 412½ grains.

Under the act of March 3d, 1853, the three-dollar gold pieces were authorized to be struck and coined, conformably to the standard of gold coins established by law, which made them 77⅔ grains in weight.

The following are the various standards of the gold and silver coins.

DATE.	GOLD EAGLE.		SILVER DOLLAR.	HALF DOLLAR.	QUARTER.	DIME.	HALF DIME.	SILVER.
	Weight. Grs.	Fineness. Thous.	Weight. Grs.	Weight. Grs.	Weight. Grs.	Weight. Grs.	Weight. Grs.	Fineness. Thous.
Act of April 2, 1792	270.	916.7	416.					892.4
" June 28, 1834	258.	899.2	416.					892.4
" January 18, 1837	258.	900.	412.5					900.
" March 3, 1853	258.	900.	412.5	192.	96.	38⅖	19¼	900.

By act of February 21st, 1857, Sec. 4, it was enacted that the standard weight of the cent coined at the Mint should be 72 grains, or three-twentieths of one ounce Troy, with no greater deviation than four grains in each piece; and said coin shall be composed of eighty-eight per centum of copper and twelve per centum of nickel, of such shape and device as may be fixed by the director of the Mint, with the approbation of the Secretary of the Treasury; and the coinage of the half-cent shall cease.

"Sec. 6. That it shall be lawful to pay out the said cent at the Mint in exchange for any of the gold and silver coins of the United States, and also *in exchange for the copper coins issued*. And it shall also be lawful for the space of two years from the passage of this act, and no longer, to pay out at the Mint the cents aforesaid, for the pieces commonly known as the quarter, eighth, and sixteenth of the Spanish pillar-dollar, and of the Mexican dollar."

Under this act, successful inducements are presented for retiring the old copper cents which had been an "institution," under the Federal government, from 1793 to 1857, or about sixty-four years. And, previous to the establishment of the present Mint, the "copper, with a multitude of devices—royal and republican—had, for more than one hundred and fifty years, been the daily companion of millions of people, and the convenient facility for the exchange of millions of value. We could mourn over the final banishment of these ancient coins and their more modern successors, were it not that their fac-similes will be preserved, and that, hence, we will still be able to contemplate their interesting faces, and gather wisdom from the many philosophic and patriotic impressions, sayings and inscriptions, which they present for our gratification and enlightenment.

"A BRIEF ACCOUNT OF THE PROCESSES EMPLOYED IN THE ASSAY OF GOLD AND SILVER COINS AT THE MINT OF THE UNITED STATES, PREPARED FOR THE USE OF THE COMMISSIONERS APPOINTED TO ATTEND THE ANNUAL ASSAYS.

"PRINCIPLES OF OPERATION.

"According to law the standard of the gold of the United States is so constituted, that in 1000 parts by weight, 900 shall be of pure gold, and 100 of an alloy composed of copper and silver.

"The process of assay requires that the copper and silver be both entirely removed from the gold; and to effect this, two separate operations are necessary.

"The first is for the removal of the copper, and this is done by a method called *cupellation*, which is conducted in an assay furnace, in a cupel composed of calcined bones. To the other metals, lead is added; this metal possesses the properties of oxidizing and vitrifying under the action of heat, of promoting at the same time the oxidation of the copper and other base metals, and of drawing with it into the pores of the cupel the whole of those metals, so as to separate entirely this part of the alloy, and to leave behind the gold and silver only.

"The separation of the silver from the gold is effected by a process founded on the property possessed by nitric acid of dissolving silver without acting upon gold. But that the gold may not protect the silver from this action, sufficient silver must first be added to make it at least two-thirds of the mass. The process to be described is based upon the rule of *quartation*, in which the proportion of silver is three-fourths.

"PROCESS OF ASSAY.

"The reserved gold coins are placed in a black lead crucible, and covered with borax, to assist the fluxing and to prevent the oxidation of the copper alloy. They are thus melted down and stirred; by which a complete mixture is effected, so that an assay piece may be taken from any part of the bar cast out. The piece taken for this purpose is rolled out for convenience of cutting. It is then taken to an assay balance (sensible to the ten-thousandth of a half gramme or less), and from it is weighed a half gramme, which is the normal assay weight for gold, being about 7.7 grains Troy. This weight is stamped 1000, and all the lesser weights (afterwards brought into requisition) are decimal divisions of the weight, down to one ten-thousandth part.

"Silver is next weighed out for the quartation, and as the assay piece, if standard, should contain 900-thousandth of gold, there must be three times this weight, or 2700-thousandths of silver, and this is accordingly the quantity used. It is true that there is already some silver in the alloy, but a little excess over the quantity required for the quartation does no injury to the process.

"The lead used for the cupellation is kept prepared in thin sheets cut into square pieces, which should each weigh about ten times as much as the gold under assays.

"The lead is now rolled into the form of a hollow cone, and into this are introduced the assay gold and the quartation silver, when the lead is closed round them, and pressed into a ball.

"The furnace having been properly heated, and the cupels placed in it, and brought to the same temperature, the leaden ball, with its contents, is put into one of the cupels, the furnace closed, and the operation allowed to proceed until all agitation is ceased to be observed in the melted metal, and its surface has become bright.

"This is an indication that the whole of the base metals have been converted into oxides and absorbed by the cupel.

"The cupellation being thus finished, the metal is allowed to cool slowly, and the disc or *button* which it forms is detached from the cupel.

"The button is then flattened by a hammer; is annealed by bringing it to a red heat; is laminated by passing it between rollers; is again annealed; and is rolled loosely into a spiral or coil called a *cornet*. It is now ready for the process of quartation.

"For this purpose it is introduced into a matrass containing about 1¼ ounces of nitric acid, at 22° of Baumè's hydrometer; and in this acid it is boiled for ten minutes, as indicated by a sand-glass.

"The acid is then poured off, and three-fourths of an ounce of stronger acid, at 32°, is substituted for it, in which the gold is boiled for ten minutes.

"This second acid is then also poured off, and another equal charge of acid of the same strength is introduced, in which the gold is kept for ten minutes longer.

"It is then presumed that the whole of the silver has been removed, and the gold is taken out, washed in pure water, and exposed in a crucible to a red heat, for the purpose of drying, strengthening, and annealing it.

"Lastly, the cornet of fine gold thus formed is placed in the assay balance, and the number of thousandths which it weighs expresses the fineness of the gold assayed, in thousandths.

"Test Assay.

"To test the accuracy of this process the following method is employed:

"A roll of gold of absolute purity, which has been kept under the seal of the chairman of the assay commissioners, is opened in their presence, and from it is taken the weight of 900 parts. To this are added 75 of copper, and 25 of silver; so as to form, with the gold, a weight of 1000 parts, of the exact legal standard.

"This is passed through the same process of assay as the other gold, and at the same time. After the assay is finished it is evident that the pure gold remaining ought to weigh exactly 900. If, however, from any cause, it be found to differ from this weight, and therefore to require a correction, it is assumed that the same correction must be made in the other assays, and this is done accordingly."

"ASSAY OF SILVER COINS.

"Principles of the Operation.

"The standard silver of the United States is so constituted that of a 1000 parts by weight, 900 shall be of pure silver, and 100 of copper.

"The process of assay requires that the exact proportion of silver in a given weight of the compound be ascertained, and this is done by a method called the *humid assay*, which may be explained as follows:

"The silver and copper may both be entirely dissolved in nitric acid; and if to a solution thus made another of common salt in water be added, the silver will be precipitated in the form of a white powder, which is an insoluble chloride, while the copper will remain unaffected.

"Now it has been ascertained that 100 parts by weight of pure salt will convert into chloride of silver just 184.25 parts of pure silver. Consequently the quantity of salt necessary to convert into chloride 1000 parts of silver is 542.74, as found by the proportion—

$$184.25 : 100 :: 1000 : 542.74.$$

"A standard solution of salt is accordingly so prepared as that a given measure (the French decilitre) shall contain 542.74 thousandths of a gramme of salt. The normal weight employed for silver assays is the gramme (equal to about 15.4 Troy grains), which is marked 1000, and has its subdivisions, in practical weighings, to the half or quarter thousandth.

"Besides this standard solution, which effects the main precipitation of chloride of silver, there is a decimal solution of one-tenth the proportion of salt, which it is expedient to use for the lesser and final precipitations.

"In the mode of assay under consideration, it is necessary that the portion of alloyed silver used shall contain as nearly as may be, 1000 parts of pure silver. The rigid standard requires that of 1000 parts by weight, 900 shall be of pure silver; but the law allows a variation from this ratio, provided that it do not exceed three-thousandths. The fineness may, therefore, be as low as 897, and as high as 903. In the practice of the assay, it is found most convenient to assume the lower extreme. Now, the weight of metal, of the fineness 897, which would contain 1000 parts of silver, is 1114.83; as found by the proportion —

$$897 : 1000 :: 1000 : 1114.83.$$

"The nearest integer to this number is employed, and the weight of metal taken for the assay is 1115.

"Process of Assay.

"The reserved silver coins are melted together in a black lead crucible, with the addition of fine charcoal within the pot, to prevent oxidation, and to allow of dipping out. After stirring, a small portion of the fluid metal is poured quickly into water, producing a *granulation;* from which the portion for assay is taken. As this differs from the mode pursued with gold, it must be specially noted, that in the case of silver alloyed with copper, there is a separation, to a greater or less degree, between the two metals in the act of gradual solidification. Thus an ingot cooled in a mould, or any single coin cut out of such ingot, though really 900 thousandths fine on the average, will show such variations, according to the place of cutting, as might even exceed the limits allowed by law. This fact has been established by many experiments, both in this Mint and the Mint of Paris, since the enactment of our Mint law; and it possesses the stubborness of a law of chemistry. But the sudden chill produced by throwing the liquid metal into water, yields a granulation of entirely homogeneous mixture, and it can be proved that the same fineness results, whether by assaying a single granule, or part of one, or a number together.

"From this sample the weight of 1115 thousandths is taken, which is dissolved in a glass bottle with nitric acid.

"Into this solution the large pipette-full of standard solution of salt is introduced, and it produces immediately a white precipitate, which is chloride of silver, and which contains, of the metallic silver, 1000 parts.

"To make this chloride subside to the bottom of the vessel and leave the liquid clear, it is necessary that it be violently shaken in the bottle; and this is accordingly done, by a mechanical arrangement, for the necessary time.

"Unless the coins have chanced to be below the allowable limit of standard, the liquid will still contain silver in solution, and accordingly a portion of the decimal solution is introduced from the small pipette, capable of precipitating a thousandth of silver, and a white cloud of chloride will show itself. More doses are added if the indications require it.

"The liquid is again shaken and cleared, and the process is thus repeated, until the addition of the salt water shows only a faint trace of chloride below the upper surface of the liquid.

"Let us suppose, for the sake of example, that three measures of the decimal solution have been used with effect. This will show that the 1115 parts of the coin contained 1003 of pure silver; and thus the proportion of pure silver in the whole alloyed metal is ascertained.

"Test Assay.

"For the foregoing process to be exact, it is necessary that the saline solution be of the true standard strength, or be such that the quantity of it, measured in the large pipette, shall be just sufficient to precipitate 1000 parts of silver. This cannot be assumed without proof, and a test assay is accordingly made as follows:

"A roll of silver, known to be of absolute purity, is kept from year to year in an envelope, under the seal of the Chairman of the Assay Commissioners. This being opened in their presence, a portion of the silver is taken, and 1004 parts carefully weighed off, and submitted to the process of assay described above. If the salt water used be of the exact standard, it is evident that as the solution in the larger pipette will precipitate 1000 parts of silver, four measures of the decimal solution will be required to precipitate the remaining four parts.

But as the normal or standard solution is affected, from day to day, by changes of temperature or other influences, the finishing decimal doses may be more or fewer; and the other assays are to be corrected by the proof-piece accordingly.

UNITED STATES.

CALCULATION OF FINENESS.

"By the assay, thus corrected, the number of parts of silver contained in 1115 of the metal under trial, is ascertained; and the fineness, in thousandths, is then found by the proportion: As 1115 is to the number of parts of fine silver, so is 1000 to the fineness of the alloyed silver, in thousandths.

"Thus, if the assay show the presence of 1005½ parts of fine silver, the fineness of the alloyed silver will be 901.8 thousandths, as found by the proportion,—

$$1115 : 1005.5 :: 1000 : 901.79.$$

"It is on this principle that the following table is constructed. The numbers at the top and the fractions at the side correspond to the measures of the decimal solution used, corrected by the test assay. The numbers in the body of the table show the corresponding fineness of the assay-piece, of which the weight was 1115 parts.

	0	1	2	3	4	5	6
0	896.9	897.7	898.6	899.6	900.4	901.3	902.2
¼	897.1	898.0	898.9	899.8	900.7	901.6	902.5
½	897.3	898.2	899.1	900.0	900.9	901.8	902.7
¾	897.5	898.4	899.3	900.2	901.1	902.0	902.9

"In the testing of single pieces, it is to be expected that any gold coin, or a cut from any part thereof, will conform faithfully to the bounds prescribed by law. But the silver coins, in addition to the source of error already pointed out (the manner of taking assay samples), are somewhat liable to show too high a result, from several causes. At certain grades of alloy, and especially the standard of 900, the gradual cooling of ingots will draw the better metal to the interior, and the worst towards the exterior and the edges. Hence the fineness of pieces cut off the central part of the ingot is higher than the average fineness of the ingot. Again, in casting ingots from a melting pot, the exposure of the metal to the air during all the time of dipping out, and at the same time, the increase of heat toward the bottom of the pot, unavoidably produces a progressive refining, so that the lower ingot is of a higher quality than the average of the whole melt; and, of course, a coin cut from it will be higher still. Yet with the precautions observed, our silver coins should very rarely exceed the superior limit assigned by law; and there is no good reason why they should fall below the legal limit, unless it be the taking of an unfair sample for assay."

GOLD COINAGE.

The *data* relative to our gold coinage, owing to the want of proper Mint records, and the great scarcity of the earlier emissions, is so limited, as to render impracticable a particular detail of the types and varieties. We must, therefore, content ourselves with giving the different types and such varieties as have come under our observation.

The early gold coinage of our government has become very scarce, and hence is exceedingly rare, being found more frequently in the southern than in the northern part of our Union.

The first coinage of gold occurred in June, 1795, in the form of eagles and half-eagles, and the fineness was 916.7 thousandths.

EAGLE.

Device.—A female head—the Goddess of Liberty—wearing the liberty-cap, and the hair flowing loosely. Around the edge of the field are fifteen six-   1795.
pointed stars—five on the right, and ten on the left of the same.
Legend.—LIBERTY.
Exergue.—1795.
Reverse.—The American Eagle with expanded wings, holding in its beak a laurel chaplet, and in the talons a palm-branch.
Legend.—UNITED STATES OF AMERICA.
(Size 9. See Plate XIV., Figure 1.)

Of this emission we have met with but one type and three varieties; number coined was 2795, and the weight 270 grains.

HALF-EAGLE.

The designs the same, weight 135 grains. Of this coin there were one type and three varieties, and the number coined was 8707. They are scarcer and   1795.
rarer than the eagles. (Size 6½. See Plate XIV., Figure 2.)

EAGLE.

The designs the same as the preceding with the addition of another star, emblematic of the admission of Tennessee into the Union. This system of the   1796.
adornment of our coinage was commenced — as will be subsequently noted —
not only upon the gold, but the silver and copper, but afterwards abandoned. We think the adding of such a symbol, upon the admission of a State, as an expressive

UNITED STATES.

and beautiful idea; and we cannot but regret that it was not continued. Of this omission there were one type and two varieties, and the number coined was 6934. They are extremely rare.

HALF-EAGLE.

1796. The designs the same, with one type and two varieties; and the number coined was 6196. Equally rare with the preceding. One of the varieties bears the effigy of a well-formed and very pretty face, which has been denominated the Martha Washington. It has been stated that she sat to the artist for this portrait. Whether true or not, the declaration has been sufficient to impress its credibility upon the imagination of some one, for the piece—based upon this idea—has been lately sold for the sum of ten dollars. If there is any foundation for this statement, we must conclude that the artist's admiration of the lady's beauty overcame all scruples relative to the propriety of the act; and if he had but chronicled the fact, he might himself have been included in the charmed circle of the immortalized.

QUARTER-EAGLE.

1796. This denomination made its first appearance this year. There were two types and three varieties, and the number coined was 963.

The designs the same as the preceding denominations, in what we designate as the first type; but in the second the stars are left off the obverse, and the eagle on the reverse is entirely changed, the wings being partially expanded; on the breast a heart-shaped shield; in its beak a scroll with the motto E. PLURIBUS UNUM; over the head of the Eagle, clouds and sixteen six-pointed stars, in one talon a bundle of barbed arrows, and in the other a laurel branch.

Legend.—UNITED STATES OF AMERICA.

Of the first type very few were issued, and the number of the second being small, they may both be said to be extremely rare. (Size 5. See Plate XIV., Figure 5.)

EAGLE.

1797. The device the same as this denomination of the preceding year, the number of stars on the obverse being sixteen, ten on the left hand, and six on the right of the effigy.

Reverse.—The Eagle changed—the wings partially expanded; on the breast a heart-shaped shield; in its beak a scroll with the motto E. PLURIBUS UNUM; over the head of the Eagle, clouds and thirteen six-pointed stars; one talon grasps a bundle of barbed arrows, and the other a laurel branch.

Legend.—UNITED STATES OF AMERICA.

(Size 7. See Plate XIV., Figure 4.)

UNITED STATES.   157

Of this emission we have met with but one type and three varieties, and the number coined was 8323. They are more numerous than any of the previous issues of this denomination, but cannot be said to be easily obtained. It has been stated that there was an issue of this year with but fifteen stars on the obverse; we can only say, that in our extensive researches we have not been fortunate enough to meet with it, and hence we cannot accede to the correctness of the statement.

Half-Eagle.

The designs the same as this denomination in the preceding year. There were of this issue one type and two varieties, and the number coined was 3609.   1797. They are now quite rare.

Quarter-Eagle.

The designs the same as the preceding, with one type and two varieties, and the number coined was 855. They are seldom met with, except in cabinet   1797. collections, and hence are extremely rare.

Eagle.

The designs the same as the preceding of this denomination, except that the number of stars is reduced from sixteen to thirteen on the obverse — seven on   1798. the left, and six at the right of the effigy. Of this issue there were one type and three varieties, and the number coined was 7974. They are quite scarce.

(Size 7. See Plate XIV., Figure 3.)

Half-Eagle.

The designs the same, with one type and three varieties, and the number coined was 24,867. Notwithstanding the comparatively large number coined,   1798. they are scarce.

Quarter-Eagle.

The designs the same, with one type and two varieties, and the number coined was 614. They are, of course, extremely rare.   1798.

Eagle.

The designs the same, with the exception of the arrangement of the stars on the obverse—eight on the left, and five on the right of the effigy. There were   1799. of this issue one type and three varieties, and the number coined was 17,483. One variety has fourteen stars on the reverse, evidently an error. This emission is more plenty than any of the same denomination for previous years, and yet they may be considered scarce.

HALF-EAGLE.

1799. The designs the same as the preceding, with one type and two varieties, and the number coined was 7451. They are not numerous at this time.

QUARTER-EAGLE.

1799. The Mint report gives a coinage of this denomination, in this year, of 480 pieces. Never having seen one of them, or heard of any one who had, it is out of our power to furnish either the designs, types or varieties of the same.

EAGLE.

1800. The designs the same as the preceding of this denomination, with one type and two varieties, and the number coined was 25,965. They are scarce.

HALF-EAGLE.

1800. The designs the same as the preceding, with one type and two varieties, and the number coined was 7451. They are considered as rare.

EAGLE.

1801. The designs the same as the preceding, with one type and two varieties, and the number coined was 29,254. They may be considered as scarce.

HALF-EAGLE.

1801. Here we have to record another instance, in the history of our coinage, in which the comparatively large number of 26,006 pieces was coined, as per report of the United States Mint, and yet every piece has escaped the eagle eyes of numismatologists; not a single piece having been seen by them, or other collectors of coins of whom we have heard. There is a mystery connected with it wholly inexplicable to us. Could "John Bull" have gotten that whole *batch*, and consigned it to the melting-pot? If so, we shall never hear of it more.

EAGLE.

1802. And still another instance in which the number of pieces is given, as coined by the Mint, 15,090, and not a solitary piece to be seen or heard of. This destruction of links in our metallic chain is anything but agreeable.

Half-Eagle.

The designs the same as upon the preceding coin of this denomination, with one type and a single variety, and the number coined was 53,176. They are more easily procured than any of the others of this denomination.   1802.

Eagle.

The designs the same as the last of this denomination described, with one type and three varieties, and the number coined was 8979. They are considered as rare.   1803.

Half-Eagle.

The designs the same as the preceding of this denomination, with one type and three varieties, and the number coined was 33,506. They are not considered as scarce.   1803.

Quarter-Eagle.

A fourth instance in which the Mint report gives us, as coined, the number of 423 pieces, not a solitary one of which, so far as we have been able to learn, has a place in any cabinet in our country — not so much to be wondered at, however, as the coinage was so small.   1803.

Eagle.

The designs the same as the preceding of this denomination, with one type and two varieties, and the number of pieces coined was 9795. They are indeed rare.   1804.

This was the last of the emission of the old-fashioned Eagle, whose diameter is so remarkable, contrasted with the same denomination since coined at our Mint. We look upon it with somewhat of a feeling of reverence, it being the pioneer of that description of currency in our country, and characterized by an appearance that partakes much of the times when our forefathers had the same quaint resemblance, but not the less allied to those solid and substantial qualities so essential in laying the foundations of a government, which for enlightened and perfect workmanship, has ever since been the model and admiration of the thinking portion of the human family.

Half-Eagle.

The designs the same as the preceding of this denomination, with one type and three varieties, and the number of pieces coined was 30,475. They are not plenty, but on the contrary show indications of scarcity.   1804.

QUARTER-EAGLE.

1804. The designs the same as the preceding of this denomination, with one type and two varieties, and the number coined was 3327. May be said to be merely scarce.

HALF-EAGLE.

1805. The designs the same as the preceding of this denomination, with one type and two varieties, and the number coined was 33,183. They are scarce.

QUARTER-EAGLE.

1805. The designs the same as the preceding of this denomination, with one type and one variety, and the number coined was 1781. This emission is rare.

HALF-EAGLE.

1806. The designs the same as the preceding of this denomination, with one type and two varieties, and the number coined was 6493. It is not difficult to procure specimens of this issue.

HALF-EAGLE.

1807. The designs the same with the preceding, except a change in the arrangement of the stars — seven on the left, and six on the right of the effigy, with one type and three varieties, and the number coined was 8493. This emission is not scarce.

QUARTER-EAGLE.

1807. The designs the same, with one type and two varieties, and the number of pieces coined was 6812. They are scarce.

HALF-EAGLE.

1808. *Device.*—A female head, with a band around the same, bearing the word LIBERTY. Around the edges of the field thirteen stars.
Exergue.—1808.
Reverse.—The Eagle with the heart-shaped shield, &c., as on previous emissions; a scroll with E. PLURIBUS UNUM inscribed upon it, being substituted for the clouds and stars over the head of the same.
Legend.—UNITED STATES OF AMERICA.
(Size 6. See Plate XIV., Figure 13.)

UNITED STATES.

Quarter-Eagle.

The designs the same as the above, with one type and three varieties, and the number coined was 2710. They are scarce.   1808.
(Size 4. See Plate XIV., Figure 8.)

Half-Eagle.

The designs the same, with one type and one variety, and the number coined was 33,875. They are scarce.   1809.

Half-Eagle.

The designs the same, with one type and four varieties, and the number coined was 100,207. Not scarce.   1810.

Half-Eagle.

The designs the same, with one type and two varieties, and the number coined was 99,581. Plenty.   1811.

Half-Eagle.

The designs the same, with one type and three varieties, and the number coined was 58,087. Becoming scarce.   1812.

Half-Eagle.

The designs the same, with one type and four varieties, and the number coined was 95,428. Plenty.   1813.

Half-Eagle.

The designs the same, with one type and two varieties, and the number coined was 15,454. They are rare.   1814.

Half-Eagle.

The mint report gives a coinage of 635 pieces for this year. We have never met with one of them — the designs of this emission were undoubtedly the same.   1815.

Half-Eagle.

The designs the same—two years having elapsed without any gold coinage—with one type and three varieties, and the number coined was 48,588. This issue is scarce.   1818.

Half-Eagle.

The designs the same, with one type and three varieties, and the number coined was 51,723. They can be easily procured.   1819.

HALF-EAGLE.

1820. The designs the same, with one type and two varieties, and the number coined was 263,806. This emission is quite plenty

HALF-EAGLE.

1821. The designs the same, with one type and two varieties, and the amount coined was 34,641. They are scarce.

QUARTER-EAGLE.

1821. The designs the same, with one type and three varieties, and the number coined was 6448. They are rare.

HALF-EAGLE.

1822. The designs the same, with one type and two varieties, and the number coined was 17,340. They are rare.

HALF-EAGLE.

1823. The designs the same, with one type and two varieties, and the number coined was 14,485. Rare.

HALF-EAGLE.

1824. The designs the same, with one type and three varieties, and the number coined was 1734. They are rare.

QUARTER-EAGLE.

1824. The designs the same, with one type and four varieties, and the number coined was 2600. Rare.

HALF-EAGLE.

1825. The designs the same, with one type and three varieties, and the number coined was 29,060. Plenty.

QUARTER-EAGLE.

1825. The designs the same, with one type and one variety, and the number coined was 4434. They are scarce.

HALF-EAGLE.

1826. The designs the same, with one type and one variety, and the number coined was 18,069. Scarce.

UNITED STATES.

QUARTER-EAGLE.

The designs the same, with one type and two varieties, and the number coined was 760. Very rare. 1826.

HALF-EAGLE.

The designs the same, with one type and three varieties, and the number coined was 24,913. Scarce. 1827.

QUARTER-EAGLE.

The designs the same, with one type and one variety, and the number coined was 2800. Rare. 1827.

HALF-EAGLE.

The designs the same, with one type and one variety, and the number coined was 28,029. Rare. 1828.

HALF-EAGLE.

The designs the same, with one type and one variety, and the number coined was 57,442. Rare. 1829.

QUARTER-EAGLE.

The designs the same, with one type and four varieties, and the number coined was 3403. Scarce. 1829.

HALF-EAGLE.

The designs the same, with one type and two varieties, and the number coined was 126,351. Plenty. 1830.

QUARTER-EAGLE.

The designs the same, with one type and three varieties, and the number coined was 4540. Merely scarce. 1830.

HALF-EAGLE.

The designs the same, with one type and three varieties, and the number coined was 140,594. This issue has become scarce, notwithstanding the large number coined. 1831.

QUARTER-EAGLE.

The designs the same, with one type and two varieties, and the number coined was 4520. Rare. 1831.

HALF-EAGLE.

The designs the same, with one type and two varieties, and the number coined was 157,487. Scarce. 1832.

UNITED STATES.

QUARTER-EAGLE.

1832. The designs the same, with one type and three varieties, and the number coined was 4400. Merely scarce.

HALF-EAGLE.

1833. The designs the same, with one type and one variety, and the number coined was 193,630. Not plenty. This was the last issue bearing the favorite motto, "E. PLURIBUS UNUM," which was given up with much regret, it having been for many years upon our coins, and daily reminding the people of their own unity, as well as the unity of the States.

QUARTER-EAGLE.

1833. The designs the same, with one type and two varieties, and the number coined was 4160. Only scarce.

HALF-EAGLE.

1834. Device the same as on the obverse of this denomination of the preceding year; the scroll with the motto, "E. PLURIBUS UNUM," on the reverse, removed. Of this issue there were two types and five varieties, and the number coined was 732,169. Notwithstanding this large coinage, they are scarce, the first type being extremely rare.

(Size 5½. See Plate XIV., Figure 9.)

QUARTER-EAGLE.

1834. The designs the same as the half-eagle, with one type and three varieties, and the number coined was 117,370. Rare.

HALF-EAGLE.

1835. The designs the same, with one type and two varieties, and the number coined was 371,534. Scarce.

QUARTER-EAGLE.

1835. The designs the same, with one type and two varieties, and the number coined was 131,402. Rare.

UNITED STATES.

HALF-EAGLE.

The designs the same, with one type and three varieties, and the number coined was 553,147. Scarce. 1836.

QUARTER-EAGLE.

The designs the same, with one type and three varieties, and the number coined was 547,986. Scarce. 1836.

HALF-EAGLE.

The designs the same, with one type and two varieties, and the number of pieces coined was 207,121. Scarce. 1837.

QUARTER-EAGLE.

The designs the same, with one type and three varieties, and the number coined was 45,080. Rare. 1837.

EAGLE.

Device.—A female head—Goddess of Liberty—facing to the left, the hair done up behind, and bound by a fillet, upon which is inscribed the word LIBERTY, curls falling down on the neck. Around the edge of the field thirteen stars. 1838.

Exergue.—1838.

Reverse.—The eagle proportionally reduced in size, otherwise the same in design as on the half-eagle of 1834.

Legend.—UNITED STATES OF AMERICA.

Exergue.—TEN D.

(Size 7. See Plate XIV., Figure 10.)

Of this issue there were one type and two varieties, and the number coined was 7200. Rare. Of this denomination there had been none coined since 1804, a period of thirty-four years.

HALF-EAGLE.

The designs the same as upon the eagle, with one type and one variety, and the number coined was 286,588; notwithstanding which, they are scarce. 1838. (Size 5. See Plate XIV., Figure 11.)

QUARTER-EAGLE.

The designs the same, with one type and two varieties, and the number coined was 47,030. Plenty. (Size 4. See Plate XIV., Figure 12.) 1838.

EAGLE.

The designs the same, with one type and two varieties, and the number coined was 38,248. Scarce. 1839.

UNITED STATES.

HALF-EAGLE.

1839. The designs the same, with one type and three varieties, and the number coined was 118,143. Scarce.

QUARTER-EAGLE.

1839. The designs the same, with one type and two varieties, and the number coined was 27,021. Scarce.

EAGLE.

1840. The designs the same, with one type and three varieties, and the number coined was 47,338. Scarce.

HALF-EAGLE.

1840. The designs the same, with one type and three varieties, and the number coined was 137,382. Scarce.

QUARTER-EAGLE.

1840. The designs the same, with one type and two varieties, and the number coined was 18,859. Scarce.

EAGLE.

1841. The designs the same, with one type and three varieties, and the number coined was 63,031. Scarce.

HALF-EAGLE.

1841. The designs the same, with one type and two varieties, and the number coined was 15,838. Scarce.

QUARTER-EAGLE.

1841. The designs the same, with the exception of the letter C on the reverse, which addition, as we are informed, referred to California, this emission being a private enterprise designed for that country. There was one type and one variety, but the Mint report does not furnish the number coined.

EAGLE.

1842. The designs the same, with one type and three varieties, and the number coined was 81,507. Scarce.

UNITED STATES.

HALF-EAGLE.

The designs the same, with one type and four varieties, and the number coined was 27,578. Rare. 1842.

QUARTER-EAGLE.

The designs the same, with one type and three varieties, and the number coined was 2823. This issue is extremely rare. 1842.

EAGLE.

The designs the same, with one type and two varieties, and the number coined was 250,624. Not scarce. 1843.

HALF-EAGLE.

The designs the same, with one type and two varieties, and the number coined was 855,085. Not scarce. 1843.

QUARTER-EAGLE.

The designs the same, with one type and two varieties, and the number coined was 530,853. Not scarce. 1843.

EAGLE.

The designs the same, with one type and two varieties, and the number coined was 125,061. Scarce. 1844.

HALF-EAGLE.

The designs the same, with one type and three varieties, and the number coined was 817,583. Scarce, though the emission was large. 1844.

QUARTER-EAGLE.

The designs the same, with one type and two varieties, and the number coined was 35,738. They are rare. 1844.

EAGLE.

The designs the same, with one type and two varieties, and the number coined was 73,653. Scarce. 1845.

HALF-EAGLE.

The designs the same, with one type and three varieties, and the number coined was 548,728. They are plenty. 1845.

UNITED STATES.

Quarter-Eagle.

1845. The designs the same, with one type and three varieties, and the number coined was 110,511. They are scarce.

Eagle.

1846. The designs the same, with one type and two varieties, and the number coined was 101,875. Not scarce.

Half-Eagle.

1846. The designs the same, with one type and two varieties, and the number coined was 547,231. Not scarce.

Quarter-Eagle.

1846. The designs the same, with one type and one variety, and the number coined was 110,709. They are rare.

Eagle.

1847. The designs the same, with one type and three varieties, and the number coined was 1,433,764. They are plenty.

Half-Eagle.

1847. The designs the same, with one type and three varieties, and the number coined was 1,080,337. Notwithstanding the large amount coined, they are getting to be scarce.

Quarter-Eagle.

1847. The designs the same, with one type and two varieties, and the number coined was 192,824. Scarce.

Eagle.

1848. The designs the same, with one type and three varieties, and the number coined was 145,484. Notwithstanding the comparatively limited amount, they are not scarce.

Half-Eagle.

1848. The designs the same, with one type and two varieties, and the number coined was 267,775. They are becoming scarce.

UNITED STATES. 169

QUARTER-EAGLE.

The designs the same, with one type and two varieties, and the number coined was 8886. They are quite scarce. 1848.

DOUBLE-EAGLE.

Device.—A bust of the Goddess of Liberty facing left; the hair done up behind the head, and falling in curls; around the same a fillet on which is the motto 1849. LIBERTY; and around the edge of the field thirteen stars.

Exergue.—1849.

Reverse.—An eagle with expanded wings; on the breast of the same a shield; on a scroll, pendent from the beak of the eagle and passing round the shield, is the motto "E PLURIBUS UNUM;" above the head of the Eagle is an oval circle formed by thirteen stars, and surmounted by a blaze; in the talons the olive-branch and arrows.

Legend.—UNITED STATES OF AMERICA.
Exergue.—TWENTY DOLLARS.
(Size 9. See Plate XIV., Figure 6.)

The first coinage of this piece occurred in this year, an evidence of expansion of ideas in relation to our currency; it being, however, induced by the development of, and accessions from the gold deposits of California, and consequent upon the increase of business, which demanded additional facilities for the increasing exchanges based thereon.

The coinage of this denomination, it will be observed, was, for a number of years, quite large; but gold bars, as soon as the means for assaying the same were given — afforded by the establishment of the Assay Office in New York in 1853—superseded in a great measure the demand for coin for export, and, hence, very materially reduced the amount coined.

There was of this piece one type and a single variety, and the weight was 517 grains.

EAGLE.

The designs the same as upon this denomination in the preceding year, with one type and three varieties, and the number coined was 653,618. Not scarce. 1849.

HALF-EAGLE.

The designs the same, with one type and two varieties, and the number coined was 133,070. Scarce. 1849.

22

QUARTER-EAGLE.

1849. The designs the same as the preceding, with one type and two varieties, and the number of pieces coined was 23,294. They are rare.

DOLLAR.

1849. This very convenient little coin, which it would now be very difficult to dispense with, made its first appearance this year. The originator is entitled to much credit for comprehending a very great convenience, which many, at first, were unwilling to acknowledge or incapable of appreciating.

1849. *Device.*—A bust of the Goddess of Liberty, facing to the left; a band around the head, bearing the word LIBERTY; around the edge of the field thirteen six-pointed stars.
Reverse.—A laurel wreath enclosing the inscription: "I DOLLAR 1849."
Legend.—UNITED STATES OF AMERICA.
(Size 2. See Plate XIV., Figure 14.)

DOUBLE-EAGLE.

1850. The designs the same as upon this denomination of the preceding year, with one type and two varieties, and the number of pieces coined was 1,170,261—amounting to $23,405,220 of a single denomination, and which has been followed, under the new state of affairs—at this period of time being initiated—by similar extraordinary results.

EAGLE.

1850. The designs the same as upon this denomination of the preceding year, with one type and two varieties, and the number coined was 291,451. Not scarce.

HALF-EAGLE.

1850. The designs the same, with one type and two varieties, and the number coined was 64,491. They are rare.

QUARTER-EAGLE.

1850. The designs the same, with one type and three varieties, and the number coined was 252,923. Plenty.

DOLLAR.

1850. The designs the same as upon this denomination of the preceding year, with one type and three varieties, and the number coined was 481,953. They are scarce.

UNITED STATES.

DOUBLE-EAGLE.

The designs of this denomination unchanged, with one type and four varieties, and the number coined was 2,087,155. They are plenty.   1851.

EAGLE.

The designs the same as previously given of this denomination, with one type and three varieties, and the number coined was 176,328. Not scarce.   1851.

HALF-EAGLE.

The design the same as the preceding, with one type and four varieties, and the number coined was 377,505. Not scarce.   1851.

QUARTER-EAGLE.

The designs the same, with one type and three varieties, and the number coined was 1,372,748. Plenty.   1851.

DOLLAR.

The designs unaltered, with one type and two varieties, and the number coined was 1,317,671. Plenty.   1851.

DOUBLE-EAGLE.

The designs unaltered, with one type and four varieties, and the number coined was 2,053,026. Not scarce.   1852.

EAGLE.

The designs unaltered, with one type and three varieties, and the number coined was 263,106. Plenty.   1852.

HALF-EAGLE.

The designs unaltered, with one type and four varieties, and the number coined was 573,901. Not scarce.   1852.

QUARTER-EAGLE.

The designs unaltered, with one type and two varieties, and the number coined was 1,159,681. They are scarce.   1852.

UNITED STATES.

DOLLAR.

1852. The designs unaltered, with one type and three varieties, and the number coined was 2,045,351. Not scarce.

DOUBLE-EAGLE.

1853. The designs unaltered, with one type and two varieties, and the number coined was 1,261,326. They are not plenty.

EAGLE.

1853. The designs unaltered, with one type and two varieties, and the number coined was 210,253. They are not scarce.

HALF-EAGLE.

1853. The designs unaltered, with one type and two varieties, and the number coined was 305,770. Not scarce.

QUARTER-EAGLE.

1853. The designs unaltered, with one type and one variety, and the number coined was 1,404,668. Plenty.

DOUBLE-EAGLE.

1854. The designs unaltered, with one type and two varieties, and the number coined was 757,899. Plenty.

EAGLE.

1854. The designs unaltered, with one type and one variety, and the number coined was 54,250. Scarce.

HALF-EAGLE.

1854. The designs unaltered, with one type and two varieties, and the number coined was 160,675. Rare.

THREE-DOLLAR PIECE.

1854. *Device.*—A female effigy, designed to represent an Indian princess, the head of which is encircled in feathers in a band around the same, on which is inscribed the word LIBERTY.
Legend.—UNITED STATES OF AMERICA.
Reverse.—3 DOLLARS 1854. Surrounded by a wreath.
(Size 5. See Plate XIV., Figure 16.)

UNITED STATES.

The weight of this piece is 77⅞ grains, and it first made its appearance in this year.

As a coin it is very unpopular, being frequently mistaken for a quarter-eagle, and often counted as a five-dollar piece. It is exceedingly annoying to that portion of the human family whose vision is dependent upon artificial aid, and we think its retirement would meet with the public approbation. Of this issue there was one type and a single variety, and the amount coined was 138,618. Scarce.

QUARTER-EAGLE.

The designs unaltered, with one type and two varieties, and the number coined was 596,258. Plenty. 1854.

DOLLAR.

Device.—A female effigy, designed to represent an Indian princess, the head of which is encircled with feathers in a band around the same, on which is inscribed the word LIBERTY. 1854.

Legend.—UNITED STATES OF AMERICA.

Reverse.—1 DOLLAR 1854. Surrounded by a wreath.

(Size 3. See Plate XIV., Figure 15.)

This, and the three-dollar piece are the most beautiful and artistic coins issued by the United States Mint. Of this dollar there was one type and a single variety, and the number coined was 1,639,445. Not scarce.

DOUBLE-EAGLE.

The designs unaltered, with one type and two varieties, and the number coined was 964,666. Not scarce. 1855.

EAGLE.

The designs unaltered, with one type and two varieties, and the number coined was 121,701. Not scarce. 1855.

HALF-EAGLE.

The designs unaltered, with one type and two varieties, and the number coined was 117,098. Scarce. 1855.

THREE-DOLLAR PIECE.

The designs unaltered, with one type and one variety, and the number coined was 50,555. Not scarce. 1855.

UNITED STATES.

QUARTER-EAGLE.

1855. The designs unaltered, with one type and two varieties, and the number coined was 235,480. Not scarce.

DOLLAR.

1855. The designs unaltered, with one type and two varieties, and the number coined was 758,269. Plenty.

DOUBLE-EAGLE.

1856. The designs unaltered, with one type and two varieties, and the number coined was 329,878. Not scarce.

EAGLE.

1856. The designs unaltered, with one type and three varieties, and the amount coined was 60,490. Plenty.

HALF-EAGLE.

1856. The designs unaltered, with one type and two varieties, and the number coined was 197,990. Not scarce.

THREE-DOLLAR PIECE.

1856. The designs unaltered, with one type and one variety, and the number coined was 26,010. Scarce.

QUARTER-EAGLE.

1856. The designs unaltered, with one type and two varieties, and the number coined was 384,240. Not scarce.

DOLLAR.

1856. The designs unaltered, with one type and two varieties, and the number coined was 1,762,936. Plenty.

DOUBLE-EAGLE.

1857. The designs unaltered, with one type and two varieties, and the number coined, up to June 30th, was 98,315. Not scarce.

EAGLE.

1857. The designs unaltered, with one type and one variety, and the number coined, up to June 30th, was 2,916. Not scarce.

PLATE XIV.

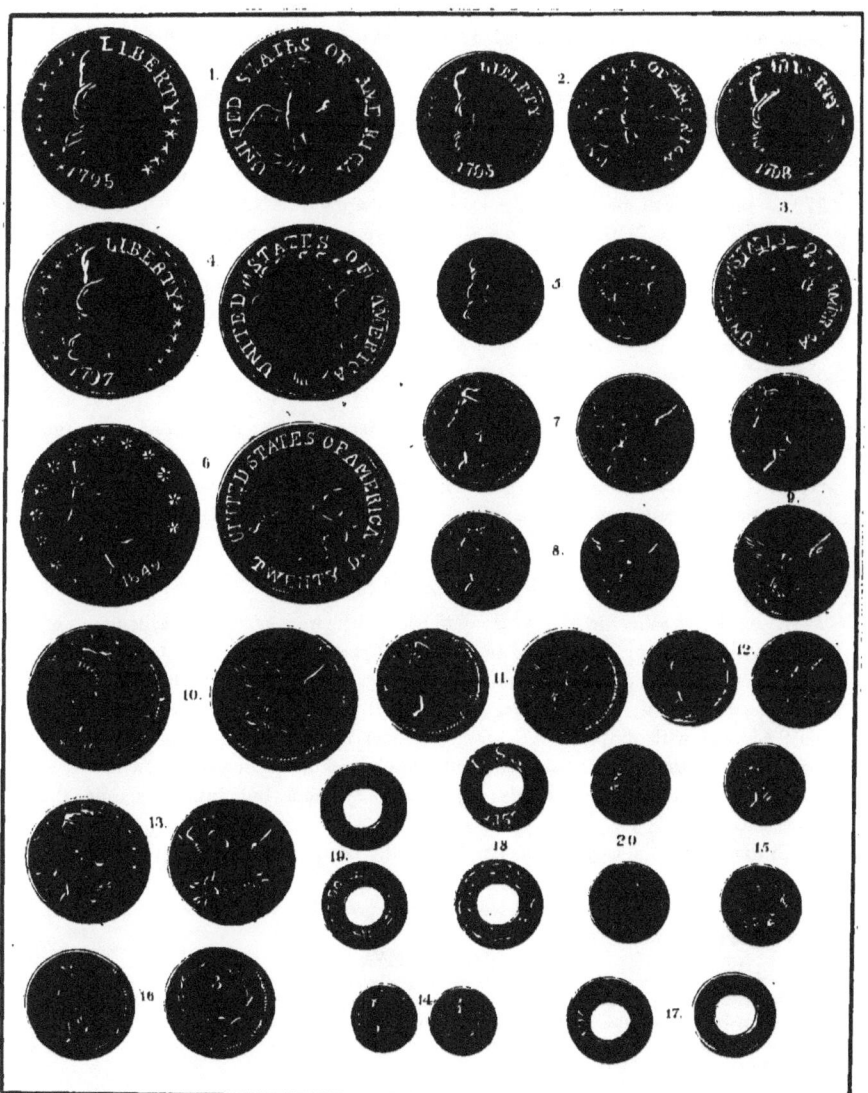

UNITED STATES.

Of the dollar of this year, we have met with but one type and four varieties;[1] the latter of which may be determined by the variation in the size of the eagle, and the arrangement and size of the leaves in the wreath. This coin has become exceedingly rare, and fair specimens command a handsome premium.

HALF-DOLLAR.

1794. The design the same as the dollar, differing only in size, which is *nine*, and the legend on the edge, which is: FIFTY ✱ ✱ ◻ ◉ ◻ CENTS ✱ ✱ ✱ OR ✱ ✱ ◻ ◉ ◻ HALF ✱ ✱ DOLLAR ✱ ✱ ◻ ◉ ◉. We have met with but one type and three varieties. The number coined we are unable to state, though it must have been much greater than of the dollar. Though getting to be scarce, they command but a small premium, being much worn. It is rare to find perfect specimens in circulation.

(Size 9. See Plate XV., Figure 2.)

HALF-DIME.

1794. The general design the same on this denomination of coin, and it was the only piece, below the half-dollar, coined in this year. We have seen but a limited number of these pieces, which are of one type and two varieties. They are particularly rare, and hence, a well preserved specimen is seldom found out of the cabinets of our oldest collectors. (Size 4. See Plate XVI., Figure 6.)

DOLLAR.

1795. Those coined in this year, up to September, were of the same design as of the preceding year; but, in the latter portion of the year, the type was changed, which formed two distinct types. Of the first of these, there are six varieties, and the second, four. In the latter, the effigy is presented with a full bust adorned with drapery; the hair is secured by a band, the bow of which is perceptible on the back of the head, and flows gracefully in ringlets below the lower part of the bust. The edge also differs slightly from the former type in the punctuation.

On the reverse the eagle is smaller, apparently floating upon clouds, the wings not extending, as in the first type, beyond the circle of the wreath. The number coined we cannot give, it being aggregated with the preceding year. Not rare, but good specimens are scarce.

(Size 12. See Plate XV., Figure 3.)

---

[1] Our statements, in relation to the number of *varieties*, are, in all cases, based upon the knowledge of them, which we have, with much care and great labor, been able personally to acquire. There may be varieties, consequently, that have escaped our notice, or which have not come under our observation, though we have striven to present them fully.

UNITED STATES.

Half-Dollar.

The design the same as of this denomination in the preceding year, with one type and four varieties. We are satisfied that the change of type of the dollar in this year did not extend to the half-dollar, as in all our researches we have not been able to find anything contradicting this conclusion. The variation on the edge is simply A * * before DOLLAR. 1795.

Half-Dime.

The design the same as upon this denomination for the preceding year, except that the wreath has lost some of its leaves, and is so united as not to display the means employed. We have seen but one type and two varieties. They are very seldom found in circulation, and may be considered rare. 1795.

Dollar.

The design the same as the last described or altered type of the same denomination of the preceding year, with one type and four varieties; the latter of which may be distinguished by variations in the wreath: seven, eight, and nine berries on the laurel portion, and the leaves also varying in number and form. The number coined in this year was 72,920; they are not considered rare, and may be found in good order. It is stated that there was another type this year, formed by an additional star. Though we have not seen it, we think a few of this description may have been coined in the latter part of the same, as Tennessee was admitted to the Union in 1796. 1796.

Half-Dollar.

The designs the same, with one type and one variety, and the number coined was 3918. They are rare. 1796.

Quarter-Dollar.

The designs the same, with one type and two varieties, and the number coined was 5894. Rare. (Size 8. See Plate XVI., Figure 1.) 1796.

Dimes.

The designs the same, with one type and a single variety, and the number coined was 22,135. They are scarce. (Size 5. See Plate XVI., Figure 18.) 1796.

Half-Dimes.

The designs the same, with one type and two varieties, and the number coined was 10,230. They are scarce. (Size 4. See Plate XVI., Figure 9.) 1796.

DOLLAR.

1797. The designs the same as in the preceding year, with three types and seven varieties. The first type having eight six-pointed stars on the left of the effigy, and seven on the right; the second, nine on the left, and seven on the right; and the third, ten on the left; and six on the right, thus emblemizing, in the last two types, the admission of Tennessee into the Union.

The varieties may be distinguished as follows: In that which we designate as number one, there are no berries below the lower leaves on the laurel; in No. 2, they appear at that point outside of the wreath; in No. 3 they occur inside of the same; in No. 4 on both sides; in No. 5 the eagle is much smaller, and in Nos. 6 and 7 the arrangement in the wreath varies in each, and from the others. It is stated that the reverse was changed in this year, and a few trial pieces struck off. We have never met with them. The number coined for 1797 was but 7776, and yet they are not considered rare.

There were no half-dollars coined in this year. The Mint statement for quarters of a dollar, gives the number coined as 252. They were, probably, not thrown into circulation, as we have never found a single specimen.

DIME.

1797. The device the same as upon the other coins of the preceding year, with one type and three varieties, and the number coined was 25,261. For the first time reference is made to the "Old Thirteen," there being upon it that number of stars. The design upon the reverse, for the first time, also underwent a change. The wreath was abandoned; the eagle enlarged with its wings extended upward, on its breast a shield, and holding in its beak a scroll upon which the motto E. PLURIBUS UNUM appears. In one talon it grasps a bundle of arrows, and in the other a laurel-branch; over its head clouds, and under them sixteen stars. These coins are now much worn and particularly rare.

(Size 5. See Plate XVI., Figure 2.)

HALF-DIME.

1797. The device the same as the dime, except that there are fifteen stars, eight on the left of the effigy, and seven on the right. The reverse of this same denomination in 1796 is continued on this coin. There were one type and three varieties, and the number coined was 44,527. They are becoming quite rare.

UNITED STATES.

DOLLAR.

The device the same as on the dollar of the preceding year, except that thirteen stars made their appearance for the first time upon the dollar—seven on the left of the effigy, and six on the right. In this year we find but one type and four varieties, and the number coined was 327,536. On the reverse of this denomination, for the first time there was a total change, which had been adopted upon the dime of 1797, and is, in that year, fully described— 1798.

Legend.—UNITED STATES OF AMERICA.

(Size 12. See Plate XV., Figure 3.)

This emission is not considered rare.

The government in this design very appropriately acknowledged, on the obverse, the corner-stone—"thirteen"—upon which we were then building up this mighty nation; and on the reverse—"sixteen"—the progress we had made in the structure; three stories having been added to the edifice of Constitutional Liberty.

DIME.

The designs the same as the preceding year, with one type and five varieties, one of the latter being simply a Mint alteration of the date 1797 to 1798—a portion of the seven being perceptible in the figure eight. The number coined was 27,550, and they are not considered rare. 1798.

DOLLAR.

The designs the same as on the dollar of the preceding year, with two types and six varieties, and the number coined was 423,515. Type No 2 is distinguished by eight stars on the left of the effigy, and five on the right—in the first type there being seven on the left, and six on the right. The varieties may be determined as follows: In that which we designate as No. 1, the laurel is without berries; No. 2, one small berry midway of the branch; No. 3, fourteen stars, evidently an error of the die-sinker, who attempted to correct it by enlarging a portion of the clouds, leaving but two perfect stars on the left of the same, when there should have been three. No. 4 has five berries on the laurel; in No. 5 the figure 9, on the obverse, touches the bust of the effigy, and in No. 6 there is one more leaf on the laurel branch. This emission is neither scarce nor rare. 1799.

There was no silver coinage in this year, except the dollar.

UNITED STATES.

DOLLAR.

1800. The designs the same as the preceding, with one type and three varieties, the latter of which can be determined by reference to the reverse. The number coined was 220,920. This coin is becoming scarce, and it is with difficulty that a well preserved specimen can be found.

DIME.

1800. The designs the same as that of 1798, except that on the reverse, there are thirteen, instead of sixteen stars. The number coined was 21,760. They are becoming rare, and can seldom be found in such a state as to render them desirable for a cabinet.

HALF-DIME.

1800. The designs the same as the dime of this year, with one type and three varieties; and the number coined was 24,000. The remarks relative to the dime will apply equally to this coin.

DOLLAR.

1801. The designs the same as on the dollar of the preceding year, with one type and four varieties, and the number coined was 54,454. The high premium paid for specimens of this emission, lately brought to light, and into the market, a very considerable number, and also of the emissions of from 1795 to 1803, which has furnished a temporary supply to collectors. Apart from this, they were getting to be scarce, and soon must again be so, as the small number coined, with the inducement to bring them out, has had the effect, we think, to develop the full supply.

HALF-DOLLAR.

1801. The designs the same as on the dollar of this year, with one type and three varieties, and the number coined was 30,289. This emission is becoming scarce. (Size 9. See Plate XV., Figure 4.)

DIME.

1801. The designs the same as on the half-dollar, with one type and two varieties, and the number coined was 34,640. This emission is scarce, and a well-preserved specimen is rarely met with.

UNITED STATES.

Half-Dime.

The designs the same as on the dime, with one type and two varieties, and the number coined was 33,910. The remarks made relative to the dime, apply equally to this coin.   1801.

Dollar.

The designs the same as on this denomination for several years, with one type and two varieties, and the number coined was 41,650. They are quite scarce here, and elsewhere are considered rare.   1802.

Half-Dollar.

The designs the same as on the dollar, with one type and three varieties, and the number coined was 29,890. This emission is becoming rare.   1802.

Dime.

The designs the same as on the preceding denomination, with one type and three varieties, and the number coined was 10,975. This coin is extremely rare.   1802.

Half-Dime.

The designs the same as upon the dime, with one type and two varieties, and the number coined was 13,010. They are considered particularly rare.   1802.

Ohio having been added to the galaxy of States that then formed the Union, we could have reasonably anticipated some acknowledgment of it upon the coins of this year's emission, as had previously been the accident if not the rule; but their effulgence was not increased by a single luminary in honor of the event.

Dollar.

The designs the same, with one type and two varieties, and the number coined was 66,064. They are becoming rare, and good specimens command a premium.   1803.

Half-Dollar.

The designs the same, with one type and four varieties, and the number coined was 31,715. This emission is generally well preserved, but getting to be scarce.   1803.

DIME.

1803. The designs the same, with one type and two varieties, and the number coined was 33,040. They are extremely rare.

HALF-DIME.

1803. The designs the same, with one type and two varieties, and the number coined was 37,850. They may be considered as approaching rarity.

DOLLAR.

1804. The designs the same, with one type and but one variety, and the number coined was 19,570. The emission was small, and they are extremely rare.

HALF-DOLLAR.

1804. The designs the same, with one type and two varieties, and the number coined was 156,519. From some cause, to us inexplicable, they are quite as rare as the dollar of this year, with its very moderate coinage.

QUARTER-DOLLAR.

1804. The designs the same, with one type and three varieties, and the number coined was 6738. This emission is barely considered rare, even with the limited amount of coinage, it being the third of this denomination—the previous issues being 5894, in 1796; and 252 pieces in 1797.

DIME.

1804. The designs the same, with one type and three varieties, and the number coined was 8265. They are considered to be particularly rare.

DOLLAR.

1805. The designs the same as the preceding year, and the Mint report gives 321 as the number coined. We have never met with a dollar of this date, and the probability is that, though coined, none were issued.

HALF-DOLLAR.

1805. The designs the same, with one type and three varieties, and the number coined was 211,722. One of the varieties is a Mint alteration from 1803. They are becoming scarce.

Quarter-Dollar.

The designs the same, with one type and two varieties, and the number coined was 121,394. They are becoming scarce.   1805.

Dime.

The designs the same, with one type and three varieties, and the number coined was 120,780. Not scarce.   1805.

Half-Dime.

The designs the same, with one type and two varieties, and the number coined was 15,000. They are considered to be very rare.   1805.

Half-Dollar.

The designs the same, with one type and four varieties, and the number coined was 839,576. One of the varieties is a Mint alteration of the die of 1805. Not scarce.   1806.

Quarter-Dollar.

The designs the same, with one type and two varieties, and the number coined was 206,124. They are scarce.   1806.

Half-Dollar.

The designs the same, with one type and three varieties, and the number coined was 1,051,576. In these coins, for the first time, the punctuation was left off the edges, leaving plain FIFTY CENTS OR HALF A DOLLAR. They are not scarce, but still command a small premium.   1807.

Quarter-Dollar.

The designs the same, with one type and two varieties, and the number coined was 220,643. They are plenty.   1807.

UNITED STATES.

HALF-DOLLAR.

1808. *Device.*—A female bust — Goddess of Liberty — the head dressed with a turban — the fashion of the time — around which is a fillet, on which is inscribed the word LIBERTY; the hair flowing in ringlets below the bust; thirteen stars — seven on the right, and six on the left of the effigy.
Exergue.—1808.
Reverse.—An eagle, new in design, over the head of which, removed for the first time from the beak of the same, is a scroll inscribed "E. PLURIBUS UNUM;" a shield on the breast; in the right talon three barbed arrows, and in the left, a laurel branch.
Legend.—UNITED STATES OF AMERICA.
Exergue.—50 c.
(Size 9. See Plate XV., Figure 7.)

Of this emission, we have found one type and three varieties, and the number coined was 1,368,600. Good specimens can be procured at this time.

HALF-DOLLAR.

1809–1814. In this series of years — the designs the same as on the preceding — there was but one type of each, and the variations on the reverse are so slight, that we do not deem it essential to designate varieties. The number coined in these years was, in the aggregate, 7,794,767. The emissions of the years 1811 and 1814 are scarce; of the other years specified, they are easily procured, in a fine state of preservation, at the ordinary commercial premium.

DIMES.

1809–1814. Were the same in the designs as the half-dollar above. The emission of 1809 had one type and three varieties, and the number coined was 44,710. They are scarce. Of 1810, there were one type and three varieties, and the number coined was 6355. Very scarce. Of 1811, one type and two varieties, and the number coined was 65,180. They have become, notwithstanding the respectable number, extremely scarce. Of 1814, one type and two varieties, and the number coined was 421,500, and though the emission was unusually large, they are becoming scarce. (Size 5. See Plate XVI., Figure 5.)

HALF-DOLLAR.

1815. The designs the same, with one type and two varieties. The Mint report does not acknowledge the coinage of this year, hence we are unable to give the number coined. Most cabinets of note contain them. The amount may have

UNITED STATES.

been small, but we have cited proof of their emission. They are rare, and command a good premium.

QUARTER-DOLLAR.

The designs the same as upon the preceding denomination, with one type and three varieties, and the number coined was 69,232 — there having been no emission of this denomination of coin since 1807. They are easily obtained. (Size 7. See Plate XVI., Figure 4.) — 1815.

HALF-DOLLAR.

The designs the same, with one type and one variety, and the number coined was 1,215,567. This was the only coinage of silver in this year. Rare. — 1817.

HALF-DOLLAR.

The designs the same, with one type and four varieties, and the number coined was 1,960,322. Scarce. — 1818.

QUARTER-DOLLAR.

The designs the same, with one type and three varieties, and the number coined was 361,174. No coinage but halves and quarters this year. Scarce. — 1818.

HALF-DOLLAR.

The designs the same, with one type and four varieties, and the number coined was 2,208,000. They are quite plenty. — 1819.

QUARTER-DOLLAR.

The designs the same, with one type and four varieties, and the number coined was 144,000. They are scarce. The silver coinage confined to halves and quarters in this year. — 1819.

HALF-DOLLAR.

The designs the same, with one type and three varieties, and the number coined was 751,122. They are scarce. — 1820.

QUARTER-DOLLAR.

The designs the same, with one type and four varieties, and the number coined was 127,444. They are plenty. — 1820.

Dime.

1820.   The designs the same, with one type and three varieties, and the number coined was 942 587. Notwithstanding the large coinage, they are quite scarce.

Half-Dollar.

1821.   The designs the same, with one type and two varieties, and the number coined was 1,305,797. Not scarce.

Quarter-Dollar.

1821.   The designs the same, with one type and four varieties, and the number coined was 216,851. Not scarce.

Dime.

1821.   The designs the same, with one type and three varieties, and the number coined was 1,186,512. This issue is quite plenty.

Half-Dollar.

1822.   The designs the same, with one type and three varieties, and the number coined was 559,573. They are plenty.

Quarter-Dollar.

1822.   The designs unaltered, with one type and one variety, and the number coined was 64,080. Scarce.

Dime.

1822.   The designs unchanged, with one type and two varieties, and the number coined was 100,000. Rare

Half-Dollar.

1823.   The designs unchanged, with one type and two varieties, and the number coined was 1,694,200. Not scarce.

Quarter-Dollar.

1823.   The designs unchanged, with one type and two varieties, and the number coined was 17,800. They are extremely rare.

PLATE XV.

UNITED STATES.

DIME.

The designs unchanged, with one type and one variety, and the number coined was 440,000. Scarce.   1823.

HALF-DOLLAR.

The designs unchanged, with one type and two varieties, and the number coined was 3,504,954. According to the Mint report, this was the only silver coinage minted in this year; which is clearly an error, as we have in our collection two other denominations — the quarter of a dollar and dime — which follow.   1824.

QUARTER-DOLLAR.

The designs unchanged, with one type and two varieties, the number coined of which we are, for the reasons previously stated, unable to give. They are rare.   1824.

DIME.

The designs unchanged, with one type and two varieties, and the number coined, as with the preceding denomination, and for the same reasons, is unknown. Scarce.   1824.

HALF-DOLLAR.

The designs unchanged, with one type and two varieties, and the number coined was 2,943,166. Not scarce.   1825.

QUARTER-DOLLAR:

The designs unchanged, with one type and three varieties, and the number coined was 168,000. Scarce.   1825.

DIME.

The designs unchanged, with one type and two varieties, and the number coined was 510,000. Not scarce.   1825.

HALF-DOLLAR.

The designs unchanged, with one type and three varieties, and the number coined was 4,004,180. This was the only denomination of silver minted in this year, and it is plenty.   1826.

HALF-DOLLAR.

The designs unchanged, with one type and three varieties, and the number coined was 5,493,400. Plenty.   1827.

UNITED STATES.

QUARTER-DOLLAR.

1827. The designs unchanged, with one type and two varieties, and the number coined was 4,000. They are extremely rare.

DIME.

1827. The designs unchanged, with one type and two varieties, and the number coined was 1,215,000. Plenty.

HALF-DOLLAR.

1828. The designs unchanged, with one type and three varieties, and the number coined was 3,075,200. Plenty.

QUARTER-DOLLAR.

1828. The designs unchanged, with one type and two varieties, and the number coined was 102,000. Not scarce.

DIME.

1828. The designs unchanged, with one type and two varieties, and the number coined was 125,000. Plenty.

HALF-DOLLAR.

1829. The designs unchanged, with one type and two varieties, and the number coined was 3,712,156. Plenty. There were no quarters of a dollar minted in this year.

DIME.

1829. The designs unchanged, with one type and two varieties, and the number coined was 770,000. Not scarce.

HALF-DIME.

1829. The designs the same of the above, with one type and two varieties, and the number coined was 1,230,000. Plenty.

HALF-DOLLAR.

1830. The designs unchanged, with one type and two varieties, and the number coined was 4,764,800. Plenty.

UNITED STATES.

DIME.

The designs unchanged, with one type and three varieties, and the number coined was 510,000. Scarce.   1830.

HALF-DIME.

The designs unchanged, with one type and two varieties, and the number coined was 1,240,000. Plenty.   1830.

HALF-DOLLAR.

The designs unchanged, with one type and four varieties, and the number coined was 5,873,660. Scarce. Here, for the first time, a milling of parallel lines was executed between the letters of the legend on the edge of the coin.   1831.

QUARTER-DOLLAR.

The obverse the same as on the previous denominations of this coin since 1808.   1831.

Exergue.—1831.
Reverse.—The eagle reduced in size, and the motto, E. PLURIBUS UNUM, left off.
Legend.—UNITED STATES OF AMERICA.
Exergue.—QUAR. DOL.
      (Size 6. See Plate XVI., Figure 7.)

Of this emission, there were one type and three varieties, and the number coined was 398,000. Scarce.

DIME.

The designs unchanged, with one type and two varieties, and the number coined was 771,350. Plenty.   1831.

HALF-DIME.

The designs unchanged, with one type and two varieties, and the number coined was 1,242,700. Not scarce.   1831.

HALF-DOLLAR.

The designs unchanged, with one type and two varieties, and the number coined was 797,000. Not scarce.   1832.

QUARTER-DOLLAR.

The designs the same as on this denomination of the previous year, with one type and one variety, and the number coined was 320,000. They are rare.   1832.

UNITED STATES.

DIME.

1832. The designs unchanged, with one type and three varieties, and the number coined was 522,500.

HALF-DIME.

1832. The designs unchanged, with one type and two varieties, and the number coined was 965,000. Scarce.

HALF-DOLLAR.

1833. The designs unchanged, with one type and three varieties, and the number coined was 5,206,000. Plenty.

QUARTER-DOLLAR.

1833. The designs unchanged, with one type and one variety, and the number coined was 156,000. Scarce.

DIME.

1833. The designs unchanged, with one type and two varieties, and the number coined was 485,000. Not scarce.

HALF-DIME.

1833. The designs unchanged, with one type and two varieties, and the number coined was 1.370,000. Plenty.

HALF-DOLLAR.

1834. The designs unchanged, with one type and four varieties, and the number coined was 6,412,004. Plenty.

QUARTER-DOLLAR.

1834. The designs unaltered, with one type and three varieties, and the number coined was 286,000. Plenty.

DIME.

1834. The designs unaltered, with one type and one variety, and the number coined was 635,000. Plenty.

UNITED STATES.

HALF-DIME.

The designs unchanged, with one type and two varieties, and the number coined was 1,480,000. Plenty.   1834.

HALF-DOLLAR.

The designs unaltered, with one type and three varieties, and the number coined was 5,352,006. Not scarce.   1835.

QUARTER-DOLLAR.

The designs unchanged, with one type and four varieties, and the number coined was 1,952,000. Not scarce.   1835.

DIME.

The designs unchanged, with one type and two varieties, and the number coined was 1,410,000. Plenty.   1835.

DOLLAR.

Device.—The Goddess of Liberty seated, supporting with her right hand a heart-shaped shield, on which, in a scroll, is the motto LIBERTY; and with the left the liberty-pole, surmounted by the cap.   1836.
Exergue.—1836.
Reverse.—An eagle, volant, in the centre of the field, over which is twenty-six large and small six-pointed stars.
Legend.—UNITED STATES OF AMERICA.
Exergue.—ONE DOLLAR.
(Size 12. See Plate XVI., Figure 19.)

This piece was gotten up by Mr. Christian Gobrecht, a native Pennsylvanian, who was at that time chief engraver of the Mint. It was not, however, adopted, and hence may be considered a pattern-piece, of which one thousand were struck off. They are extremely rare and command a large premium. We observe twenty-six stars on the reverse, which, as emblems or ornaments, are unmeaning—Arkansas being admitted into the Union this year, and making but twenty-five States. In the succeeding year, 1837, Michigan came in, which would have completed the galaxy of the artist. Perhaps the error may have been fatal to its approval.

UNITED STATES.

HALF-DOLLAR.

1836. The designs unchanged, with one type and three varieties, and the number coined was 6,546,200. Not scarce.

QUARTER-DOLLAR.

1836. The designs unchanged, with one type and one variety, and the number coined was 472,000. Scarce.

DIME.

1836. The designs unchanged, with one type and four varieties, and the number coined was 1,190,000. Plenty.

HALF-DIME.

1836. The designs unchanged, with one type and four varieties, and the number coined was 1,900,000. Plenty.

HALF-DOLLAR.

1837. The change made upon the quarter of a dollar in 1831, was adopted this year upon this denomination — the effigy upon the obverse being slightly reduced in size; the stars decreased in magnitude one-third — and six of the thirteen placed on the left hand of the effigy instead of seven, as in the former type; the legend disappears entirely from the edge, which is substituted by graining.

On the reverse the eagle of diminished size, and the scroll with E. PLURIBUS UNUM dispensed with.

(Size 9. See Plate XV., Figure 8.)

QUARTER-DOLLAR.

1837. The designs unchanged, with one type and four varieties, and the number coined was 252,400. Scarce.

DIME.

1837. *Device.*—The Goddess of Liberty seated, supporting with her right hand a heart-shaped shield, on which in a scroll is the motto, LIBERTY, and with the left, the liberty pole, surmounted by the cap.
Exergue.—1837.
Reverse.—ONE DIME, surrounded by a wreath.
Legend.—UNITED STATES OF AMERICA.
(Size 4. See Plate XVI., Figure 8.)

UNITED STATES. 193

Of this coinage there were two types and six varieties, and the number coined was 1,042,000. Both types are plenty; and it is said the Branch at New Orleans had the honor of their first mintage.

HALF-DIME.

The designs the same of the previous denomination, with two types and five varieties, and the number coined was 2,276,000. Plenty.   1837.
(Size 3. See Plate XVI., Figure 12.)

DOLLAR.

Device.—The Goddess of Liberty seated, supporting with her right hand the shield, on which is a scroll with the motto, LIBERTY, and with the left the   1838. liberty pole, surmounted by the cap. Around the edge of the upper portion of the field thirteen six-pointed stars.
Exergue.—1838.
Reverse.—The eagle, volant, in the centre of the field.
Legend.—UNITED STATES OF AMERICA.
Exergue.—ONE DOL.
(Size 12.)

The Mint report does not notice this coinage. Only eighteen were struck off, and hence they are peculiarly rare.

HALF-DOLLAR.

The designs unchanged, with one type and three varieties, and the number coined was 3,546,000. Plenty.   1838.

QUARTER-DOLLAR.

The designs unchanged, with one type and three varieties, and the number coined was 832,000. Plenty.   1838.

DIME.

The designs the same as on this denomination of the preceding year, with the exception of the addition of thirteen six-pointed stars around the upper   1838. part of the obverse, with one type and two varieties, and the number coined was 1,992,500. Scarce.
(Size 4. See Plate XVI., Figure 11.)

HALF-DIME.

The designs the same as upon the denomination preceding, with one type and three varieties, and the number coined was 2,255,000. Scarce.   1838.

UNITED STATES.

DOLLAR.

1839. The designs the same as on this denomination of the preceding year, with one type and one variety, and the number coined was 300. They are extremely rare.

HALF-DOLLAR.

1839. The designs unaltered, with one type and three varieties, and the number coined was 3,334,561. Plenty.

QUARTER-DOLLAR.

1839. The designs unaltered, with three types and four varieties, and the number coined was 491,146. Scarce; the first type being very rare.

DIME.

1839. The designs unchanged, with one type and two varieties, and the number coined was 1,053,115. Rare.

HALF-DIME.

1839. The designs unchanged, with one type and two varieties, and the number coined was 1,069,150. Plenty.

DOLLAR.

1840. *Device.*—The Goddess of Liberty seated, supporting a shield with the right hand, and with the left the pole, surmounted by the liberty cap. Around the upper portion of the field thirteen six-pointed stars.
Exergue.—1840.
Reverse.—The eagle with expanded wings, holding in its talons the arrows and laurel branch.
Legend.—UNITED STATES OF AMERICA.
Exergue.—ONE DOL.
(Size 12. See Plate XV., Figure 7.)

Of this emission there was one type and a single variety, and the number coined was 61,005. Scarce.

UNITED STATES.

HALF-DOLLAR.

The designs the same as upon the dollar of this year, the exergue being HALF DOL., with one type and two varieties, and the number coined was 1,435,008. Plenty.   1840.

(Size 9. See Plate XV., Figure 9.)

QUARTER-DOLLAR.

The designs the same as upon the half-dollar of this year, with one type and two varieties, and the number coined was 188,137. Scarce.   1840.

DIME.

The designs unchanged, with one type and two varieties, and the number coined was 1,358,580. Plenty.   1840.

HALF-DIME.

The designs unchanged, with one type and two varieties, and the number coined was 1,344,085. Plenty.   1840.

DOLLAR.

The designs unchanged, with one type and two varieties, and the number coined was 173,000. Plenty.   1841.

HALF-DOLLAR.

The designs unchanged, with one type and three varieties, and the number coined was 310,000. Rare.   1841.

QUARTER-DOLLAR.

The designs unchanged, with one type and two varieties, and the number coined was 120,000. Rare.   1841.

DIME.

The designs unchanged, with one type and three varieties, and the number coined was 1,622,500. Plenty.   1841.

HALF-DIME.

The designs unchanged, with one type and two varieties, and the number coined was 1,150,000. Plenty.   1841.

UNITED STATES.

DATE.	DESIGNS.	DENOMINATION.	TYPES.	VARIETIES.	COINAGE.	REMARKS.
1842	Unaltered.	Dollar.	1	3	184,618	Plenty.
"	"	Half-Dollar.	1	2	2,012,764	"
"	"	Quarter-Dollar.	1	4	88,000	Rare.
"	"	Dime.	1	2	1,887,500	Plenty.
"	"	Half-Dime.	1	1	815,000	Scarce.
1843	"	Dollar.	1	1	165,000	Plenty.
"	"	Half-Dollar.	1	1	6,112,000	"
"	"	Quarter-Dollar.	1	2	1,613,600	"
"	"	Dime.	1	1	1,520,000	"
"	"	Half-Dime.	1	1	1,165,000	"
1844	"	Dollar.	1	1	20,000	Rare.
"	"	Half-Dollar.	1	1	3,771,000	"
"	"	Quarter-Dollar.	1	2	1,161,200	Scarce.
"	"	Dime.	1	4	72,500	"
"	"	Half-Dime.	1	3	650,000	Plenty.
1845	"	Dollar.	1	1	24,500	Scarce.
"	"	Half-Dollar.	1	1	2,683,000	"
"	"	Quarter-Dollar.	1	1	922,000	"
"	"	Dime.	1	2	1,985,000	Plenty.
"	"	Half-Dime.	1	3	1,565,000	"
1846	"	Dollar.	1	1	169,600	Scarce.
"	"	Half-Dollar.	1	2	4,514,000	Plenty.
"	"	Quarter-Dollar.	1	1	510,000	Rare.
"	"	Dime.	1	1	31,300	"
"	"	Half-Dime.	1	1	27,000	"
1847	"	Dollar.	1	1	140,750	Plenty.
"	"	Half-Dollar.	1	1	3,740,000	"
"	"	Quarter-Dollar.	1	1	1,102,000	Scarce.
"	"	Dime.	1	2	245,000	"
"	"	Half-Dime.	1	2	1,270,000	Plenty.
1848	"	Dollar.	1	1	15,000	Scarce.
"	"	Half-Dollar.	1	2	580,000	Plenty.
"	"	Quarter-Dollar.	1	3	146,000	Rare.
"	"	Dime.	1	2	451,000	Scarce.
"	"	Half-Dime.	1	2	668,000	"
1849	"	Dollar.	1	1	62,600	"
"	"	Half-Dollar.	1	1	1,252,000	Plenty.
"	"	Quarter-Dollar.	1	2	340,000	Scarce.
"	"	Dime.	1	3	830,000	Plenty.
"	"	Half-Dime.	1	4	1,309,000	"

UNITED STATES.

DATE.	DESIGNS.	DENOMINATION.	TYPES.	VARIETIES.	COINAGE.	REMARKS.
1850	Unaltered.	Dollar.	1	1	7500	Scarce.
"	"	Half-Dollar.	1	1	227,000	"
"	"	Quarter-Dollar.	1	2	190,800	"
"	"	Dime.	1	1	1,931,500	Plenty.
"	"	Half-Dime.	1	3	955,000	"
1851	"	Dollar	1	2	1300	Extremely rare.
"	"	Half-Dollar.	1	2	200,750	Scarce.
"	"	Quarter-Dollar.	1	3	160,000	"
"	"	Dime.	1	2	1,026,500	Plenty.
"	"	Half-Dime.	1	2	78,100	"

THREE-CENT PIECE.

Device.—A six-pointed star, in the centre of which is a shield.   1851.
Legend.—UNITED STATES OF AMERICA.
Exergue.—1851.
Reverse.—An ornamented C, in the centre of which are the numerals III.; above is the olive branch, and beneath are the arrows; and around the edge of the field are thirteen six-pointed stars.
(Size 3. See Plate XVI., Figure 17.)

Much odium was visited upon this little coin when it first made its appearance. It has, however, survived it, and is now a great favorite. There were one type and two varieties of this coin, and the number coined was 5,447,400. Plenty.

DATE.	DESIGNS.	DENOMINATION.	TYPES.	VARIETIES.	COINAGE	REMARKS.
1852	Unaltered.	Dollar.	1	1	1100	Rare.
"	"	Half-Dollar.	1	2	77,130	Scarce.
"	"	Quarter-Dollar.	1	3	177,060	"
"	"	Dime.	1	3	12,173,010	Plenty.
"	"	Half-Dime.	1	2	13,345,020	"
"	"	Three-Cent.	1	2	11,400,000	"
1853	"	Dollar.	1	1	46,000	Scarce.

UNITED STATES.

HALF-DOLLAR.

1853. The designs unchanged, except by the addition of a barbed arrow on each side of the exergue, on the obverse, and the rays in the background of the eagle — covering the entire field on the reverse. There were of this emission two types and three varieties, and the number coined was 2,892,000. They are plenty.

DATE.	DESIGNS.	DENOMINATION.	TYPES.	VARIETIES.	COINAGE.	REMARKS.
1853	Unaltered.	Quarter-Dollar.	1	3	15,254,200	Plenty.
"	"	Dime.	1	3	12,173,010	"
"	"	Half-Dime.	1	2	13,345,020	"
"	"	Three-Cent.	1	2	11,400,000	"
1854	"	Dollar.	1	1	33,140	Rare.
"	"	Half-Dollar.	1	3	2,982,000	The rays of the previous issue abandoned. Plenty.
"	"	Quarter-Dollar.	1	2	2,380,000	Plenty.
"	"	Dime	1	3	4,470,000	"
"	"	Half-Dime.	1	3	5,740,000	"
"	"	Three-Cent.	1	2	671,000	"
1855	"	Dollar.	1	1	26,000	Scarce.
"	"	Half-Dollar.	1	2	750,500	Plenty.
"	"	Quarter-Dollar.	1	2	2,857,000	"
"	"	Dime.	1	3	2,075,000	"
"	"	Half-Dime.	1	3	1,750,000	"
"	"	Three-Cent.	1	2	139,000	Rare.
1856	"	Dollar.	1	2	63,500	Scarce.
"	"	Half-Dollar.	1	2	938,000	The arrows removed from the sides of the exergue. Plenty.
"	"	Quarter-Dollar.	1	2	7,264,000	Plenty.
"	"	Dime.	1	4	5,780,000	"
"	"	Half-Dime.	1	2	4,880,000	"
"	"	Three-Cent.	1	1	1,458,000	"
1857[1]	"	Dollar.	1	1	94,000	"
"	"	Half-Dollar.	1	1	142,000	"
"	"	Dime.	1	2	4,890,000	"
"	"	Half-Dime.	1	2	3,940,000	"

[1] To June 30th.

PLATE XVI.

UNITED STATES. 199

COPPER COINAGE.

Following will be found the types and varieties of this currency, with such history and incidents in relation thereto as we have been able to gather. Though a despised coin—too often, we fear, the consequence of affectation—it has been, and continues to be a very useful one; enabling him who affects to disregard trifles, to gratify to the utmost the natural cupidity, which, in pecuniary transactions, is often enchanted with the advantage of a penny.

For our own part, we deem it an important medium, between man and man, which not only subserves the purposes of a fractional currency, but sometimes quiets the fractional ideas which otherwise might result in differences that a larger denomination of coin could not heal.

Chain Cent.

Device.—Goddess of Liberty, the hair streaming backward, freely and unbound. 1793.
Legend.—LIBERTY.
Exergue.—1793.
Reverse.—A circle composed of fifteen links, forming a chain.
Inscription.—ONE CENT $\frac{1}{100}$
Legend.—UNITED STATES OF AMERICA
Edge.—Stars and stripes.
(Size 7. See Plate XVII., Figures 1 and 2.)

Of the above described coin, we have found in circulation but four types and six varieties, which may be distinguished by the punctuation of the legend on the obverse, and termination of the base line of the bust, as follows:

Legends.	Types.	Varieties.
1. LIBERTY	Base Curved Line	1.
2. LIBERTY	"	2.
3. LIBERTY	Point	1.
4. LIBERTY	"	2.

The varieties may be determined by the variation of the legends on the reverse; the edges plain or figured; the inscriptions, and the configuration of the chain. In one type the legend on the reverse reads AMERI instead of AMERICA; of this there are two varieties. In one variety the edge is plain, and in others, there is a variation in the size of the chain. We have noticed other peculiarities on the reverse, but we have not deemed them of sufficient importance to extend the number of the varieties.

In type No. 1, neither the legend nor exergue is punctuated, and the base line of the bust connects with the hair without forming a point; in No. 2 the legend and exergue are punctuated, and the base line joins the hair in the same manner; in No. 3 there is no punctuation of the legend, and at the point where the base line joins the hair, the angles form a figure resembling the letter W, and No. 4 differs from No. 3 only in being punctuated.

The impressions from the die, in types No. 1 and 2, were imparted very faintly, hence it is very rare to find good specimens of these types; in No. 3 and 4 they were much better, and consequently they are found well preserved.

In no instance have we found the palm leaves on either of the types bearing the chain. We are disposed to assume, although we have no positive evidence to that effect, that the type bearing the abbreviated legend, was the first struck off after the adoption of the Constitution.

Wreath Cent.

1793.   *Device.*—Goddess of Liberty, the hair flowing loosely back, and beneath the bust, three leaves.
Legend.—LIBERTY.
Exergue.—1793.
Reverse.—A wreath enclosing the words ONE CENT.
Legend.—UNITED STATES OF AMERICA.
Exergue.— $\frac{1}{100}$
Edge.—Stripes and stars.
(Size 7. See Plate XVII., Figures 3 and 4.)

Of this cent we have found in cabinet collections and circulation, two types and twenty-one varieties, as follows:

Type.	Varieties.
Head, small	17.
" large	4.

The varieties are distinguished either by the arrangement of the hair, form of the head, or size and form of the palm leaves, &c. The palm leaves aid very materially in establishing the varieties, and may be particularized as follows:

Large Palm Leaves	7	varieties.
Medium "	5	"
Small "	3	"
Double Stem Palm Leaves	4	"
Single Stem "	2	"

UNITED STATES.   201

The varieties may be determined, as far as our classification of them extends, by comparing them with these divisions. They were probably issued in the order described. Though the number of dies, at so early a period in our coinage, may excite some surprise, yet we believe that further research would increase it.

HALF-CENT.

Device.—A bust of the Goddess of Liberty, the hair flowing loosely back, facing left, and supporting, from the shoulder, the liberty-pole surmounted by the cap.   1793.
Legend.—LIBERTY.
Exergue.—1793.
Reverse.—A laurel wreath surrounding the words HALF CENT.
Exergue.—$\frac{1}{200}$
Edge.—TWO HUNDRED FOR A DOLLAR.
(Size 5¼. See Plate XVII., Figure 17.)

Though it has very frequently been asserted that this denomination of coin was issued, bearing the chain, to correspond with the cent with that device, still we have never been able to find any reliable authority for it. This emission of the half-cent, therefore, may be considered as the first coined by our government. It possesses, we think, on that account, a peculiar interest. We have found one type and six varieties. They are rare, as it is difficult to find them in a good state of preservation.

LIBERTY-CAP CENT.

Device.—The Goddess of Liberty, facing to the right, the hair flowing loosely back, and supporting the pole surmounted by the liberty-cap.   1793.
Legend.—LIBERTY.
Exergue.—1793.
Reverse.—A wreath inclosing the words ONE CENT.
Legend.—UNITED STATES OF AMERICA.
Exergue.—$\frac{1}{100}$
Edge.—ONE HUNDRED FOR A DOLLAR.
(Size 8. See Plate XVII., Figure 5.)

Of this cent we have seen but few, owing to their scarcity. In our researches we have discovered but one type and four varieties.

We think the coins of this type were designed and struck off in the latter part of this year as trial pieces, for the Mint authorities adopted them, as described, for the emission of cents and half-cents of the succeeding three years.

UNITED STATES.

The varieties can be distinguished by the variations in the effigy, wreath, and spaces between the figures of the date. In one of the varieties there must have been a flaw in the die, which disfigured the effigy by a raised line through it lengthwise. The copper planchets used for this cent were of such pure material that they suffered from the slightest abrasion; and, therefore, perfect specimens are both rare and valuable.

Cent.

1794. *Device.*—The Goddess of Liberty, facing to the right, the hair flowing loosely back, and supporting the pole surmounted by the liberty-cap.
Legend.—LIBERTY.
Exergue.—1794.
Reverse.—A wreath inclosing the words ONE CENT.
Legend.—UNITED STATES OF AMERICA.
Exergue.—$\frac{1}{100}$
Edge.—ONE HUNDRED FOR A DOLLAR.
(Size 8. See Plate XVII., Figure 6.)

Of this emission we have discovered but one type; of which twenty-six varieties have come under our notice, which may be determined mainly by reference to the variations of those of 1793.

These cents were somewhat thicker than those that preceded them, the weight of each being increased about seventeen grains; the hair of the goddess, also, does not recede so much from the forehead.

The planchets from which they were struck were of good copper, and the milling of the edges being more prominent has protected them from the effect of abrasion, and hence they are frequently found in a fine state of preservation.

They are quite plenty, the number issued by the Mint amounted, according to the official statement, to 12,513,300; and the number of dies in a single year, excites surprise, the preparation of each die involving much expense.

Half-Cent.

1794. The same as the cent in design, except in the denomination, which is expressed $\frac{1}{200}$. We have found but one type and five varieties; they are in a fine state of preservation and are not rare.
(Size 5½. See Plate XVII., Figure 18.)

UNITED STATES. 203

Cent.

The design the same as those coined in the latter part of the year 1794, which have a small curved line above the date. Of these cents there were two types and eight varieties.   1795.

(Size 8. See Plate XVII., Figure 7.)

The pieces coined in the early part of this year, which we denominate as the first type, were the same in weight and thickness as those of 1794, being about 208 grains in weight. They bear on their edge ONE HUNDRED FOR A DOLLAR; but in the type which we designate as No. 2, subsequently coined, we find, by weighing them, that there was a reduction in weight of from 38 to 40 grains in each cent, and that the edge was so narrow as to exclude the legend which occurs in type No. 1.

The President issued a proclamation, January 29, 1796, based upon an Act of Congress of the 3d of March, 1795, in which, for the reasons therein urged, of "the increased price of copper and the expense of coinage," he had ordered the cent to be reduced in weight, one pennyweight and sixteen grains, and the half-cent in like proportion, from the 27th day of December, 1795, which weight was continued down to the last issue of the old whole and half-cents.

Half-Cents.

The design the same as the cents, and like them of two types. Of the first type we have seen but a single specimen, consequently we can convey no information relative to varieties. Being so scarce, they are necessarily very rare.   1795.

Of the second type there are four varieties. The effigy was altered in this type by reducing the size, which was probably suggested by the diminution of the weight, corresponding to that of the cent, of some twenty grains. The change of the size of the effigy, according to our taste, rendered it much less artistic and interesting.

(Size 5½. See Plate XVII., Figure 19.)

Cent.

The design of the first issue of this year was the same as of the cent of the reduced weight that followed the proclamation. But in the latter portion of this year the type was wholly changed; for, instead of the naked bust and liberty-cap, the hair was formed into a cue on the back of the head, and around the lower part of the same it was supplied with ringlets. The bust was also much enlarged, and republican modesty, for the first time, substituted drapery for nudity.   1796.

This change gave for this year two types and fourteen varieties, six of the first, and eight of the second type. The number coined 974,700.

(Size 8. See Plate XVII., Figures 8 and 9.)

HALF-CENT.

1796. The design the same as of the cent last issued and described. In our very extensive researches, though there were 115,480 pieces of this design and denomination issued in this year, we have only been able to find ten pieces in the whole; and our investigations have resulted in but one type and two varieties. There may be more, but we have not been able to discover them.

Taking into view the number coined, it is difficult to account for this scarcity. But, probably being defective, from the imperfect tempering of the dies, as the greater number of the very few pieces we have found indicate, they may have been deemed unworthy of care or preservation. But three cabinets in Philadelphia contain a specimen of this coin; they are consequently both rare and valuable.

CENT.

1797. The design is the same as the preceding, or of the second type of the cent, bearing the cue in the last named year. Of this issue there are but one type and eleven varieties, and though the number (897,510) coined was comparatively small, they are not considered scarce.

HALF-CENT.

1797. The design corresponds with the reduced liberty-cap head of the cent of 1796. There are but one type and four varieties of this coin. The impressions on them are rather faint, which render good specimens very difficult to be procured. They are neither scarce nor rare; number coined, 107,048.

(Size 5¼. See Plate XVII., Figure 20.)

CENT.

1798. The design the same as of the cent of 1797, with but one type and seventeen varieties; the latter of which may be distinguished by examining the legend, bust, wreath, date, &c. The die of one of these varieties was altered from that of 1797 — the first Mint alteration, we believe, that occurred in the copper coinage. The number of cents issued this year was 979,700. most of which must have been kept

UNITED STATES.

in circulation from the great number of them about but a short time since. They are mostly in a good state of preservation, the material of which they were composed having been a happy combination for resistance to abrasion.

Cent.

1799.
The design the same with one type and four varieties. This cent is deemed by Numismatologists as being very rare and valuable; fine specimens of which will command a greater premium than those of the cent of 1793 of the same condition of preservation, to which, from their extreme scarcity, much value is attached. The number of this coin issued amounted to 904,585 — no insignificant sum. Their scarcity, however, is attributed to a shipment to the coast of Africa, by a Salem, Mass., firm, of several hundred thousand on an order from that country, where, being punched with holes, they were bartered away, probably to the chiefs—certainly not for negroes — and subsequently used as ornaments by the natives, being depended from the neck by a string, and showing to what good account so slightly valuable a thing as a copper cent may be applied by the sagacity of our countrymen.

Of the few of these cents to be found, it is very difficult to procure perfect specimens. The copper of which they were composed was rendered very inferior by too much alloy, which gave them a very rough and uneven surface—perhaps the result of the copper being burnt in smelting.

The great value of these cents among numismatologists, has led to an attempt at counterfeiting them, by altering those issued in 1798 by means of acid or the graver—the former being the most successful. Both are readily exposed by the use of the lens.

Half-Cent.

1799.
The Mint report gives the issue of this coin for the year at 12,167—a very inconsiderable number truly; and which, if there were any issue at all, may account in a measure, but not conclusively, for their non-existence now, so far as we have been able to discover. We have discovered errors in other instances, and this also may be one. In 1815, the Mint statistics give no coinage of half-dollars; and also, in 1841, no quarter-eagle, although specimens of these pieces are in the hands of collectors, they having been coined in those years, if the date is any proof of the same. In the case of the half-cent of this year, we must conclude there was no coinage, or the peculiarity exists of their total disappearance.

UNITED STATES.

CENT.

1800. The design the same as the preceding year, with one type and twelve varieties, two of the latter of which were struck off upon the dies of 1799, altered at the Mint to 1800. Some collectors have, in consequence of seeing the circle of the upper part of the nine very distinctly in the naught, placed this cent in their cabinets as belonging to the former year. The number coined this year was larger than any preceding one. They are plenty, very much worn from the copper being too soft, and it is difficult to find perfect specimens.

HALF-CENT.

1800. In this year, the liberty-cap on the half-cents was superseded by the new design which has prevailed upon the cent from the latter portion of the year 1796. Of these coins there were one type and three varieties; they are easily obtained and are found in a good state of preservation. Issue 211,530.
(Size 5¼. See Plate XVII., Figure 21.)

CENT.

1801. No change in design of the cent, except for the first time, we notice a dot thus $_{\text{CENT}}^{\text{ONE}}$. There were one type and fifteen varieties, of the latter of which we give the following peculiarities: say, first, with $\frac{1}{000}$, and a raised line, from a defect in the die, extending across the piece; second, the legend thus, IINITED STATES OF AMERICA — the die otherwise defective in this piece, than in the first letter in the legend, there being a line from a crack running diagonally across the II, and also but a single end to the ribbon where the wreath is tied together; third, $\frac{1}{000}$, and one of the ends of the ribbon extending to the U in the legend; and fourth, without ribbon ends on either side. The other varieties may be distinguished by the position of the wreath to the legend. The number of cents coined this year was 1,362,837; they are plenty enough, but good specimens are in demand.

Half-cents altered from those of 1804, and hence purporting to be of this year's issue, are frequently sold as such, though no coinage of them occurred.

CENT.

1802. The design the same, with one type and twenty-one varieties, and the number coined was 3,435,100. These cents are abundant and in a good state of preservation.

UNITED STATES.

As in the preceding year, some of the varieties are marked with the same errors, such as $\frac{1}{000}$; the ribbon extending to the U in the legend, and evidently the same die, with alteration of date, as the preceding year; $\frac{1}{000}$, die not cracked, and, also, $\frac{1}{000}$, with but one end of the ribbon, and with no ends; exhibiting great carelessness, or a total disregard of criticism, which was inexcusable even in the coinage of the lowest denomination in our currency. It is said a trial piece in brass was got up in this year.

HALF-CENT.

The design the same, with one type and three varieties, and the number coined very small, being but 14,366, which has rendered them very rare. 1802. One of the varieties is from the die of 1800 altered, and portions of the naught are perceptible around the figure 2, which is smaller than the other figures. They command a good price when perfect, which is very rarely the case.

CENT.

The design unaltered, with one type and fourteen varieties, and the number coined was 2,471,353. More care exercised in the coinage this year, and we 1803. consequently find none of the errors which characterized the two former years. Recourse must be had to the legend, wreath, and figures, for determining the varieties. No scarcity of this emission, and they are found well preserved.

HALF-CENT.

The design the same as the cent, with one type and three varieties. Though the number coined (97,300) was not large, there is no scarcity of them, and 1803. they are found in good condition.

CENT.

The design the same as the preceding year, with one type and six varieties, and the number issued amounted to 756,838. From some cause which we 1804. cannot explain, though the number coined was very considerable, these cents have become very rare, and command the next highest premium to those of 1799. This has induced the counterfeiting of them, and to effect it the coinage of other years has been trespassed upon; that most successfully altered being of 1801. The counterfeit may be detected when the glass fails, by noticing the cue in two of the varieties, which sets unusually low; two are broken on the edges, and one has on the reverse $\frac{1}{000}$.

UNITED STATES.

Half-Cent.

1804. The design the same as the cent, with one type and five varieties, and the number coined, 1,055,312. Plenty, and found in a fine state of preservation.

Cent.

1805. The design the same as the preceding, with one type and five varieties. Although the number coined this year (941,116) was not largely in excess of those coined in 1804, the average proportion found in circulation at the time of the issue of the new cent was at least 30 to 1, and mostly well preserved.

Half-Cent.

1805. The design the same as the cent, with one type and five varieties; the number coined was 814,664. They are not by any means rare.

Cent.

1806. The design the same as the previous year, with one type and six varieties; the number coined (348,000), though small compared with the issue of 1805, has not prevented them from being more abundant than those of that year. We have seen one variety of this cent which was struck from the altered die of 1805, which must have been broken or discarded, as it is the only specimen we have met with. We have also seen another variety on which $\frac{1}{100}$ occurs.

Half-Cent.

1806. The design the same as the cent, with one type and two varieties; the number coined 356,000. Compared with the cent, it is very difficult to procure them.

Cent.

1807. The design the same as the preceding year, with one type and nine varieties; the number coined was 727,221. A Mint alteration of the die from 1806 to 1807, constitutes one of the varieties. They are abundant and generally well preserved.

Half-Cent.

1807. The design the same as the cent, with one type and four varieties; the number coined, 476,000. They can be found in good order.

UNITED STATES.

CENT.

The design the same in the first portion of this year; but in the latter, the devices were changed — the Goddess of Liberty facing to the left for the first 1808. time; across the head of the same is a band on which "LIBERTY" is inscribed, and to the right of the effigy are six, and to the left seven, stars. The wreath on the reverse is united and more elaborate in workmanship, and $\frac{1}{100}$ is omitted. The bust is deprived of its drapery, and reduced almost to the original size. In both of these types we have found but seven varieties; the number coined was 1,109,000, and yet they are considered to be scarce, as it is difficult to find good specimens. The line below ONE CENT appeared for the first time upon this denomination of coin.

(Size 8. See Plate XVII., Figure 10.)

HALF-CENT.

The design the same with the cents of the earliest emission of this year, with one type and three varieties. The number coined was 400,000. They 1808. are well preserved, but getting to be scarce.

CENT.

The design the same as the new emission of the preceding year, with one type and four varieties, the number coined, small, being but 222,867; in 1809. consequence of which they are scarce. The rim of this cent is very imperfectly executed, which has exposed a portion of the effigy and exergue to serious wear. There are many cents in cabinets which have been altered from 1808 to 1809; this has been effected principally by acids, but may be readily detected by the use of the glass. The most perfect specimens in Philadelphia collections were taken from the corner-stone of the "Mansion House" by Mr. Hoxie when it was demolished.

HALF-CENT.

The devices of the cent were adopted in this emission, with one type and four varieties, and the number coined was 1,154,572. 1809.

(Size 6. See Plate XVII., Figure 22.)

CENT.

The design the same as the preceding cent, with one type and seven varieties, and the number coined was 1,458,500. We notice in this emission the 1810. alteration of the dies of 1809 to 1810, from which we form one of the varieties.

These cents are plenty enough, but owing to the imperfect rim, previously noticed, it is difficult to find them perfect

HALF-CENT.

1810. The design the same, with one type and four varieties, and the number coined was 215,000. So small as to render them scarce.

CENT.

1811. The design the same, with one type and eight varieties, and the number coined was 218,025. We have to notice the alteration of the dies of 1810 to 1811 in this emission, which supplies one of the varieties. Good specimens are seldom found in circulation. We are indebted for ours to an unopened keg returned to the Mint from Charleston, South Carolina. Collectors must be careful to avoid the cent of 1814, with a portion of the last figure removed.

HALF-CENT.

1811. The design the same, with one type and two varieties, and the number coined was only 63,140. They are considered rare and valuable, as they are to be found but in few cabinets.

CENT.

1812. The design the same, with one type and nine varieties, and the number coined was 1,075,500. They are abundant.

CENT.

1813. The design the same, with one type and nine varieties, and the number coined was 418,000. So many of the best of this emission have been altered to 1815, that it is difficult to obtain good specimens.

CENT.

1814. The design the same, with one type and eight varieties, and the number coined was 357,830. The number of these cents altered to 1811 has aided very materially to supply cabinets with their specimens of that year. Additional value has been attached to the issues of that year, in consequence of a rumor that it contained gold lost at the Mint at that time. Many cling to them with much tenacity on that account — the slightest basis for credulity being ardently responded to.

UNITED STATES.   211

CENT.

In this year, we are satisfied there was no coinage of either cents or half-cents, or even a pattern-piece gotten up for either. Most numismatologists and others concur in this opinion, though a few contend that pattern-pieces were struck off at the Mint, and urge as a reason for their not being coined in volume and circulated, the destruction of the Mint by fire in this year. It will be found, by referring to the newspapers of that time, that the fire did not occur till January, 1816, and that it then only destroyed a portion of the shed adjoining the mint-house, in which the rolling was done. The true reason for the non-coinage was, we believe, the want of copper, occasioned by the European agents not sending it forward in time for use. A few amateur collectors, however, boast of genuine specimens, and cite tests and proofs; but if the coins could tell their own history, they would not impute their origin to the United States Mint. Those *we* have examined, bearing the date of this year, are clearly alterations of the cent of 1813, rendered scarce, as we have heretofore remarked, by this very operation. 1815.

CENT.

The device on the obverse in this emission was changed by the adjustment of the hair, which was tied up with two bands into a tuft upon the head, according to the fashion of the day. The stars were arranged equidistant from each other, and from the exergue. The reverse remained unaltered. Of this cent, there were one type and eleven varieties, and the number coined was 2,820,982, being large in consequence of the non-coinage of the preceding year. They are quite plenty, and can be procured looking as fresh as when they first came from the Mint. 1816.

(Size 8. See Plate XVII., Figure 11.)

CENT.

The design the same as the preceding, with two types and twenty-two varieties, and the number coined was 3,948,400. One of the types contains thirteen, and the other, fifteen stars. The metal of which they were composed is well milled and very hard, which protects the face of the coin. They are hence in a good state of preservation. 1817.

(Size 8. See Plate XVII., Figure 12.)

CENT.

The design the same, with one type and ten varieties, and the number coined was 3,167,000. Plenty and well preserved. 1818.

UNITED STATES.

CENT.

1819. The design the same, with one type and ten varieties, and the number coined was 2,671,000. In the latter part of this year, we notice the absence of the dot between ONE and CENT in some of the varieties. Equally plenty, and in good order with the preceding emission out.

CENT.

1820. The design the same, with one type and sixteen varieties, and the number coined was 4,407,550. The dot, previously referred to, occurs but on a portion of the varieties. The slight milling of the edges of these coins render good specimens difficult to be obtained.

CENT.

1821. The design the same, with one type and five varieties, and the number coined was 389,000. The small number originally issued renders these cents scarce, and good specimens are obtained with much difficulty — the few remaining in circulation being very poor, owing to the imperfect milling of the edges.

CENT.

1822. The design the same, with one type and nine varieties, and the number coined was 2,072,339. They are plenty, but it is difficult to obtain good specimens.

CENT.

1823. The design the same, with one type and three varieties, two of which varieties are mint alterations of the date upon the die of the preceding year. The number coined—obtained through letters from Washington—was 12,250.[1] This coinage is not acknowledged in the Mint report, it being, from that authority, one of the years of non-coinage. The copper of this emission is pure and soft, hence the cents are much worn, and can be rarely found in a condition worthy of preservation. They command a premium.

CENT.

1824. The design the same, with one type and seven varieties, and the number coined was 1,262,000. Plenty, but much worn.

---

[1] See State papers, 1st Session, 18th Congress, vol. ii. Doc. 152.

UNITED STATES.   213

CENT.

The design the same, with one type and nine varieties, and the number coined was 1,461,000. Not scarce, but much worn.   1825.

HALF-CENT.

The design the same, with one type and three varieties, and the number coined, 63,000. Notwithstanding this small emission, they are plenty and *well preserved*, showing that, in the fourteen years during which there had been no issue, the people had acquired the habit of disregarding fractions, and felt no disposition to renew them in making change. We can recollect, however, when, in some portions of our country, the half-cent was rigidly exacted, and where many a war of words, and sometimes of fists, grew out of such a controversy.   1825.

CENT.

The design the same, with one type and ten varieties, and the number coined was 1,517,425. This emission not scarce, but much worn.   1826.

HALF-CENT.

The design the same, with one type and four varieties, and the number coined was 234,000. They are easily procured, though seldom circulated.   1826.

CENT.

The design the same, with one type and eleven varieties, and the number coined was 2,357,732. Well preserved and abundant.   1827.

CENT.

The design the same, with one type and ten varieties, and the number coined was 2,260,624. Plenty and well preserved.   1828.

HALF-CENT.

The design the same, with two types and five varieties, and the number coined was 606,000. One of these types has, on the obverse, twelve instead of thirteen stars—seven on the left, and five on the right hand. This number of stars undoubtedly originated in error, as nothing less than thirteen had any intelligible reference to our country, as adopted upon our coinage. This emission is by no means rare.   1828.

(Size 6. See Plate XVII., Figure 23.)

UNITED STATES.

Cent.

1829. The design the same, with one type and seven varieties, and the number coined was 1,414,500. Not difficult to be obtained.

Half-Cent.

1829. The design the same, with one type and three varieties, and the number coined was 487,000. It is difficult to obtain specimens.

Cent.

1830. The design the same, with one type and nine varieties, and the number coined was 1,711,500. They are much worn.

Cent.

1831. The design the same, with one type and eight varieties, and the number coined was 3,359,260. Good specimens can easily be obtained.

Half-Cent.

1831. The design the same, with one type and one variety, and the number coined was 2,200. This emission is extremely rare, even in cabinet collections.

Cent.

1832. The design the same, with one type and seven varieties, and the number coined was 2,362,000. They are plenty and perfect.

Half-Cent.

1832. The design the same, with one type and four varieties, and the number coined we are unable to state. Though the Mint report states there was no coinage of the half-cent in this year, they are quite as plenty as the same denomination of coin of the succeeding year.

Cent.

1833. The design the same, with one type and five varieties, and the number coined was 2,739,000. Plenty and well preserved.

UNITED STATES. 215

Half-Cent.

The design the same, with one type and two varieties, and the number coined was 154,000. Well preserved and easily obtained. 1833.

Cent.

The design the same, with one type and nine varieties, and the number coined was 1,855,100. Plenty and well preserved. 1834.

Half-Cent.

The design the same, with one type and four varieties, and the number coined was 120,000. No scarcity, and they are easily procured. 1834.

Cent.

The design the same, with one type and five varieties, and the number coined was 3,878,400, which would indicate profusion, in a good state of preservation. 1835.

Half-Cent.

The design the same, with one type and four varieties, and the coinage numbered 141,000. They are quite plenty and are found in good condition. 1835.

Cent.

The design the same, with one type and three varieties, and the coinage numbered 2,111,000. Not scarce, and are found in good order. 1836.

Half-Cent.

The design the same, with one type and two varieties, and the number coined (398,000), though much larger than in preceding years, failed to render them plenty, as they are now extremely rare and command a premium. 1836.

Cent.

The design the same, with two types and eight varieties, and the number coined was 5,558,300. They are very plenty, and there is no difficulty in finding perfect specimens. One of the types is distinguished by the hair being held together by a string of beads instead of the cord. 1837.

UNITED STATES.

CENT.

1838. The design the same, with two types and four varieties, and the number coined was 6,370,200. They were perfectly milled, the copper was hard, and hence they are found in a prime state of preservation. The types may be designated by the cord and beads.

CENT.

1839. Of this coinage, amounting in number to 3,128,661, there were four types and seven varieties. The design the same, upon the two first types, as in the preceding year, having on them the cord and beads. In the third type there is a somewhat different arrangement of the hair, which gives to the effigy a simple expression. Here, for the first time, both the dot under the ONE, and the line under CENT, are omitted, which shows that this type was issued last. In the fourth type, the head is smaller than in the others. Still another has been claimed for this year's coinage, but our examination makes the variation so slight, that we class it among the varieties. Of the two first types, specimens are easily obtained, but of the third, it is not so, as we know of but four specimens, with one exception, that can be considered as fair, and that is now in the possession of J. J. Mickley, Esq. The fourth type is quite plenty, but soft, poorly milled, and difficult to be found good.

(Size 8. See Plate XVII. Figures 13, 14, and 15.)

CENT.

1840. The design the same as the fourth type of the preceding year, with one type and five varieties, and the number coined was 2,462,700. These cents are composed of fine copper, hence they are much worn. They were esteemed very highly, as were the issues of 1840, '41, '42 and 43, by the silver-smiths for alloy, which has aided in rendering them scarce. It is very unusual to find perfect specimens. The destruction of ancient buildings in this city, has been the source to us of rare and valuable specimens of the years above mentioned.

HALF-CENT.

1840. The design the same, with only 200 in number coined as proof specimens. They are necessarily very rare.

(Size 6. See Plate XVII., Figure 24.)

UNITED STATES.

CENT.

The design the same, with one type and two varieties, and the number coined was 1,597,367. They are much worn, and it is with difficulty that good specimens can be obtained. 1841.

HALF-CENTS.—Only a small number coined this year as specimens.

CENT.

The design the same, with one type and four varieties, and the number coined was 2,428,320. Even fair specimens are scarce. 1842.

HALF-CENT.—The coinage limited to a small number of specimen pieces.

CENT.

The design the same, with one type and three varieties, and the number coined was 2,428,320. Good specimens quite rare. 1843.

HALF-CENTS.—A few coined as in preceding years, and for the same purpose.

CENT.

The design the same, with one type and three varieties, and the amount coined was 2,398,752. Good specimens of this emission are very scarce. 1844.

HALF-CENT.—A merely nominal coinage—a few specimens.

CENT.

The design the same, with one type and four varieties, and the number coined was 3,894,804. Specimens, that have been at all well preserved, very scarce. 1845.

HALF-CENT.—A few coined only, as for several years past.

CENT.

The design the same, with one type and eight varieties, and the amount coined was 4,120,800. Good specimens very rare. 1846.

HALF-CENT.—The emission of this year the same as the previous one.

CENT.

The design the same, with one type and five varieties, and the number coined was 6,183,669. Good specimens scarce, notwithstanding the large issue. 1847.

HALF-CENT.—A very limited number coined as usual.

UNITED STATES.

Cent.

1848. The design the same, with one type and six varieties, and the number coined was 6,415,799. Good specimens are scarce.

Half-Cent.—The coinage, merely a few specimens.

Cent.

1849. The design the same, with one type and six varieties, and the number coined was 4,178,500. The material of which these cents were coined was harder, and the specimens are consequently better preserved.

Half-Cent.

1849. The design the same as the cent, with one type and two varieties, and the amount coined was 39,864. This issue, though of some magnitude compared with the issues for the past twelve years, is fast disappearing, and will soon become rare except in the cabinets of collectors.

Cent.

1850. The design the same, with one type and five varieties, and the number coined was 4,426,844. Good specimens plenty.

Half-Cent.

1850. The design the same, with one type and two varieties, and the number coined was 39,812. This emission, like the previous of the same denomination, is rapidly disappearing from the public view.

Cent.

1851. The design the same, with one type and six varieties, and the number coined was 9,889,707. Good specimens, of course, at this time, are plenty.

Half-Cent.

1851. The design the same, with one type and three varieties, and the number coined was 147,672. Good specimens plenty at present.

PLATE XVII.

UNITED STATES.

CENT.

The design the same, with one type and six varieties, and the number coined was 5,063,094. Plenty and good.   1852.

HALF-CENT.—Only proofs, which command a high premium.

CENT.

The design the same, with one type and nine varieties, and the number coined was 6,641,131. Specimens plenty, but much defaced, owing to the softness of the copper.   1853.

HALF-CENT.

The design the same, with one type and two varieties, and the number coined 129,694. Specimens good and plenty.   1853.

CENT.

The design the same, with one type and ten varieties, and the number coined was 4,236,156. Copper soft, hence defaced.   1854.

HALF-CENT.

The design the same, with one type and two varieties, and the number coined was 55,358. Getting to be scarce.   1854.

CENT.

The design the same, with one type and nine varieties, and the number coined was 1,574,829. One of the varieties made by a defective die, which shows itself above the ear of the effigy. Plenty.   1855.

HALF-CENT.

The design the same, with one type and two varieties, and the number coined was 56,500. Not very plenty.   1855.

CENT.

The design the same, with one type and seven varieties, and the number coined was 2,690,463. Plenty of this emission. The nickel cent, one type and variety, issued as a specimen, is now quite rare.   1856.

HALF-CENT.

1856. The design the same, with one type and variety, and the number coined was 40,430. They are becoming quite scarce.

CENT.

1857. The design the same, and the last coinage of the copper cent. The number issued was small, many of them have been returned to the Mint, and the demand, by collectors, will soon make them rare.

The number of cents coined this year, of both nickel and copper, was 6,333,456. The Mint reports do not furnish the proportion of each. We suppose the greater number were of nickel.

HALF-CENT.

1857. The design the same, and the coinage, up to June 30th of this year, was 35,180. Private initials stamped upon this issue — fame, in one of its little phases, identifying itself by such letters upon the last of this coinage. Perfect specimens will soon be very rare.

CENT.

1858. The Nickel Cent; One type exclusively coined in this year, but the number we have not been able to learn. We have noticed it fully and more particularly elsewhere.

(Size 6. See Plate XVII., Figure 16.)

NORTH CAROLINA GOLD COINS.

The States of North Carolina, Georgia, and Virginia, at one time attracted much attention on account of their gold deposits; but since the discovery of gold in California, they have been superseded and neglected. The enterprise of working the gold mines of these States was never very marked; the rich gold deposits of North Carolina being chiefly developed in the shape of millions of scrip, manufactured and issued by the denizens of Wall street, New York.

With views of profits, proportioned in some degree to the cost of the property before it became expressed by corporation values, money could undoubtedly be made in North Carolina and the other auriferous districts we have named, which is sustained by cases of individual enterprise in mining and coining.

The following is derived from the works of Messrs. Eckfeldt and Du Bois. "In the year 1830, when gold began to be raised, the project was set on foot of coining it so to speak 'at the pit's mouth.' Three denominations of coin, ten, five, and two and a half dollar pieces were struck, bearing the name of 'Templeton Reed, Assayer,' and the designation, 'Georgia Gold.' On two occasions they were brought to this mint in quantities, but not since 1831. They were soon discontinued, and probably by this time are forgotten even at home. The following is the weight, assay, and value of two kinds — the five dollar piece has not been tried.

DENOMINATION.	WEIGHT. Grs.	FINENESS. Thous.	VALUE. D. C.
Piece of ten dollars.[1]	248	942	10·06
Piece of two and a half dollars.	60.5	932	2·43

"Mr. Bechtler's mint, which is located at Rutherfordton, North Carolina, is of much greater importance. Its operations were commenced in 1831, the coins circulated freely at the South and West, but are rarely seen north of Washington.

"There were of these coins two series; the first, bearing no date, but issued earlier than 1834, of the three denomination of five, two and a half, and one dollar, professedly 20 carats fine, and 150 grains to the piece of five dollars. The second series bears the date of 1834. In that year there was an important reduction of standards in the national gold coins, to which Mr. Bechtler conformed, and by way of distinction, has used the uniform date of that year ever since. The denominations were the same, but there were three grades of fineness and weight; thus, at 20 carats, the five dollar piece was to weigh 140 grains; the same at 21 carats, to weigh 134 grains; and at 22 carats, to weigh 128 grains.[2] The pieces of 20 carats were stamped 'North Carolina Gold,' those of 21 carats, 'Carolina Gold,' and those of 22 carats, 'Georgia Gold.' It is probable that all the gold was the product of North Carolina, and that these stamps were only to assist in indicating the different qualities, as they were generally understood in that region; Georgia gold being usually the best, and North Carolina the poorest.

"The following is the result of numerous trials of these coins at the Mint.

---

[1] Our eagle of that date would be worth $10·66.

[2] "The calculations are not strict. These three pieces at their rates would be worth, by the law of 1834, $5·02¼, $5·04$\frac{7}{10}$, and $5·05, respectively."

UNITED STATES.

DENOMINATION.	PROFESSED WEIGHT. Grs.	PROFESSED FINENESS. IN CARATS.	PROFESSED FINENESS. IN THOUS.	AVERAGE WEIGHT. Grs.	AVERAGE FINENESS. Thou.	AVERAGE VALUE. D. C. M.	VALUE PER DWT. C. M.	VARIATIONS IN FINENESS. Thous.	VARIATIONS IN VALUE.
Five dollar piece, before 1834.	150	20	833	148	833	5.34	86.6	829 to 846	$5.28 to $5.39
Five dollar piece, since 1834. "North Carolina gold."	140	20	833	139.8	815	4.90.7	84.2	813 to 819	$4.89 to $4.93
Five dollar piece. "Carolina gold."	134	21	875	134.4	845	4.89	87.3	833 to 852	$4.82 to $4.93
Five dollar piece. "Georgia gold."	128	22	917	127.6	882	4.84.6	91.2	856 to 899	$4.70 to $4.84
Two and a half. "N. C. gold."	70	20	833	70	819	2.47	84.6		
Two and a half. "Georgia gold."	64	22	917	63.6	872	2.39	90.1		
One dollar. "N. C. gold."	28	20	833	27.6	810	96.2	83.7	804 to 816	95¼ to 97 cts.

"There is not much variation in the weight, but the fineness, as shown above, is exceedingly irregular and inferior, causing an average loss of 2½ per cent. on the nominal value. A safe estimate of five dollar pieces as they come would be $4.84.

"The North Carolina Mint, formerly conducted by C. Bechtler, passed into the hands of A. Bechtler subsequent to 1842, and there is a marked difference of value between the C and A. The five dollar pieces of the former were deficient from 1 to 6 per cent. upon the alleged value, averaging three per cent., or $4.85; the one dollar pieces were worth from 95½ to 97 cents. The five dollar pieces of the latter vary from the alleged value to a deficit of 1½ per cent. There are no dates on the coins however, to enable us to mark the difference, but the pieces assayed in 1843 were better than those assayed in 1849. The last and newest lot gave $4.94 to the five dollar piece. As Bechtler's pieces are alloyed with silver, they will produce about a half of one per cent. more, if offered in sufficient quantities. The dollars, so far as tried, are two per cent. below their nominal value."

(See Plate XVIII., Figures 15, 16, and 17.)

PLATE XVIII.

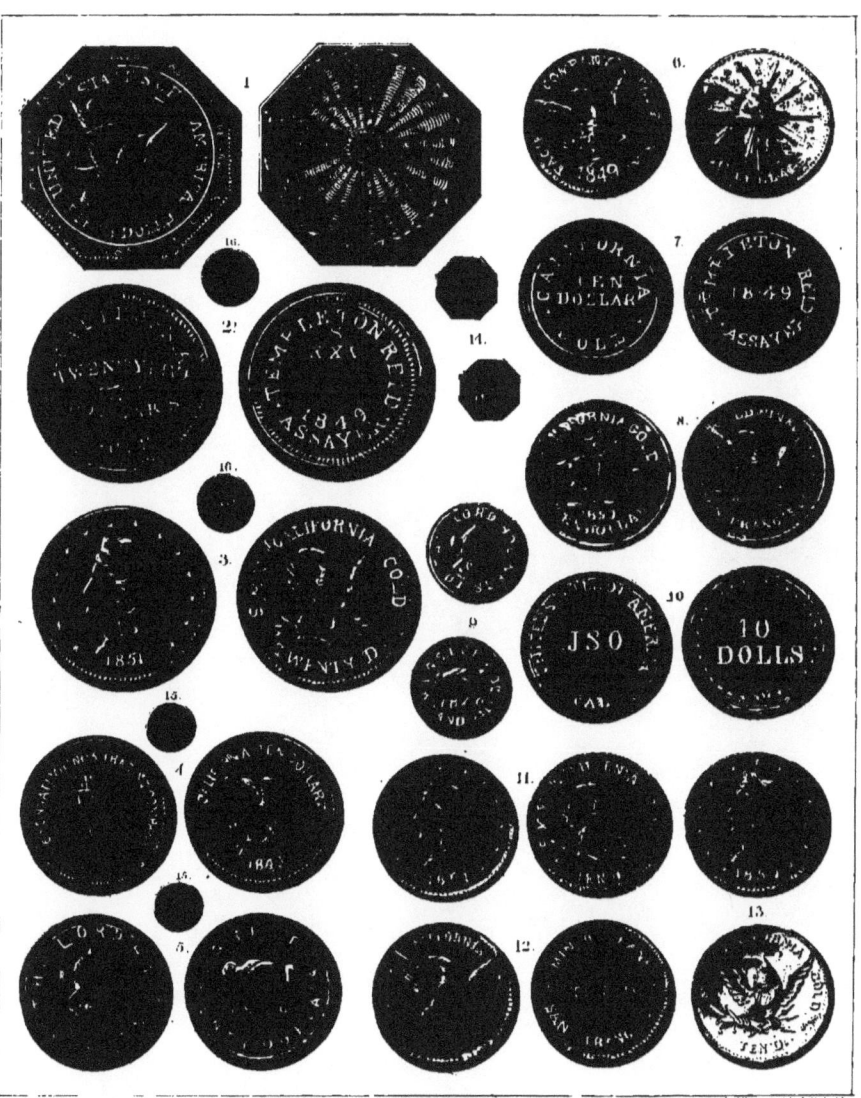

CALIFORNIA COINS.

Soon after the discovery of gold in California, the great difficulty, risk, and frequent losses, consequent upon its retention or transportation, and the schemes devised, and often successful, for cheating the miner, relative to the weight or fineness of the product of his labor, inaugurated the necessity for assaying and coining there. Thus grew up numerous private mints, whose coinage was characterized by skill, honor, and remarkable enterprize.

Messrs. Eckfeldt and Du Bois, in their supplemental work of 1851, to their Manual of 1842, say: "The number of private mints in California, as indicated by specimens here, is fourteen. Some of them have issued but a single denomination of coin, others two, and the Mormons four. Besides these, there are the stamped ingots of Moffatt & Co., and F. D. Kohler, State Assayer; and, lastly, the coin of Augustus Humbert, an United States assayer under a legal provision of 1850.

"1. The coin of 'N. G. & N.'—half-eagle—claims to be full weight, and it is proved by a number of trials, that the variation does not exceed one grain in any case; but the legend on the reverse, CALIFORNIA GOLD WITHOUT ALLOY, allows a pretty wide range. As far as our assays go, the truth of this stamp is proved; there is no alloy, other than that already introduced by the hand of nature, and which is generally more than sufficient. Three pieces severally, the fineness of 870, 880, and 892 thousandths, were within the scope of 'California gold.' They, consequently, are worth $4.83, $4.89, and $4.95½ respectively, without the silver; and including that, 2½ cents more.

"The coin is neatly executed, and, besides the two legends above quoted, bears an eagle, a circle of stars, the date 1849, and the name SAN FRANCISCO.
"(See Plate No. XVIII., Fac Simile No. 7.)

"2. The mint of the "Oregon Exchange Company' issued two denominations, ten and five dollars. They respectively profess 260 and 130 grains' weight of 'native gold.' One five-dollar piece was found to weigh 127½ grains, was 878 thousandths fine, and contained only the natural alloy: resulting value, $4.82; with the silver—in sufficiently large lots—2½ cents more.

"These coins are not well struck, but are pleasantly distinguished by the picture of a beaver, a good emblem of mining industry and of Western life.
"(See Plate No. XVIII., Fac Similes Nos. 1 and 8.)

"3. The mintage of the 'Miners' Bank of San Francisco,' a ten-dollar piece of plain appearance. The average weight is 263½ grains, the fineness about 865 thousandths; part of the alloy being copper. Average value $9.87, with a risk of having it as low as $9.75.

"(See Plate No. XIX., Fac Simile No. 12.)

"4. Coinage of Moffatt & Co., 1849, 1850; pieces of ten and five dollars, in imitation of the national coinage. Several of the coining establishments adopted the same device, but evidently without evil intent, as most of the coins were worth what they professed to be, and some even more. The fineness, however, is in every case inferior to the standard of the Mint. A large promiscuous lot of both kinds of Moffatt & Co.'s coins, dates 1849, 1850, showed an average of 897; average weight to the ten-dollar piece, 258½ grains; average value, $9.97.7. The S. M. V. on these coins is said to mean 'Standard Mint Value.'

"(See Plate No. XVIII., Fac Similes Nos. 2 and 12.)

"5. Ten-dollar piece of 'J. S. O.'—said to be Dr. Ormsby, of Pennsylvania; one piece assayed gave 842 fine; weight, 258½ grains; value, $9.37.

"(See Plate No. XIX., Fac Simile No. 10.)

"6. Twenty-five and ten-dollar pieces of Templeton Reed, whose name appears as assayer upon the emissions of 'Georgia Gold,' in North Carolina, in 1830; weights, respectively, 649 and 260 grains. These, being the only two specimens received are still in the Mint, were not cut for assay, but appear to be of California gold without artificial alloy. Assuming this, the value would be about $24.50 for the first, and $9.75 for the second.

"(See Plate No. XIX., Fac Similes Nos. 2 and 7.)

"7. Ten and five-dollar pieces of the 'Cincinnati Mining and Trading Company,' 1849. These have, also, not been cut, on account of their rarity, but appear to be of native gold, and at the weights of 258 and 132 grains, may be rated at $9.70 and $4.95, respectively.

"(See Plates Nos. XVIII. and XIX., Fac Similes Nos. 4 and 4.)

"8. Ten and five-dollar pieces of the 'Pacific Company,' 1849; very irregular in weight, and debased in fineness; a ten-dollar piece weighed 229 grains, a five-dollar piece 130; assay of a third, 797 thousandths. At those rates, the larger piece would be worth $7.86, the smaller, $4.48; but the valuation is altogether uncertain.

"(See Plates Nos. XVIII. and XIX., Fac Similes Nos. 3 and 6.)

UNITED STATES.

"9. Five-dollar piece of the 'Massachusetts and California Company,' 1849; a very pretty coin, but apparently debased with copper; only one specimen; it weighed 115½ grains; has not been assayed.

"(See Plate No. XVIII., Fac Simile No. 6.)

"10. Coins of Baldwin & Co., four varieties: 1. a ten-dollar piece, 1850, distinguished by a horse and his rider, with a lasso; 2. twenty-dollar piece; 3. ten-dollar piece, 1851; 4. five-dollar piece, 1850; the last two in imitation of United States coinage. Of the first, one piece tried weighed 263 grains; fineness, 880; value $9.96. Of the second, four pieces tried varied from 861 to 871; average fineness, 868½; average value $19.33. Of the third, ten pieces averaged 259½ grains; average fineness, 870; average value, 972. Of the fourth, average value, $4.92. These coins contain some copper—about twenty-thousandths.

"(See Plates Nos. XVIII. and XIX., Fac Similes Nos. 10, 8, 3, and 13.)

"11. Ten and five-dollar pieces of Dubosq & Co., 1850; also in imitation of the National coinage. The larger piece averages 262 grains, and three specimens gave the fineness of 899½, which is a mere shade below standard; consequent value $10.15. A single five-dollar piece yielded $4.92; but a mixed parcel, counting a thousand dollars, gave the fineness of 887, and the close value of $1000.20. Consequently the pieces may be averaged at par.

"(See Plates XVIII. and XIX., Fac Similes Nos. 9 and 11.)

"12. Five-dollar pieces of Shultz & Co., 1851. Average weight 128½ grains; fineness of three pieces, 879; value, $4.97.4. The devices in imitation of United States coin.

"(See Plate No. XVIII., Fac Simile No. 11.)

"13. The Mormon coinage, although executed in the Territory of Utah, is classed among the California coins, being in the neighborhood, and the source whence the material is derived. The denominations are twenty, ten, five, and two and a half dollar pieces. Although there is much irregularity of weight and fineness, the denominations are tolerably in proportion to each other. A parcel made up of all sizes, and counting $562.50, yielded at the Mint, 479.20; say $8.52 to the ten-dollar piece. The fineness was 886.

"(See Plates Nos. XVIII. and XIX., Fac Similes Nos. 5, 14, 5, and 9.)

"14. Five-dollar piece of Dunbar & Co., in imitation of the United States coin. lot of 111 pieces averages 131 grains weight; 883 fineness; value $4.98.

"(See Plate No. XVIII., Fac Simile No. 13.)

"15. Fifty-dollar piece of the United States Assay Office at San Francisco, established by act of Congress of 1850. It first appeared here in 1851. The coin was prepared and issued by Messrs. Moffatt & Co., as contractors, and bears the stamp of Augustus Humbert, assayer. The two professed rates of fineness, 880 and 887 thousandths, are found upon assay here to be fully maintained, whether in single pieces or large quantities. But some irregularity in the weight of so heavy a piece, alloyed with silver only, and offering eight corners to wear, is to be expected. When presented in quantities sufficient to allow for parting the silver, say seventy ounces, the average Mint value is about $50.10; in less quantities, the silver not being allowed for, the average value is about $49.90. But even without the silver they occasionally come up to the full value. This coinage is understood to have put a stop to all private issues in California.

"(See Plates No. XVIII. and XIX., Fac Similes No. 18 and 1.)

"INGOTS.

"1. The ingots of Moffatt & Co., of various sizes, from about $9.00 to $260.00. It may be stated, in general, that some were found to be rated too high, and others too low. The $16.00 ingot yields about $15.75, but is irregular.

"(See Plate No. XVIII., Fac Similes No. 20 and 21.)

"BARS.

"2. The issue of bars by F. D. Kohler, assayer of the State of California, commenced in May, 1850. They are of various sizes, from about $40 to $150. We found a slight undervaluation in his basis of calculation, and generally an error of assay in the same direction; so that on an average his bars were worth at the Mint one per cent., perhaps one and a half per cent., more than the value stamped upon them.

"(See Plate No. XVIII., Fac Simile No. 19.)"

DOLLAR.

This coin is of octagon shape, with the bust of the Goddess of Liberty for a device, around which are eight stars. On the reverse is a wreath, in which are the denomination $\frac{1}{\text{DOLLAR}}$, and the date, 1853.

Legend.—CALIFORNIA GOLD DERI.

HALF-DOLLAR.

This piece is round, with the same device of the previous denomination, and surrounded by thirteen stars. A wreath on the reverse, within which is the date, 1852.

Legend.—HALF-DOLLAR. CALIFORNIA GOLD.

UNITED STATES. 227

QUARTER-DOLLAR.

The device on this is the same as that upon the half-dollar, with a wreath on the reverse enclosing the denomination $\frac{1/4}{\text{DOLLAR}}$.

(See Plate XIV., Figures 14, 15, and 16.)

These pieces conclude our task of describing, and presenting representatives of the private coining enterprize of California; and the contrast of bars and ingots with these tiny denominations, covers the whole ground of local enterprise, necessity or convenience — indicating the powers of invention of the race, which has given tone and character to every industrial or utilizing feature of the American Union, and exhibiting an adaptability of the American mind to any condition or circumstances in which the subject of it, either designedly or unpremeditatedly, may happen to be placed.

By Act of Congress of July 3, 1852, a Branch Mint was established at San Francisco, California, and it was provided therein, that, as soon as said Mint went into operation, "so much of the act making appropriations for the civil and diplomatic expenses of the government for the year ending 30th June, 1851, and for other purposes, as provides for the appointment of an United States Assayer, and the contracting for the assaying and fixing the value of gold in grains or lumps, and for forming the same into bars, be, and the whole of the clause, containing such provisions, shall be hereby repealed."

Thus the much longer continuance of the temporary expedients of the government or private enterprize, in aid of, or to facilitate the operations of the laborers in this vineyard of gold, was rendered unnecessary, by being superseded by a new law, which promised, what has since been accomplished — a pleasing and profitable subjection to order.

We have attempted to present fac-similes, in an acceptable style, of the coinage of California, as in a few years it will be a matter of history; for although specimens of the same may be found in the National Mint, which is open to all, still we must remember that it is convenient of access but to a few of the many millions who comprise our population, and feel an interest in whatever there has been that is either rare or curious.

We leave the reader to travel in imagination to where the gold is found; to thus participate in the processes to which it is subjected — from the washing of the dirt, or the grinding of the quartz that contains it, to its vigilant transportation, in chamois skins, through the valleys and over the mountains, till it is deposited with the United States Assayer, or in the hands of those who, in days past, converted it into "eagles" and "half-eagles."

From the immense discoveries of gold within the last ten years, that period of time, in the history of the world, may properly be denominated the era of gold; and from the first discovery of the auriferous particles, down to the present day, the energy of man, in whatever quarter of the world the intelligence relative to the same had penetrated, has been directed and stimulated to general physical discovery; the effect of which, in the future, opens a wide field for thought and calculation.

Our wonder at the discoveries of gold has hardly been lulled into repose by the extraordinary reality of the past, when rumors from new localities, which promise additional and inexhaustible supplies, are thrust upon us, to stimulate still more the enterprise and cupidity of man for gold — more gold. That there is to be — out of the general order of knowledge and reasoning in regard to the future — an effect of all this, upon the industrial energies of mankind and the progress of the world, we think is foreshadowed — a mighty impetus to be given to everything under the sun, till material development — the hobby of mankind, as mankind is now shaped and directed — shall equal in magnitude the results of physical discovery and science.

We leave to the casuist and Christian philosopher the task of calculating and foretelling the progress of the human mind — in contradistinction to worldly gain — in its connection with the foreshadowed events of the future. That the laborer in this vocation must be early at his post, and vigilant in arranging and leading on his forces, in order to combat successfully with "Mammon" in the human affections, and also to secure some of the laurels with which he is proposing to crown his followers, requires no index but a knowledge of the past.

PLATE XIX.

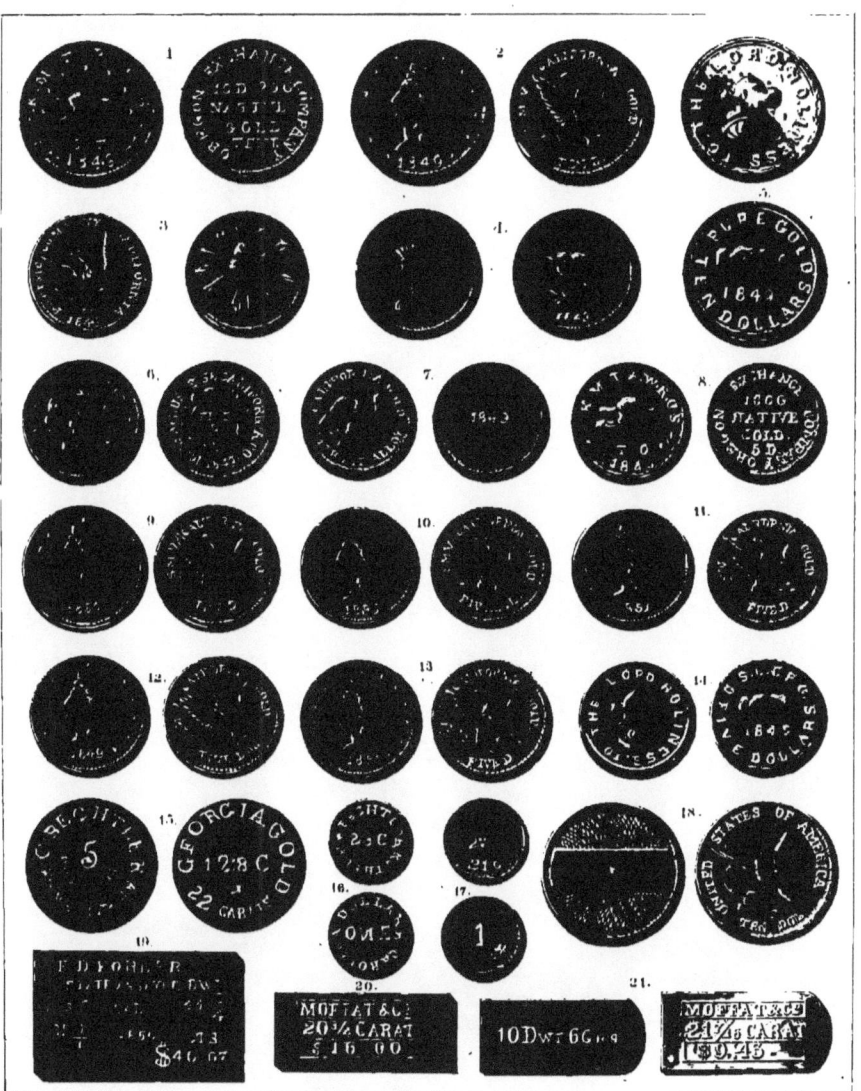

"PATTERN-PIECES."

Following, we have described and presented fac-similes of the various "pattern-pieces" gotten up by, or under the authority of our government and rejected; and, also, some which evidence a commendable zeal and marked progress in art and beauty, and which have been adopted, or are to make their appearance as part of our currency. Comparing our coins, however, with those of France, England, and other European governments, we must conclude that there is still room for emulation and improvement. To the naked eye, but particularly under the *lens*—to illustrate—the wreath upon the pieces, issued by Napoleon III., is presented with all the perfection and beauty of nature; while the wreath on our three-dollar pieces—the most artistic of our whole series of coins—appears, in comparison, like a composition stuck on the same, instead of being the result of the *graver*.

Occupying, as a nation, equal prominence with any other in the world for contiguously geographical extent, mineral wealth, agricultural resources, commerce, and — as soon as we can harmonize upon the policy necessary to establish and protect them — manufactures and the mechanic arts; with no slight claims to science, and the vitality that gives force to intellectual and physical power; it is our duty, as it should be our laudable ambition, to permit no nation to surpass ours in works either of utility or art — nor in anything else, that can justly be made to redound to our intelligence, taste, skill, energy, enterprise, or prosperity.

In the establishment of the Mint, President Washington took so deep an interest as to be almost a daily visitor to it. On one occasion he brought with him one hundred dollars in bullion, with the request that it might be coined into *half-dismes;* and, from the various patterns gotten up for the inspection and decision of the government, the following was selected for the purpose.

Device.—A portrait of the Goddess of Liberty, hair flowing naturally, and facing to the left; and said to have been intended for Mrs. Martha Washington.   1792.
Legend.—LIB. PAR. OF SCIENCE & INDUSTRY.
Exergue.—1792.
Legend.—UNITED STATES OF AMERICA.
Exergue.—HALF DISME. Beneath which is a five-pointed star.
(Size 4. See Plate XVI., Figure 3.)

This coinage was not intended for general circulation, but was a private enterprise of Washington's, and distributed by him among his friends in this country and Europe. It is now particularly rare, commands a large price, and is to be found in but four cabinets in our country.

DISME.

1792. *Device.*—The Goddess of Liberty, facing to the left, with the hair flowing loosely.
Legend.—LIBERTY PARENT OF SCIENCE & INDUS.
Exergue.—1792.
Reverse.—Eagle volant,—in the centre of the field.
Legend.—UNITED STATES OF AMERICA.
Exergue.—DISME.
(Size 6. See Plate XIII., Figure 9.)

CENT.

1792. *Device.*—A bust of the Goddess of Liberty, with loosely flowing hair, and facing to the right.
Legend.—LIBERTY PARENT OF SCIENCE & INDUSTRY.
Exergue.—1792.
Reverse.—A wreath inclosing a ring, in which is the inscription ONE CENT.
Legend.—UNITED STATES OF AMERICA.
Exergue.—$\frac{1}{100}$
(Size 10. See Plate XIII., Figure 7.)

Nothing but the modesty of our fathers could, it seems to us, have prevented the adoption of this coin; they, perhaps, thinking it was too early a period in the history of the Republic, to proclaim upon their currency, what has since been exemplified, that liberty is the parent of science and industry. For if science does not particularly flourish under a free government, the freedom of thought is at least essential to its progress, and liberty is the very breath of industry.

CENT.

1792. The same as that previously described, with the exception of the legend—LIBERTY PARENT OF SCIENCE & INDUST:
(Size 5. See Plate XIII., Figure 10.)

1792. Another, same as the preceding, except that a round piece of silver is inserted in the centre of the field — the letter N in CENT, being stamped on the silver — $\frac{ONE}{CENT.}$
(Size the same. See Plate XIII., Figure 11.)

UNITED STATES.   231

These pieces being about the size of the half-cent, the insertion of the small piece of silver was probably to give it the standard value of that coin.

CENT.

Device.—A bust, whether masculine or feminine, it would be difficult to determine, facing right.   1792.
Legend.—LIBERTY.
Exergue.—1792.
Reverse.—An eagle with partially expanded wings, standing upon, apparently, the upper portion of the globe.
Legend.—UNITED STATES OF AMERICA.
(Size 8. See Plate XIII., Figure 13.)

We have denominated this as a pattern-piece for a cent, in the absence of positive information in relation to the purpose for which it was gotten up. It may have been designed for some other denomination, however, as the eagle never appeared upon the authorized cent of the Federal government, till it made its appearance in nickel.

PIECES.

Device.—An eagle with wings closed, perched upon the upper portion of the globe, apparently in meditation, and surveying, at the same time, the scene from 1792. thence.
(Size 7. See Plate XIII., Figure 12.)

Another: the device being an eagle with expanded wings, as if in the act of alighting upon a shield presented sideways.
(Size 7. See Plate XIII., Figure 15.)
Neither of the above have a reverse.

DOLLAR.

There were one type and two varieties of this pattern or trial-piece, subsequently adopted, for which   1836.
(See Plate XVI., Figure 19.)
There was, also, a pattern piece as follows:

GOLD DOLLAR.

Device.—The liberty-cap, with its motto LIBERTY, in the centre of a blaze covering the whole field.   1836.
Reverse.—A palm wreath enclosing the numeral I., under which is D.
Legend.—UNITED STATES OF AMERICA.
Exergue.—1836.
(Size 3. See Plate XIV., Figure 20.)

UNITED STATES.

Dollar.

1838. The device the same as of this denomination of 1836. The thirteen stars placed around the edge of the field.

This piece is extremely rare and valuable — sixteen only having been struck off. Also, in this year, a half-dollar with four varieties.

1838. In this year there were two types and four varieties struck off — one with an eagle volant, and the other with the wings extended. They are both very rare and valuable, and to be found but in few cabinets.

Dollar and Half-Dollar.

1839. *Device.*—The eagle with expanded wings, &c., adopted in 1840.
(See Plate XV., Figures 7 and 9.)

Double-Eagle.

1849. See regular description, 1850.
(See Plate XIV., Figure 6.)

Three-Cent Pieces.

1849. *Device.*—The Goddess of Liberty seated, &c., as upon half-dimes.
Exergue.—1849.
Reverse.—The figure 3 in the centre of the field.
(Size 3. See Plate XIII., Figure 22.)

1849. *Device.*—The same as the preceding.
Exergue.—1849.
Reverse.—The numerals III.
(Size 3. See Plate XIII., Figure 24.)

1850. *Device.*—The liberty-cap with its motto LIBERTY in the centre of a blaze covering the whole field.
Reverse.—A palm wreath enclosing the numerals III.
Legend.—UNITED STATES OF AMERICA.
Exergue.—1850.
(Size 3. See Plate XIII., Figure 23.)

UNITED STATES.

Ring-Cent.

Device.—On the upper part of the piece the inscription CENT; midway, each side of the ring, a star. 1850.
Exergue.—1850.
Reverse.—On the upper part of the piece U. S. A.
Legend.—ONE TENTH SILVER.
(Size 4. See Plate XIII., Figure 21.)

This piece is a flat ring, the centre being open, and as the legend shows a composition.

Cent.

Device.—The Goddess of Liberty seated, &c., as in the present silver currency. 1851.
Exergue.—1851.
Reverse.—An oak wreath inclosing the numeral I., and the word CENT under it.
(Size 5. See Plate XIII., Figure 20.)

This coin was also a composition.

Gold-Ring-Dollar.

Device.—A wreath crossing at the lower ends and extending upward. On the upper part of the flat circle DOLLAR. 1852.
Reverse.—A serpentine line around the inner edge of the circle — the centre being open.
Legend.—UNITED STATES OF AMERICA.
Exergue.—1852.
(Size 4. See Plate XIV., Figure 17.)

Another type with a wreath around the inner circle, and outside of that the legend UNITED STATES OF AMERICA. 1852.
(Size 4.)

A Gold Ring Half-Dollar. — Same as the above.
(Size 3. See Plate XIV., Figure 18.)

Silver Ring-Dollar.

Device.—A series of seven laurel branches around the circle, each of which bears two berries. 1852.
Reverse.—U. S. A., on the upper portion of the circle.
Exergue.—1852.
(Size 4. See Plate XIV., Figure 19.)

In silver, but intended as a pattern for a gold dollar.

UNITED STATES.

CENT.

1853. *Device.*—The Goddess of Liberty, with a fillet around the head bearing the motto LIBERTY—with thirteen stars around the field.
Exergue.—1853.
Reverse.—A laurel wreath enclosing the words ONE CENT.
(Size 4. See Plate XIII., Figure 17.)

CENT.

1854. The designs the same as the last emission of the copper cents, except that the thirteen stars surrounding the first are omitted.
Exergue.—1854.
(Size 7. See Plate XIII., Figure 16.)

This pattern-cent is about two-thirds the size of the ordinary cent, and exceedingly well executed.

CENT.

1855. *Device.*—The eagle, volant, with thirteen stars around the edge of the field.
Exergue.—1855.
Reverse.—The same as on the last emission of the copper cents.
(Size 7. See Plate XIII., Figure 8).

This cent is composed of copper and nickel in such proportions as to give it a brassy appearance.

CENTS.

1856. The nickel — since adopted.
Another: the designs the same as upon the latest copper cents, and struck off from the die of the half-cent — the size 6.

This piece was a composition of copper and nickel, in such proportions as to give it nearly the tint of gold.

HALF-DOLLAR.

1858. *Device.*—The Goddess of Liberty, &c., as upon that denomination of coin.
Reverse.—An eagle with expanded wings; upon its breast a shield, and falling over the same, from the beak of the eagle is a scroll bearing the motto E PLURIBUS UNUM. In its talons the laurel branch and arrows.
Legend.—UNITED STATES OF AMERICA.
Exergue.—HALF DOLLAR.
(Size 9. See Plate XIII., Figure 14.)

UNITED STATES.

After a long suspension — broken only by its adoption upon the double-eagle — the motto "E PLURIBUS UNUM," is revived upon this beautiful piece by Hon. James Ross Snowden, the present Director of the Mint. Its adoption will be hailed with gratification by the people, who yielded reluctantly to the change that gave them a symbol without it.

CENT.

Device.—The head of an Indian princess.   1858.
Legend.—UNITED STATES OF AMERICA.
Exergue.—1858.
Reverse.—An oak wreath, meeting at the top a shield surrounded by a scroll, and enclosing the denomination ONE CENT.
(Size 4. See Plate XIII., Figure 18.)

For this decided improvement of design and workmanship upon the cent, we are also indebted to the present Director of the Mint, who in this piece, and the dollar and three-dollar pieces of 1854, has already departed from the track so long trodden by his predecessors; — thus affording evidences of a spirit of progress which cannot but redound to his own reputation and the honor of the government.

STEAM-COINAGE.

Device.—The liberty-cap with its motto LIBERTY, in the centre of a blaze covering the whole field.   1836.
Reverse. — A circle containing the inscription — FIRST STEAM-COINAGE MARCH 23.
Legend.—UNITED STATES MINT.
Exergue.—1836.

This piece was issued in copper, to commemorate the application of steam-power to coining.

"FEUCHTWANGER CENT."

Device.—An eagle strangling with its talons, a serpent.   1837.
Exergue.—1837.
Reverse.—A wreath enclosing the denomination ONE CENT.
Legend.—FEUCHTWANGER'S COMPOSITION.
(Size 5. See Plate XIII., Figure 19.)

This was gotten up as a specimen of a composition; submitted to the government for its consideration, and rejected. If in a coin of so small value as a cent, it were desirable to consult cleanliness and durability, this composition would have subserved the purpose, as it will neither corrode nor wear; the piece from which we take the foregoing description being as bright and perfect as on the day it was issued.

The distinguished metallurgist and chemist whose name it bears, may console himself for its rejection, with the reflection that his effort to serve the government was a creditable, if not a successful one.

Having completed the task of presenting to the public whatever there has been that is antiquated or rare, as well as that which now exists in the metallic money of our country, and with as much diversity and adornment of description as the subject-matter would permit, we submit this work with the hope that charity will cover up the short-comings and defects which, in all probability, exist in this our effort.

In our thoughts and deductions we have felt nationally, and in that spirit—according to our comprehension—have expressed them; but with no purpose to excite emotions incompatible with that entire freedom of opinion we have exercised for ourselves.

INDEX OF DATES, DEGREES OF RARITY, &c., OF THE GOLD, SILVER, AND COPPER COINAGE.

	GOLD.						SILVER.						COPPER.	
DATE.	DOUBLE EAGLES.	EAGLES.	HALF-EAGLES.	THREE DOLLARS.	QUARTER-EAGLES.	DOLLARS.	DOLLARS.	HALF-DOLLARS.	QUARTER-DOLLARS.	DIMES.	HALF-DIMES.	THREE CENTS.	CENTS.	HALF-CENTS.
1793	......	......	......	......	......	......	......	......	......	......	......	......	+ • •	+ • •
1794	......	......	......	......	......	......	+ • • •	+ •	......	......	+ • • •	......	+ •	+ •
1795	......	+ • •	+ • •	......	......	......	+ •	+ •	......	......	+ • •	......	+ •	+ •
1796	......	+ • •	+ • • •	......	+ • • •	......	+ •	+ • •	+ • •	+ •	+ •	......	+ •	+ • • •
1797	......	+ •	+ • • •	......	+ • •	......	+ • •	+ • • •	*	+ • • •	+ • •	......	+	+ •
1798	......	+ • •	+ •	......	+ • •	......	+	......	......	+ •	......	......	+	......
1799	......	+ •	+ • •	......	*	......	+	......	......	......	......	......	+ • • •	......
1800	......	+ •	+ •	......	......	......	+ •	......	......	+ • •	+ •	......	+	+ •
1801	......	+ •	*	......	......	......	+ •	+ • •	......	+ • •	+ • •	......	+	......
1802	......	*	+ •	......	+ • •	......	+ •	+ •	......	+ • • •	+ • • •	......	+	+ • •
1803	......	+ • •	+	......	*	......	+ • •	+ •	......	+ • • •	+ • • •	......	+	+
1804	......	+ • •	+ •	......	+ •	......	+ • • •	+ • • •	+ • •	+ • • •	......	......	+ • • •	+
1805	......	......	+	......	+ • •	......	*	+ •	+ •	+ •	+ • •	......	+ •	+ •
1806	......	......	+	......	+ • •	......	......	+	+ •	......	......	......	+ •	+ • •
1807	......	......	+	......	+ •	......	......	+	+	+ •	......	......	+ •	+ •
1808	......	......	+	......	+ •	......	......	+ •	......	......	......	......	+ • •	+ •
1809	......	......	+ •	......	......	......	......	+	......	+ •	......	......	+ • •	+
1810	......	......	+	......	......	......	......	+	......	*	......	......	+	+ •
1811	......	......	+	......	......	......	......	+ •	......	+ • • •	......	......	+ •	+ • •
1812	......	......	+ •	......	......	......	......	+	......	......	......	......	+	......
1813	......	......	+	......	......	......	......	+	......	......	......	......	+ •	......
1814	......	......	+ • •	......	......	......	......	+ •	......	+ •	......	......	+	......
1815	......	......	*	......	......	......	......	+ • • •	+	......	......	......	......	......
1816	......	......	......	......	......	......	......	*	*	......	......	......	+	......
1817	......	......	......	......	......	......	......	+ • •	......	......	......	......	+	......
1818	......	......	+ •	......	......	......	......	+	+	......	......	......	+	......
1819	......	......	+	......	......	......	......	+	+	......	......	......	+	......
1820	......	......	+ • •	......	......	......	......	+ •	+	+ •	......	......	+	......
1821	......	......	+ •	......	+ • •	......	......	+	+	+	......	......	+ •	......
1822	......	......	+ • • •	......	......	......	......	+	+ •	+ • •	......	......	+	......
1823	......	......	+ • •	......	......	......	......	+	+ • • •	+ •	......	......	+ •	......
1824	......	......	+ • •	......	+ •	......	......	+	+ • •	+ •	......	......	+	......
1825	......	......	+	......	+ •	......	......	+	+ •	+	......	......	+	+
1826	......	......	+ •	......	+ • • •	......	......	+	......	......	......	......	+	+ •
1827	......	......	+ •	......	+ • •	......	......	+	+ • • •	+	......	......	+	......
1828	......	......	+ • •	......	......	......	......	+	+	+ •	......	......	+	+
1829	......	......	+ • •	......	+ •	......	......	+	......	+	+	......	+	+
1830	......	......	+	......	+ •	......	......	+	......	+ •	+	......	+	......
1831	......	......	+	......	+ • •	......	......	+ •	+ •	+	+	......	+	+ • • •
1832	......	......	+ •	......	+ •	......	......	+	+ • •	+	+ •	......	+	+
1833	......	......	+ •	......	+	......	......	+	+ •	+	+	......	+	+
1834	......	......	+ •	......	+ • •	......	......	+	+	+	+	......	+	+
1835	......	......	+ •	......	+ • •	......	......	+	+	+	+	......	+	+
1836	......	......	+	......	+ •	......	+ O • • •	+	+ •	+	+	......	+	+ • • •
1837	......	......	+ •	......	+ • •	......	......	+	+ • •	+	+	......	+	......
1838	......	+ • •	+ •	......	+	......	+ O • • •	+	+	+ •	+ •	......	+	......
1839	......	+ •	+ •	......	+ •	......	+ O • • •	+	+ •	+ • •	+	......	+	......
1840	......	+ •	+	......	+ •	......	+ •	+	+ •	+	+	......	+	+ O • • •
1841	......	+ •	+ •	......	+ • • •	......	+	+ • •	+ • •	+	+	......	+	+ O • • •
1842	......	+ •	+ • •	......	+ • • •	......	+	+	+ • •	+	+ •	......	+	+ O • • •
1843	......	+	+	......	+	......	+	+	+	+	+	......	+	+ O • • •
1844	......	+ •	+ •	......	+ • •	......	+ • •	+ • •	+ •	+ •	+	......	+	+ O • • •
1845	......	+ •	+	......	+ •	......	+ •	+ •	+ •	+	+	......	+	+ O • • •
1846	......	+	+	......	+ • •	......	+ •	+	+ • •	+ • •	+ • •	......	+	+ O • • •
1847	......	+	+ •	......	+	......	+	+	+ •	+	+	......	+	+ O • • •
1848	......	+	+ •	......	+ •	......	+ •	+	+ • •	+ •	+ •	......	+	+ O • • •
1849	+ O ∽	+	+ •	......	+ • •	+ •	+ •	+	+ •	+	+	......	+	+
1850	+	+	+ • •	......	+	+ •	+ •	+ •	+ •	+	+	......	+	+
1851	+	+	+	......	+	+	+ • • •	+ •	+ •	+	+	+	+	+
1852	+	+	+	......	+ •	+	+ • • •	+ •	+ •	+	+	+	+	+ O • • •
1853	+	+	+	......	+	+	+ •	+	+	+	+	+	+	+
1854	+	+ •	+ • •	+ •	+	+	+ • •	+	+	+	+	+	+	+
1855	+	+	+ •	+	+	+	+ •	+	+	+	+	+ • •	+	+ •
1856	+	+	+	+ •	+	+	+ •	+	+	+	+	+	+	+ •
1857	+	+	+	+	+	+	+ •	+	+	+	+	+	+	+ •
1858	+	+	+	+	+	+	+ •	+	+	+	+	+	+	......

+ Coined.
• Scarce.
* Coinage reported by Mint — none in cabinet collections.
• • Rare.
O Trial pieces.
• • • Very rare.
∽ Unique.
...... Not coined.

UNITED STATES.

TYPES AND VARIETIES OF THE CENTS.

DATES.	CHAIN.	WREATH.	LIBERTY CAP.	CUE.	TURBAN.	FILLET.	FACING	TYPES.	VARIETIES.	DATES.	FILLET.	FACING	TYPES.	VARIETIES.
1793	Do.	...	...	...	...	...	Right.	4	6	1824	Do.	Left.	1	7
"	...	Do.	...	...	...	...	"	2	21	1825	Do.	"	1	9
"	...	...	Do.	...	...	...	"	1	3	1826	Do.	"	1	10
1794	...	...	Do.	...	...	...	"	1	26	1827	Do.	"	1	11
1795	...	...	Do.	...	...	...	"	2	7	1828	Do.	"	1	10
1796	...	...	Do.	...	...	...	"	1	8	1829	Do.	"	1	7
"	...	...	...	Do.	...	...	"	1	9	1830	Do.	"	1	9
1797	...	...	...	Do.	...	...	"	1	14	1831	Do.	"	1	8
1798	...	...	...	Do.	...	...	"	1	20	1832	Do.	"	1	7
1799	...	...	...	Do.	...	...	"	1	4	1833	Do.	"	1	5
1800	...	...	...	Do.	...	...	"	1	12	1834	Do.	"	1	9
1801	...	...	...	Do.	...	...	"	1	14	1835	Do.	"	1	5
1802	...	...	...	Do.	...	...	"	1	21	1836	Do.	"	1	3
1803	...	...	...	Do.	...	...	"	1	14	1837	Do.	"	2	8
1804	...	...	...	Do.	...	...	"	1	6	1838	Do.	"	2	4
1805	...	...	...	Do.	...	...	"	1	5	1839	Do.	"	4	7
1806	...	...	...	Do.	...	...	"	6	4	1840	Do.	"	1	5
1807	...	...	...	Do.	...	...	"	1	9	1841	Do.	"	1	2
1808	...	...	...	Do.	...	...	"	1	1	1842	Do.	"	1	4
"	...	...	...	...	Do.	...	Left.	1	4	1843	Do.	"	1	3
1809	...	...	...	...	Do.	...	"	1	4	1844	Do.	"	1	3
1810	...	...	...	...	Do.	...	"	1	7	1845	Do.	"	1	4
1811	...	...	...	...	Do.	...	"	2	6	1846	Do.	"	1	8
1812	...	...	...	...	Do.	...	"	1	9	1847	Do.	"	1	5
1813	...	...	...	...	Do.	...	"	1	5	1848	Do.	"	1	5
1814	...	...	...	...	Do.	...	"	1	6	1849	Do.	"	1	6
1816	...	...	...	...	...	Do.	"	1	11	1850	Do.	"	6	5
1817	...	...	...	...	...	Do.	"	1	22	1851	Do.	"	1	6
1818	...	...	...	...	...	Do.	"	1	10	1852	Do.	"	1	6
1819	...	...	...	...	...	Do.	"	1	9	1853	Do.	"	1	9
1820	...	...	...	...	...	Do.	"	1	14	1854	Do.	"	1	10
1821	...	...	...	...	...	Do.	"	1	5	1855	Do.	"	1	9
1822	...	...	...	...	...	Do.	"	1	9	1856	Do.	"	1	7
1823	...	...	...	...	...	Do.	"	1	3	1857	Do.	"	2	3

UNITED STATES.

TYPES AND VARIETIES OF THE HALF-CENTS.

DATES.	LIBERTY CAP.	CUE.	TURBAN.	FACING	TYPES.	VARIETIES.	DATES.	FILLET.	FACING	TYPES.	VARIETIES.
1793	Do.	......	......	Left.	1	6	1840	Do.	Left.	1	1
1794	Do.	......	......	Right.	1	5	1841	Do.	"	1	1
1795	Do.	......	......	"	1	4	1842	Do.	"	1	1
1796	Do.	......	......	"	1	2	1843	Do.	"	1	1
1797	Do.	......	......	"	1	4	1844	Do.	"	1	1
1800	......	Do.	......	"	1	2	1845	Do.	"	1	1
1802	......	Do.	......	"	1	2	1846	Do.	"	1	1
1803	......	Do.	......	"	1	2	1847	Do.	"	1	1
1804	......	Do.	......	"	1	5	1848	Do.	"	1	1
1805	......	Do.	......	"	1	4	1849	Do.	"	1	3
1806	......	Do.	......	"	1	2	1850	Do.	"	1	2
1807	......	Do.	......	"	1	4	1851	Do.	"	1	3
1808	......	Do.	......	"	1	3	1852	Do.	"	1	1
1809	......	......	Do.	Left.	1	8	1853	Do.	"	1	2
1810	......	......	Do.	"	1	4	1854	Do.	"	1	2
1811	......	......	Do.	"	1	2	1855	Do.	"	1	2
1825	......	......	Do.	"	1	3	1856	Do.	"	1	1
1826	......	......	Do.	"	1	4	1857	Do.	"	1	2
1828	......	......	Do.	"	1	5					
1829	......	......	Do.	"	1	3					
1831	......	......	Do.	"	1	1					
1832	......	......	Do.	"	1	4					
1833	......	......	Do.	"	1	2					
1834	......	......	Do.	"	1	3					
1835	......	......	Do.	"	1	4					
1836	......	......	Do.	"	1	2					

DIRECTORS OF THE MINT.

1. DAVID RITTENHOUSE (the eminent Philosopher), July, 1792, to July, 1795.

2. HENRY WILLIAM DE SAUSSERE (*vice* Mr. Rittenhouse, resigned), July 11th, to October 28th, 1795 (afterwards, and for many years, Chancellor of South Carolina).

3. ELIAS BOUDINOT (in place of Judge De Saussere, resigned), October, 1795, to July, 1805 (previously President of Congress under the Confederation).

4. ROBERT PATTERSON (on the resignation of Dr. Boudinot), July, 1805, to July, 1824 (Vice-Provost of the University of Pennsylvania, and President of American Philosophical Society).

5. DR. SAMUEL MOORE (in place of Mr. Patterson, deceased), July, 1824, to July, 1835 (member of Congress from Bucks County, Pa.).

6. DR. ROBERT M. PATTERSON (on the resignation of Dr. Moore), July, 1835, to July, 1851 (Professor of Natural Philosophy in University of Virginia, and President of American Philosophical Society).

7. DR. GEORGE N. ECKERT (*vice* Dr. Patterson, resigned), July, 1851, to April, 1853 (member of Congress from Lebanon County, Pa.).

8. THOMAS M. PETTIT (in place of Dr. Eckert, resigned), April to June, 1853 (Judge of District Court, Philadelphia).

9. The present incumbent, JAMES ROSS SNOWDEN (previously Speaker of the House of Representatives of Pennsylvania, Treasurer of Pennsylvania, and Treasurer of the Mint), was appointed in June, 1853, in the place of Judge Pettit, who died on the 31st of May in that year, having held the office of Director but a few weeks.

UNITED STATES.

TABULAR STATEMENT

OF THE AMOUNT OF

COINAGE AT THE MINT OF THE UNITED STATES

SINCE THE COMMENCEMENT OF ITS OPERATIONS.

GOLD COINAGE.

DATE.	DOUBLE EAGLE PIECES.	EAGLE PIECES.	HALF EAGLE PIECES.	THREE DOLLAR PIECES.	QUARTER EAGLE PIECES.	DOLLAR PIECES.
1793	}	2,795	8,707	....	....	....
1794						
1795						
1796	....	6,934	6,196	....	963	....
1797	....	8,323	3,609	....	859	....
1798	....	7,974	24,867	....	614	....
1799	....	17,483	7,451	....	480	....
1800	....	25,965	11,622	....	....	....
1801	....	29,254	26,006	....	....	....
1802	....	15,090	53,176	....	2,612	....
1803	....	8,979	33,506	....	423	....
1804	....	9,795	30,475	....	3,327	....
1805	....	....	33,183	....	1,781	....
1806	....	....	64,093	....	1,616	....
1807	....	....	84,093	....	6,812	....
1808	....	....	55,578	....	2,710	....
1809	....	....	33,875	....	....	....
1810	....	....	100,287	....	....	....
1811	....	....	99,581	....	....	....
1812	....	....	58,087	....	....	....
1813	....	....	95,428	....	....	....
1814	....	....	15,454	....	....	....
1815	....	....	635	....	....	....
1816	....	....	....	....	....	....
1817	....	....	....	....	....	....
1818	....	....	48,588	....	....	....

242   UNITED STATES.

GOLD COINAGE—Continued.

DATE.	DOUBLE EAGLE PIECES.	EAGLE PIECES.	HALF EAGLE PIECES.	THREE DOLLAR PIECES.	QUARTER EAGLE PIECES.	DOLLAR PIECES.
1819			51,723			
1820			263,806			
1821			34,641		6,488	
1822			17,796			
1823			14,485			
1824			17,340		2,600	
1825			29,060		4,434	
1826			18,069		760	
1827			24,913		2,800	
1828			28,029			
1829			57,442		3,403	
1830			126,351		4,540	
1831			140,594		4,520	
1832			157,487		4,400	
1833			193,630		4,160	
1834			732,169		117,370	
1835			371,534		131,402	
1836			553,147		547,986	
1837			207,121		45,080	
1838		7,200	286,558		47,030	
1839		38,248	118,143		27,021	
1840		47,338	137,362		18,859	
1841		63,131	15,833			
1842		81,507	27,578		2,823	
1843		250,624	855,085		530,853	
1844		125,001	817,583		35,738	
1845		73,653	548,728		110,511	
1846		101,875	547,231		110,709	
1847		1,433,764	1,080,337		192,824	
1848		145,484	267,775		8,886	
1849	../..ONLY	653,618	133,070		23,294	688,567
1850	1,170,261	291,451	64,491		252,923	481,953
1851	2,087,155	176,328	377,505		1,372,748	3,317,671
1852	2,053,026	263,106	573,901		1,159,681	2,045,351
1853	1,261,326	201,253	305,770		1,404,668	4,076,051
1854	757,899	54,250	160,675	138,618	596,258	1,639,445
1855	364,666	121,701	117,098	50,555	235,480	758,269
1856	329,878	60,490	197,990	26,010	384,240	1,702,936
1857[1]	98,315	2,916	69,115	7,832	106,722	578,356

[1] To June 30th.

SILVER COINAGE.

DATE.	DOLLARS. PIECES.	HALF-DOLLARS. PIECES.	QUARTER-DOLL'S. PIECES.	DIMES. PIECES.	HALF-DIMES. PIECES.	THREE CENTS. PIECES.
1793						
1794	204,791	323,144	....	....	86,416	....
1795						
1796	72,920	3,918	5,894	22,135	10,230	....
1797	7,776	....	252	25,261	44,527	....
1798	327,536	....	....	27,550	....	....
1799	423,515	....	....	....	....	....
1800	220,920	....	....	21,760	24,000	....
1801	54,454	30,289	....	34,640	33,910	....
1802	41,650	29,890	....	10,975	13,010	....
1803	66,064	31,715	....	33,040	37,850	....
1804	19,570	156,519	6,738	8,265	....	....
1805	321	211,722	121,394	120,780	15,600	....
1806	....	839,576	206,124	....	....	....
1807	....	1,051,576	220,643	165,000	....	....
1808	....	1,368,600	....	....	....	....
1809	....	1,405,810	....	44,710	....	....
1810	....	1,276,276	....	6,355	....	....
1811	....	1,203,644	....	65,180	....	....
1812	....	1,628,059	....	....	....	....
1813	....	1,241,903	....	....	....	....
1814	....	1,039,075	....	421,500	....	....
1815	....	....	69,232	....	....	....
1816	....	47,150	20,003	....	....	....
1817	....	1,215,567	....	....	....	....
1818	....	1,060,322	361,174	....	....	....
1819	....	2,208,000	144,000	....	....	....
1820	....	751,122	127,444	942,587	....	....
1821	....	1,305,797	216,851	1,186,512	....	....
1822	....	1,559,573	64,080	100,000	....	....
1823	....	1,694,200	17,800	440,000	....	....
1824	....	3,504,954	....	....	....	....
1825	....	2,943,166	168,000	510,000	....	....
1826	....	4,004,180	....	....	....	....

UNITED STATES.

SILVER COINAGE—Continued.

DATE.	DOLLARS. PIECES.	HALF-DOLLARS. PIECES.	QUARTER-DOLL'S. PIECES.	DIMES. PIECES.	HALF-DIMES. PIECES.	THREE CENTS. PIECES.
1827	....	5,493,400	4,000	1,215,000	....	....
1828	....	3,075,200	102,000	125,000	....	....
1829	....	3,712,156	....	770,000	1,230,000	....
1830	....	4,764,800	....	510,000	1,240,000	....
1831	....	5,873,660	398,000	771,350	1,242,700	....
1832	....	4,797,000	320,000	522,500	965,000	....
1833	....	5,206,000	156,000	485,000	1,370,000	....
1834	....	6,412,004	286,000	635,000	1,480,000	....
1835	....	5,352,006	1,952,000	1,410,000	2,760,000	....
1836	1,000	6,546,200	472,000	1,190,000	1,000,000	....
1837	....	3,629,820	252,400	1,042,000	2,276,000	....
1838	16	3,546,000	832,000	1,992,500	2,255,000	....
1839	300	3,334,561	491,146	1,053,115	1,069,150	....
1840	61,005	1,435,008	188,127	1,358,580	1,344,085	....
1841	173,000	310,000	120,000	1,622,500	1,150,000	....
1842	184,618	2,012,764	88,000	1,887,500	815,000	....
1843	165,100	6,112,000	1,613,600	1,520,000	1,165,000	....
1844	20,000	3,771,000	1,161,200	72,500	650,000	....
1845	24,500	2,083,000	922,000	1,985,000	1,565,000	....
1846	169,600	4,514,000	510,000	31,000	27,000	....
1847	140,750	3,740,000	1,102,000	245,000	1,274,000	....
1848	15,000	580,000	146,000	451,500	668,000	....
1849	62,600	1,252,000	340,000	839,000	1,309,000	....
1850	7,500	227,000	190,800	1,931,500	955,000	....
1851	1,300	200,750	160,000	1,026,500	781,000	5,447,400
1852	1,100	77,130	177,060	1,535,500	1,000,500	18,663,500
1853	46,110	3,532,708	15,254,220	12,173,010	13,345,020	11,400,000
1854	33,140	2,982,000	12,380,000	4,470,000	5,740,000	671,000
1855	26,000	759,500	2,857,000	2,075,000	1,750,000	139,000
1856	63,500	938,000	7,264,000	5,780,000	4,880,000	1,458,000
1857[1]	94,000	142,000	2,304,000	4,890,000	3,940,000	....

[1] To June 30th.

COPPER COINAGE.

RECAPITULATION.

DATE.	CENT PIECES.	HALF CENT PIECES.	WHOLE COINAGE IN PIECES.	WHOLE COINAGE IN VALUE.
1793	} 1,066,033	142,534	1,834,420	$453,541.60
1794				
1795				
1796	974,700	115,480	1,219,370	192,129.40
1797	897,510	107,048	1,095,165	125,524.29
1798	979,700	....	1,368,241	545,698.00
1799	904,585	12,167	1,365,081	645,906.68
1800	2,822,175	211,530	3,337,972	571,335.40
1801	1,362,637	....	1,571,390	510,956.37
1802	3,435,100	14,366	3,615,869	516,075.83
1803	2,471,353	97,900	2,780,830	370,698.53
1804	756,838	1,055,312	2,046,839	371,827.94
1805	941,116	814,464	2,260,361	333,239.48
1806	348,000	356,000	1,815,409	801,084.00
1807	727,221	476,000	2,731,345	1,044,595.96
1808	1,109,000	400,000	2,935,888	982,055.00
1809	222,867	1,544,572	2,861,834	884,752.53
1810	1,458,500	215,000	3,056,418	1,155,868.50
1811	218,025	63,140	1,649,570	1,108,740.95
1812	1,075,500	....	2,761,646	1,115,219.50
1813	418,000	....	1,755,331	1,102,271.50
1814	357,830	....	1,833,859	642,535.80
1815	....	....	69,867	20,483.00
1816	2,820,982	....	2,888,135	56,785.57
1817	3,948,400	....	5,163,967	647,267.50
1818	3,167,000	....	5,537,084	1,345,064.50
1819	2,671,000	....	5,074,723	1,425,325.00
1820	4,407,550	....	6,492,509	1,864,786.20
1821	389,000	....	3,139,249	1,018,977.45
1822	2,072,339	....	3,813,788	915,509.89
1823	12,250	....	2,166,485	967,975.00

COPPER COINAGE—Continued.

RECAPITULATION.

PERIOD.	CENT PIECES.	HALF CENT PIECES.	WHOLE COINAGE IN PIECES.	WHOLE CURRENCY IN VALUE.
1824	1,262,000	....	4,786,894	1,858,297.00
1825	1,461,100	63,000	5,178,760	1,735,894.00
1826	1,517,425	234,000	5,774,434	2,110,679.25
1827	2,357,732	....	9,097,845	3,024,342.32
1828	2,260,624	606,000	6,196,853	1,741,381.24
1829	1,414,500	487,000	7,674,501	2,306,875.50
1830	1,711,500	....	8,357,191	3,155,620.00
1831	3,359,260	2,200	11,792,284	3,923,473.60
1832	2,362,000	....	9,128,387	3,401,055.00
1833	2,739,000	154,000	10,307,790	3,765,710.00
1834	1,855,100	120,000	11,637,643	7,388,423.00
1835	3,878,400	141,000	15,996,342	5,668,667.00
1836	2,111,000	398,000	13,719,333	7,764,900.00
1837	5,558,300	....	13,010,721	3,299,898.00
1838	6,370,200	....	15,336,311	4,206,540.00
1839	3,128,661	....	9,260,345	3,576,467.61
1840	2,462,700	....	10,558,240	3,426,632.50
1841	1,597,367	....	8,811,968	2,240,321.17
1842	2,383,390	....	11,743,153	4,190,754.40
1843	2,428,320	....	14,640,582	11,967,830.70
1844	2,398,752	....	9,051,834	7,687,767.52
1845	3,894,804	....	11,806,196	5,668,595.54
1846	4,120,800	....	10,133,515	6,633,965.50
1847	6,183,669	....	15,392,344	22,657,671.69
1848	6,415,799	....	8,691,444	3,265,137.99
1849	4,178,500	39,864	9,519,513	8,913,266.32
1850	4,426,844	39,812	10,030,535	28,210,513.00
1851	9,889,707	147,672	24,985,736	52,050,878.43
1852	5,063,094	....	32,612,940	52,403,079.44
1853	6,641,131	129,694	69,775,537	60,111,249.72
1854	4,236,156	55,358	33,910,921	43,108,977.93
1855	1,574,829	56,500	10,885,610	12,045,952.93
1856	2,690,463	40,430	25,876,288	14,346,702.90
1857[1]	6,333,456	35,180	18,602,020	4,737,601.60

[1] To June 30th.

UNITED STATES. 247

COINAGE
OF
THE UNITED STATES MINT.

The annexed Table shows the Coinage of the Mint of the United States (and the Branches, from the commencement of their operation in 1838), from 1793 to the close of 1857.

DATE.	GOLD. VALUE.	SILVER. VALUE.	COPPER. VALUE.	WHOLE COINAGE. NO. OF PIECES.	WHOLE COINAGE. TOTAL VALUE.
1793	} $71,485.00	$370,683.80	$11,373.00	1,834,420	$453,541.80
1794					
1795					
1796	102,727.50	79,077.50	10,324.40	1,219,370	192,129.40
1797	103,422.50	12,591.45	9,510.34	1,095,165	125,524.29
1798	205,610.00	330,291.00	9,797.00	1,368,241	545,698.00
1799	213,285.00	423,515.00	9,106.68	1,365,681	645,906.68
1800	317,760.00	224,296.00	29,279.40	3,337,972	571,335.40
1801	422,570.00	74,758.00	13,628.37	1,571,390	510,956.37
1802	423,310.00	58,343.00	34,422.83	3,615,869	516,075.83
1803	258,377.50	87,118.00	25,203.03	2,780,830	370,698.53
1804	258,642.50	100,340.50	12,844.94	2,046,839	371,827.94
1805	170,365.50	149,388.50	13,483.48	2,260,361	333,239.48
1806	324,505.00	471,319.00	5,260.00	1,815,409	801,084.00
1807	437,495.00	597,448.75	9,652 21	2,731,345	1,044,595.96
1808	284,665.00	684,300.00	13,090.00	2,935,888	982,055.00
1809	169,375.00	707,376.00	8,001.53	2,861,834	884,752.53
1810	501,435.00	638,773.50	15,660.00	3,056,418	1,155,868.50
1811	497,905.00	608,340.00	2,495.95	1,049,570	1,108,740.95
1812	290,435.00	814,029.50	10,755.00	2,761,646	1,115,219.50
1813	477,140.00	620,951.50	4,180.00	1,755,331	1,102,271.50
1814	77,270.00	561,687.50	3,578.30	1,833,859	642,535.80
1815	3,175.00	17,308.00		69,867	20,483.00
1816		28,575.75	28,209.82	2,888,135	56,785.57
1817		607,783.50	39,484.00	5,163,967	647,276.50
1818	242,940.00	1,070,454.50	31,670.00	5,537,084	1,345,064.50
1819	258,615.00	1,140,000.00	26,710.00	5,074,723	1,425,325.00
1820	1,319,030.00	501,680.70	44,075.50	6,492,509	1,864,786.20
1821	189,325.00	825,762.45	3,890.00	3,139,249	1,018,977.45
1822	88,980.00	805,806.50	20,723.39	3,813,788	915,509.89
1823	72,425.00	895,550.00		2,166,485	967,975.00
1824	93,200.00	1,752,477.00	12,620.00	4,786,894	1,858,297.00

COINAGE OF THE UNITED STATES MINT — Continued.

DATE.	GOLD. VALUE.	SILVER. VALUE.	COPPER. VALUE.	WHOLE COINAGE. NO. OF PIECES.	WHOLE COINAGE. TOTAL VALUE.
1825	$156,385.00	$1,564,583.00	$14,926.00	5,178,760	$1,735,894.00
1826	92,245.00	2,002,090.00	16,344.25	5,774,434	2,110,679.25
1827	131,565.00	2,869,200.00	23,577.32	9,097,845	3,024,342.32
1828	140,145.00	1,575,600.00	25,636.24	6,196,853	1,741,381.24
1829	295,717.50	1,994,578.00	16,580.00	7,674,501	2,306,875.50
1830	643,105.00	2,495,400.00	17,115.00	8,357,191	3,155,620.00
1831	714,270.00	3,175,600.00	33,606.60	11,792,284	3,923,473.60
1832	798,435.00	2,579,000.00	23,620.00	9,128,387	3,401,055.00
1833	978,550.00	2,759,000.00	28,160.00	10,307,790	3,765,710.00
1834	3,954,270.00	3,415,002.00	19,151.00	11,637,643	7,388,423.00
1835	2,186,175.00	3,443,003.00	39,489.00	15,996,342	5,668,667.00
1836	4,135,700.00	3,606,100.00	23,100.00	13,719,333	7,764,900.00
1837	1,148,305.00	2,096,010.00	55,583.00	13,010,721	3,299,898.00
1838	1,809,595.00	2,333,243.00	63,702.00	15,780,311	4,206,540.00
1839	1,355,885.00	2,189,296.00	31,286.61	11,811,594	3,576,467.61
1840	1,675,302.50	1,726,703.00	24,627.00	10,558,240	3,426,632.50
1841	1,091,597.50	1,132,750.00	15,973.67	8,811,968	2,240,321.17
1842	1,834,170.50	2,332,750.00	23,833.90	11,743,153	4,190,754.40
1843	8,108,797.50	3,834,750.00	24,283.20	4,640,582	11,967,830.70
1844	5,427,870.00	2,235,550.00	23,977.52	9,051,834	7,687,397.52
1845	3,756,447.50	1,873,200.00	38,948.04	1,806,196	5,668,595.54
1846	4,034,177.00	2,558,580.00	41,208.00	10,133,515	6,633,965.00
1847	20,221,385.00	2,374,450.00	61,836.69	15,392,344	22,657,671.69
1848	3,775,512.50	2,040,050.00	64,157.99	12,649,790	5,879,720.49
1849	9,038,414.50	2,114,950.00	41,984.32	12,666,659	11,195,348.82
1850	31,981,918.50	1,866,100.00	44,467.50	14,588,220	33,892,486.00
1851	62,614,492.50	774,397.00	99,635.43	28,701,958	63,488,524.93
1852	56,846,187.50	999,410.00	50,630.94	34,224,619	57,896,228.44
1853	55,213,906.94	9,077,571.00	67,059.78	76,484,062	65,358,537.72
1854	49,206,656.29	8,619,270.00	42,638.35	44,644,189	57,868,564.64
1855	32,353,043.57	3,501,245.00	16,030.79	16,991,595	35,870,919.36
1856	39,947,318.46	5,189,877.54	27,106.78	33,866,187	45,164,302.78
1857 to June 30th, 1858	16,140,474.68	3,222,327.46	63,510.46	19,437,767	19,426,312.60
	$429,084,090.94	$108,731,662.90	$1,762,916.55	604,887,016	$540,078,670.39
				Assay Office, New York,	52,191,443.33
					$592,270,113.72

INTRODUCTION TO THE SUPPLEMENT.

The succeeding pages are the result of further investigations into the subject of this work, which I have thus endeavored to render as complete, instructive and interesting as possible. An additional plate has been added, illustrating some very novel coins, which can hardly prove to be otherwise than interesting to the Numismatologist. I have, also, added the types of others by additional tables, and an analysis of them, thus embodying and presenting increased useful matter, and throwing additional light upon particular coins.

I am indebted to the lovers of Numismatic Science, throughout the Union, for suggestions, corrections, new coins, types and varieties; and I here seize the opportunity to acknowledge, with much gratitude, the services so kindly rendered to me.

At a heavy expense of time, labor and means, I have accomplished what has previously been, and is now, presented in this work. I, therefore, submit its merits and value to the Numismatologist, curious and general reader, to whom I again make my compliments.

M. W. D.

MODEL SAFE.

The accompanying Plate, representing a Model Safe of much artistic merit and beauty, was designed and is manufactured by Messrs. Evans & Watson, Salamander Safe Manufacturers, No. 304 Chestnut Street, Philadelphia, Pa.

Appreciating the value of such a Safe, perfectly arranged for the reception and protection of coins which, in the event of loss, cannot be replaced—many in our cabinet collections being unique—I have, with much pleasure, permitted the illustration of it to occupy a page in this work, it being an appropriate accompaniment of its subject-matter.

Messrs. Evans & Watson enjoy a very extended reputation as Iron Safe manufacturers, the article they make being really fire-proof, and equal if not superior to any manufactured in the world. This last origination, which places a new and much-wanted article within the reach of those requiring such an adaptation of their mechanical skill and integrity, for the certain preservation of what the Numismatist would last hazard or part with among his earthly stores, merits the thanks, as I trust it will receive the patronage, of those who would feel secure against the arts of the burglar, as well as the devouring element of fire. It can be made capacious enough to permit of such an arrangement as to render it valuable as a depository for jewelry, silver-ware, &c.; thus combining an utility, as a piece of household furniture, which will make it particularly desirable.

SUPPLEMENT

TO THE

AMERICAN NUMISMATIC MANUAL.

PINE TREE SHILLING.

1652. *Device.*—The American pine tree in the field, surrounded by a circle of dots.
Legend.—MASATVSETS.
Reverse.—A circle of dots; in the area 1652., and under it the numerals XII.
Legend.—NEW ENGLAND . AN . DOM
(Size 8. See Plate XX., Figure 1.)

OAK TREE SHILLING.

1652. *Device.*—The oak tree in the field, surrounded by a circle of dots.
Legend.—MASATHVETS IN.
Reverse.—A circle of dots; in the area 1652, and under it the numerals XII.
Legend.—NEW ENGLAND. A DO ∴
(Size 8. See Plate XX., Figure 2.)

These very curious pieces, added to those, of the same period of time, I have illustrated in this work, show that the people of the then province were far from being united in the orthography of what has since settled down to be Massachusetts.

I am indebted for these very valuable accessions to the colonial coinage, to Jeremiah Colburn, Esq., of Boston, Mass., the originals of which are in his collection; and I can avail myself of no more appropriate time or place, than in this connection, to acknowledge my indebtedness to him for the aid I have derived from his general intelligence, and critical knowledge of Numismatics.

PINE TREE SHILLING.

1652. *Device.*—The American pine tree in the field, surrounded by a circle of dots.
Legend.—MASSATVSETS . IN.
Reverse.—A circle of dots; in the area 1652., and under it the numerals XII.
Legend.—NEW ENGLAND.
(Size 5. See Plate XX., Figure 4.)

SUPPLEMENT.

This piece differs from all others of the Massachusetts colonial coins I have seen, the legend of the obverse being "MASSATVSETS," and the reverse "NEW ENGLAND." This comes from its old home, a few miles only from where the Mint, that gave it form and value, stood. I am indebted for it, and other coins noticed in this Supplement, to Dr. Augustus Shurtleff, of Brookline, Mass., in whose collection the originals are preserved.

NEW ENGLAND COPPER.

Device.—Two lions rampant, facing right and left.
Legend.—I . V . S . C.
Reverse.—Inscription, NEW ENGLAND.
Exergue.—N

(Size 4. See Plate XX., Figure 14.)

This curious little piece is in the cabinet collection of Joseph J. Mickley, Esq., of Philadelphia, Pa. The description and the fac-simile convey all that can be said of it, so far as my knowledge, or any I have been able to obtain relative to it, extends. Though without date, it is antiquated enough in design and execution to warrant its being placed among the earliest of the colonial issues.

PINE TREE COPPER.

1652. *Device.*—The American pine tree in the field, inclosed in a circle of dots.
Legend.—MASATHVSETS IN ∴
Reverse.—1652, in a circle of dots, with the numerals XII. under it.
Legend.—NEW ENGLAD AN · DO ∴

(Size 7. See Plate XX., Figure 8.)

This unique piece carries us back to the period of the coinage of the New England shillings, etc., bearing the same date, of which it was undoubtedly a cotemporary. It bears the impress of being a genuine origination of the date inscribed upon it, though with its history I am not acquainted. It is now in the possession of John H. Curtis, Esq., of New York city, to whom I am indebted for the fac-simile.

"NORTH CAROLINA COPPER."

Device.—A small heart-shaped shield, with six parallel lines across it, in the centre of the field, and surrounded by thirteen five-pointed stars.
Reverse.—A ship under full sail.

(Size 5. See Plate XX., Figure 5.)

In the beginning of the present century, this piece was, I am informed, plentiful in

PLATE XX.

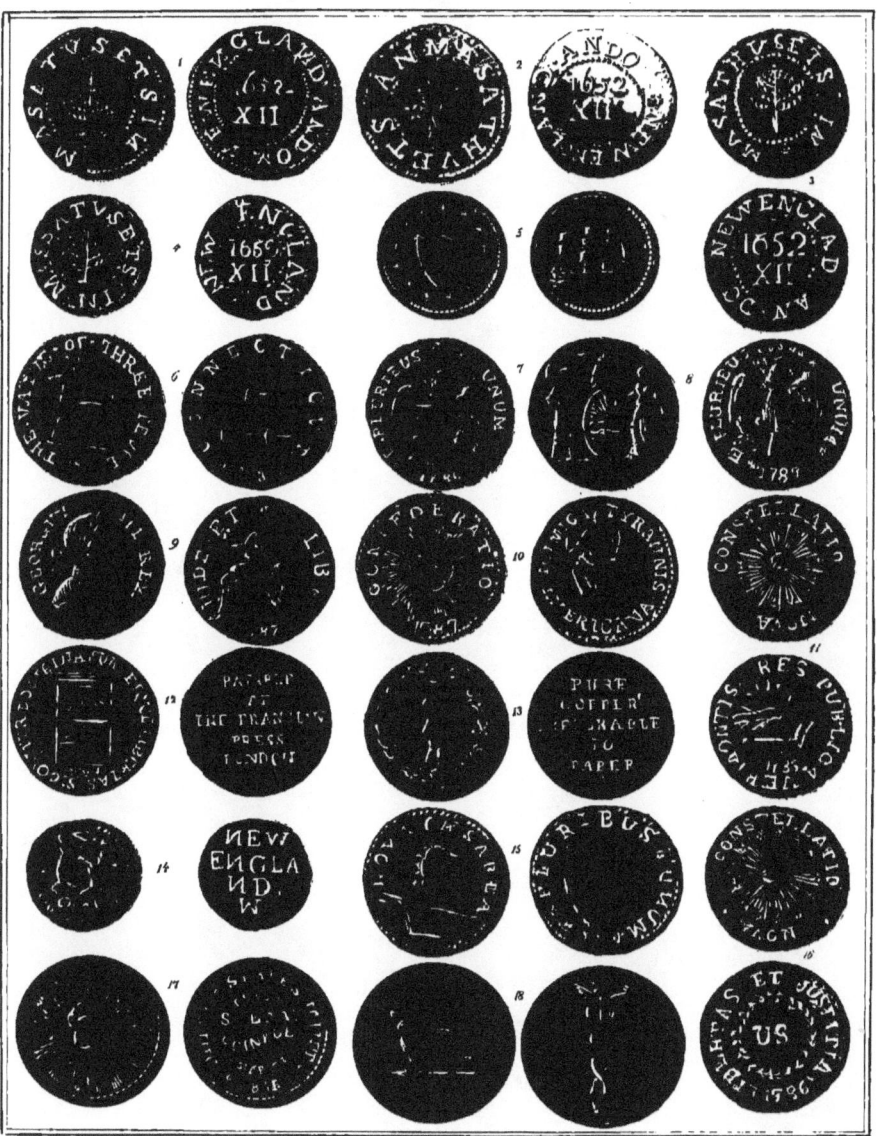

SUPPLEMENT.   253

North Carolina; having no knowledge of its appearance elsewhere, I have given it the appellation which this circumstance, in connection with it, seemed to favor.

NEW YORK COPPERS.

1786.   *Device.*—The arms of the State of New York, the figures of Liberty and Justice supporting the shield, surmounted by an eagle.
   Reverse.—A badly designed eagle with wings partially expanded, the beak open, the head surrounded by thirteen stars, on its breast a shield, an olive branch in the left talon, and arrow in the right.
   Legend.—✶ E ✶ PLURIBUS UNUM ✶
   Exergue.—1786.
                (Size 8. See Plate XX., Figure 7.)

1787.   *Device.*—The arms of the State of New York, the figures of Liberty and Justice supporting the shield, surmounted by an eagle.
   Reverse.—A badly designed eagle with wings partially expanded, the head surrounded by eleven stars, on the breast a shield, an olive branch in the right talon, and arrows in the left.
   Legend.—✶ E ✶ PLURIBUS UNUM ✶
   Exergue.—1787.
                (Size 8. Plate XX., Figure 8.)

These issues of 1786 and '87, bear a very great resemblance to each other, though an examination will show they are distinct in a number of particulars. The workmanship of these pieces is very inferior, but they are very rare.

NOVA CONSTELLATIO.

1786.   *Device.*—An eye, symbolical of supreme power, reflecting its rays upon thirteen six-pointed stars, emblematic of the States of the Confederacy.
   Legend.—NOVA CONSTELLATIO.
   Reverse.—A laurel wreath enclosing the letters US.
   Legend.—LIBERTAS ET JUSTITIA.
   Exergue.—1786.
                (Size 8. See Plate XX., Figure 16.)

This piece, which is unique so far as my knowledge, or any I have been able to acquire, extends, is in the collection of Dr. Augustus Shurtleff, of Brookline, Mass. The peculiarities are the date, and the capitals U.S., which in every other piece bearing the legend LIBERTAS ET JUSTITIA, are in italics.

SUPPLEMENT.

VERMONTIS RES PUBLICA.

1785. *Device.*—An eye, symbolical of supreme power, reflecting its rays upon thirteen six-pointed stars, emblematic of the States of the Confederacy.
Legend.—QUARTA . DECIMA . STELLA.
Reverse.—The sun rising from behind the mountains; in the foreground a plow.
Legend.—VERMONTIS RES PUBLICA.
Exergue.—1785.
(Size 7. See Plate XX., Figure 11.)

This piece, in the opinion of many very familiar with colonial coins, had no existence in fact. As no collection in this city contained it, and I had never seen it, nor been advised where it could be seen, I declined illustrating it in my work. The question is, however, now definitely settled; and I am indebted for it, and the fac-simile in this Supplement, to Dr. Augustus Shurtleff, of Brookline, Mass., whose cabinet contains the original of this rarest of the Vermont copper issues. It differs from the Vermonts and the Vermontensium, in the legend extending wholly around the field of the coin.

NOVA CÆSAREA.

1786. *Device.*—A shield in the shape of a heart, with stripes thereon, running longitudinally.
Legend.— * E * PLURIBUS * UNUM.
Reverse.—A plow surmounted by a horse's head.
Legend.—NOVA CÆSAREA.
Exergue.—1786.
(Size 7. See Plate XX., Figure 15.)

The planchet of this piece is small, and the horse's head more diminative than in any other type in the whole series of these coins. The body of the plow is very thick and heavy; the handles unusually short, beam short and curved at both ends, and the singletree runs at an angle almost parallel with the beam. The coulter is omitted, and the date 1786 occupies its place, immediately under the beam of the plow. This very rare and valuable piece, and which I venture to denominate as unique, is in the collection of Jeremiah Colburn, Esq., of Boston, Mass., to whom I am under obligations for the fac-simile that appears in this Supplement.

TORY COPPER.

1787. *Device.*—The bust of George III., head laureated and facing to the right.
Legend.—GEORGIVS III. REX.
Reverse.—The goddess of Liberty seated, holding in her right hand the liberty pole, and the olive branch in her left.

SUPPLEMENT.

Legend.—INDE ✶ ET LIB
Exergue.—1787.
(Size 7. See Plate XX., Figure 9.)

This piece differs from any previously illustrated, and hence I have given it a place. While the obverse is the same as the English half-penny of the date it bears, the reverse is of the general issues of the Vermont coppers.

FRANKLIN COPPER.

1794. *Device.*—An old Ramage press in the field.
Legend.—SIC ORITUR DOCTRINA SURGET QUE LIBERTAS. Thus Learning arises, and Liberty flourishes.
Exergue.—1794.
Reverse.—Inscription, PAYABLE AT THE FRANKLIN PRESS LONDON.
(Size 7. See Plate XX., Figure 12.)

This curious copper coin is in the collection of Timothy C. Day, Esq., of Cincinnati, Ohio, to whom I am indebted for the fac-simile. That it was gotten up in London, and intended for circulation, is evident; but further, in relation to it, I know not.

THE FOLLOWING DESCRIBED PIECE

is noticed in the London catalogues of coins as belonging to America. This must be our authority for giving it a place here. It is certainly very novel, and I am indebted for the fac-simile to Timothy C. Day, Esq., of Cincinnati, Ohio.

Device.—A full-length figure of a man dressed in the old style in the field, which is surrounded by a wreath of oak-leaf and grape vine, holding a sprig of shalelah in the right hand, and a shamrock in the left.
Reverse.—Inscription, PURE COPPER PREFERABLE TO PAPER.
(Size 7. See Plate XX., Figure 13.)

THE FOLLOWING DESCRIBED COPPER PIECE,

for the fac-simile of which I am indebted to R. T. Bonsall, Esq., of Springborough, Ohio, is about the thickness of the 1794 cent, and of a very dark color. It was evidently struck off, among others, with reference to the difficulties that existed between the American colonies and the mother country, as its legends are fully up to the standard of feeling that then prevailed.

It is said it was gotten up in Birmingham, Eng., which does not, however, qualify the sentiments expressed, as the commonalty of England is still judiciously struggling to extricate itself from the Norman grasp of its government.

Device.—A spaniel dog, apparently running, with open mouth and protruding tongue.
Legend.—MUCH GRATITUDE BRINGS SERVITUDE.
Reverse.—The staff of Mercury surmounted by a crown, and terminating in a liberty-cap.
Legend.—WE WERE BORN FREE AND WILL NEVER DIE SLAVES.
(Size 8. See Plate XX., Figure 18.)

VERMON AUCTORI.

1786. In preparing the first edition of this work for the press, I was unable to determine, from any specimens of this coin I possessed or could obtain, any date anterior to those of 1787. Since, however, I have been placed in possession by collectors, of both coins and rubbings, which have enabled me to extend my tables; and hence, there is herewith presented four types of this coin of 1786. They are as follows:

1786.	LEGEND.	VARIETIES.	DEGREES OF RARITY.	POSITION.	DECORATION.
1	VERMON AUCTORI	1	•••	Facing right.	Laureated.
2	VERMON . AUCTORI.	1	•••	" left.	"
3	AUCTORI. VERMON :	1	•••	" right.	Fillet-Festooned.
4	VERMON : AUCTORI :	1	•••	" left.	Laureated.

The most of the early Vermon Auctori are so much worn, that it is only by the application of a powerful glass that the date can be determined. The planchet upon which they were struck was the old English half-penny, which accounts for legends and dates being often so blended as to defy accuracy, except by patient examination and great care.

Types.—No. 1. This was impressed upon an unusually small planchet of soft copper, whose shape is lenticular. At first sight it has the appearance of having been cast. The effigy is uncouth, head laureated, facing to the right, ill-formed, and apparently intended to represent a bald head. The chin long, large, and double, with nothing but the legend to extricate it from the class of half-finished trial pieces so familiar to collectors.

No. 2. This is much like the preceding, except in the punctuation of the legend, the planchet, however, being larger and more regular in form.

No. 3. The legend on this piece is reversed as per table, and is known to numismatologists as the "Baby Head." It was probably among the latest of the emissions of 1786, as a similar type was issued in the succeeding year. Its chief merit is its rarity, there being but two, to my knowledge, in cabinet collections.

SUPPLEMENT.

No. 4. This type is considered very rare, and an important acquisition to the science to which it relates; as it not only determines the date of its peculiar effigy, but shows what has not been previously known, that in design it is identical with the common laureated Connecticut effigy on the issue of 1787. The only specimen of this type I have ever seen or heard of, is in this city.

VERMON AUCTORI.

An examination of about eight hundred pieces of this year's emission, ena- 1787. bles me to add to my previous number but four types. They are as follows:

1787.	LEGEND.	VARIETIES.	DEGREES OF RARITY.	POSITION.	DECORATION.
4	VERMON. AUCTORI.	2	•••	Facing right.	Laureated.
5	VERMON: AUCTORI	1	•••	"	"
6	AUCTORI. VERMON:	1	•••	"	Fillet-Festooned.
7	VERMON: AUCTORI.	1	•••	"	"

Types.—No. 4 is struck upon a much larger planchet than is common to this coin; the bust is correspondingly large, and the cheeks of the effigy quite full. The I in AUCTORI crowds the punctuation closely, upon the head of the effigy. In one of the varieties, the cap line of the L, in LIB, is extended back so far as to give it the appearance of a Z. I have seen but two varieties of this type, both of which are in my cabinet.

No. 5. This is the only specimen I have met with that is so punctuated. The planchets used may have been originally designed for the Auctori Connec of 1785, as they are materially larger than most of those used for this coin. It is very rare, and now in my cabinet.

No. 6. In this, the "Baby Head" again makes its appearance. A critical examination, by a powerful glass, discloses no difference in the obverse; and even the reverse, in one variety, is the same as on the emission of 1786.

No. 7. This is an isolated type which has lately come under my notice in the form of a rubbing, from a gentleman of Baltimore, Md., on whom I can rely for its genuineness. It bears the general appearance of the preceding type. In both tables of this year—1787—it will be found I have given but a single type facing left, and no legend of LIB ET INDE.

SUPPLEMENT.

Vermon Auctori.

1788. My extensive researches among the issues of this year have resulted in the addition of but two types to those previously given. They are as follows:

Legend.	Varieties.	Degrees of Rarity.	Position.	Decoration.
14. VERMON. AUCTORI ☆	1	...	Right	Fillet-Festooned.
15. VERMON. AUCTORI ∴	1	...	"	"

Types.—No. 14. This differs from No. 10 in the former table only in the number of points in the star or punctuation. I have seen but two types, one of which is in the valuble collection of Henry F. Geyer, Esq., of this city, and is very rare and valuable.

No. 15. This differs from the preceding only in the punctuation or formation of the star, and is a type rarely met with.

Auctori Connec.

Though very desirous of adding something to what I had given in the body of this work, I have found but a single additional type, and as that is in most particulars of the common effigy of 1787, it serves as an index to it, which fully compensates me for my labor. It is as follows: 1785.

Device.—A bust in the Roman toga, head laureated and facing to the left.
Legend.—AUCTORI CONNEC
Reverse.—The goddess of Liberty seated on the globe, facing to the left, the liberty-pole surmounted by the cap, in the left hand; the olive branch in the right.
Legend.—INDE : ∴ ET LIB :
Exergue.—1785.

In this type the legend is not punctuated, the letters being quite large, and hence is similar to Type 2 in the table of issues of 1785. It is in my possession; I have not heard of it elsewhere.

Auctori Connec.

I have thought it advisable to describe a few of the types occurring in the 1786. table on page 105, to aid the student in the classification of his coins.

Types.—No. 1. The effigy presents a very ludicrous appearance, all natural lines of the human form having apparently been disregarded. The chin is double, the lower portion being offensively square, and the eye a mere round dot, regardless of proportion. The legend on the reverse is, ET – LIB – INDE. This type is very rare, and to be met with but in few cabinets.

SUPPLEMENT.

No. 2. This was the first emission of this year, and the second in the Connecticut series of this style of effigy. The mechanical execution is better than usual, the lettering being more perfect than of the issues that precede it. The leaves of the laurel wreath are quite small, and the ends of the ribbon that fall from it are mere strings.

No. 3. This varies from the preceding only in the punctuation in the middle of the legend.

No. 4. This is deemed the most rare of this year's coinage, and bears the appellation of the "round head," the features being quite small and delicately proportioned. The hair is brought out artistically, and the wreath around the head is well arranged. The reverse ET – LIB – INDE on the reverse is the same as on Type 1 of this year. It is very rare.

No. 5. This is remarkable for nothing but the punctuation of the legend.

No. 6. The variation of this from No. 4 is, that the head is longer, the hair apparently rougher, and the tags to the wreath unusually long. I have seen but a single specimen of this type.

No. 7. Differing from No. 5 only in the punctuation.

No. 8. Same as the preceding, except in punctuation.

No. 9. Same as the preceding, except in punctuation.

No. 10. Extremely rare, because fillet-festooned instead of being laureated.

No. 11. Nothing to distinguish this but the punctuation, the effigy being of the old style.

No. 12. Though the punctuation is the same as the preceding, it is a new type, as the workmanship differs from any of the whole series, the die being deeper, and hence the muscular development of feature surpasses any other issue. To distinguish it, I have called it the type Hercules. It is extremely rare, and was evidently the work of a superior artist of the period it was gotten up.

AUCTORI CONNEC.

Since the appearance of the first edition of this work, I have been able to 1787. add twenty additional types to those previously given of this year; hence, my labors have been attended with more than usual success. They will be found in the table I have herewith arranged, which discloses so much of that fruitful ingenuity in varying a currency by punctuation, and which increases the number of types from 73 in the former table, to 93 in this.

1787.	LEGENDS.		DEGREES OF RARITY.	POSITION.	DECORATION.	VARIETIES.
74	AUCTORI	CONNEC	•••	Left	Fillet-Festooned.	1
75	AUCTORI	CONNEC	•••	Right	Laureated.	2
76	AUCTORI	CONNEC	•••	"	"	1
77	AUCTORI :.:	:: CONNEC: ∴	•••	Left	"	1
78	AUCTORI + +	CONNEC +	•••	"	Fillet-Festooned.	2
79	AUCTORI : + +	CONNEC : +	•••	"	Laureated.	1
80	+ AUCTORI : + +	CONNEC : +	•••	"	"	1
81	. AUCTORI : ✶	CONNEC : ✶	•••	"	"	1
82	✶ AUCTOPI : ✶	CONNEC .	•••	"	"	1
83	✶ AUCTORI :	CONNEC : ✶	•••	"	"	2
84	✶ AUCTORI : ✶	CONNEC : ✶	•••	"	"	1
85	✶ AUCTORI . ✶ ✶	CONNEC . ✶	•••	"	"	1
86	✶ AUCTORI : ✶ ✶	CONNEC . ✶	•••	"	"	1
87	✶ AUCTORI : ✶ ✶	CONNEC : ✶	•••	"	"	1
88	AUCTOPI ✶ ✶	CONNEC	•••	"	"	1
89	✶ AUCTORI ✶ ✶	CONNEC ✶	•••	"	Fillet-Festooned.	1
90	✶ AUCTORI ✶ ✶	CONNEC ✶	•••	"	"	1
91	← AUCTORI : ←	CONNEC : ←	•••	"	Laureated.	1
92	← AUCTORI : ←→	CONNEC :	•••	"	"	1
93	← AUCTORI ←←→	CONNEC . ←	•••	Right	Fillet-Festooned.	1

Types.—No. 74. The planchet too small for effigy, which nearly covers it. Roughly executed, and bears the appearance of having been a trial piece.

No. 75. The effigy unusually small and very unartistic, the profile being nearly on a straight line.

No. 76. The obverse of this die must have been rough, and the effigy out of proportion to the planchet. It is known as the "Bull's Head." The figure on the reverse, in full dress, with low neck, and exposing a very full bust, is better executed.

No. 77. A full bust, with a peculiar punctuation.

Nos. 78, 79, 80 and 81. Distinguished for their punctuations.

No. 82. The peculiarity is in the legend.

No. 83. Can be determined by its punctuation.

No. 84. Very curious in the representation of the hair, which resembles the negro's, hence called "Woolly Head."

No. 85. The same punctuation as the preceding, but with a different effigy.

No. 86. This is determined by the punctuation.

No. 87. This can be determined by its peculiar punctuation.

SUPPLEMENT.

No. 88. The legend is **Auctopi Connec.**
Nos. 89, 90, 91, 92, and 93. Differ from each other, only in the punctuation. They are all rare.

AUCTORI CONNEC.

1788. The following, the result of much research, have been added to the previously described types of this year.

1788.	LEGENDS.		DEGREES OF RARITY.	POSITION.	DECORATION.	VARIETIES.
26	AUCTORI :	CONNEC :	...	Right.	Fillet-Festooned.	2
27	✶ AUCTORI .	CONNEC ✶	...	"	"	1
28	✶ AUCTORI : ✶ ✶	CONNEC :	...	Left.	Laureated.	1
29	✶ AUCTORI ✶ ✶	CONNEC . ✶	...	"	"	1
30	✶. AUCTORI ✶ ✶	CONNEC : ✶	...	"	"	2
31	✶ AUCTORI : ✶ ✶	CONNEC : ✶	...	"	"	1
32	✶ AUCTORI ✶ ✶	CONNEC ✶	...	"	Fillet-Festooned.	1
33	AUCTORI ✶ ✶	CONNEC ✶	...	"	"	1
34	AUCTORI ✶ ✶	CONNEC ✶	...	Right.	"	1
35	⚜ AUCTORI ✶ ✶	CONNEC ✶	...	"	"	1

Types.—No. 26. This may be determined by the large head, irregular features, and eyes and lips protruding like a negro's. The laurel leaf, forming the wreath, is very large, and the hair is indicated by a series of oblong dots. Though there is some resemblance in this to type No. 76, of 1787, on the reverse, it will be observed, it is not as well clad; the upper part of the body being less covered, the hair formed into a top-knot, and the figure—probably the goddess of Liberty—supports in her right hand the liberty-pole and cap.

No. 27. The effigy in this is small, with a bow at the lower end of the fillet. The head resembles that of George III. in the English half-penny of the same year.

Nos. 28, 29, 30, and 31. These can be determined by the punctuations.

Nos. 32, 33, and 34. These bear the ordinary effigy, fillet-festooned.

No. 35. The hair is arranged rather fantastically in this type; but the punctuation will serve as an unerring guide.

NOVA CÆSAREA.

1787. Of this issue, I am enabled to give four additional types, as follows:

No. 31. This represents one of the straight-beam plows, the beam being nearly on a direct line with the handles, one of which is rather longer than the other. The singletree runs parallel with the coulter, and is much nearer to the plow than in any other type of this year. The shield is of medium size, and points to the thick line of the letter U in the legend in the reverse.

No. 32. This represents the ball-handled plow, and may be determined by the handles approaching nearer to each other than in any other type. The handles at the point of attachment of the balls, are scolloped out, which gives them the appearance of being quite thin.

No. 33. This is, also, of a ball-handled plow; but the balls are large, quite as much so as in No. 8, though they approach nearer to the N in NOVA, than in that type.

No. 34. This is a very valuable specimen. The planchet is large, but thin; the horse's head small, neck large, the mane exceedingly well executed. The handles of the plow are thin, of different thickness, and the space between them extends down to the line at the bottom of the plow, and terminating squarely on the base line, which is the case in no other type of the different issues of the Nova Cæsarea. The curve in the beam is double, and the beam decreases in size to the end. The singletree is very indistinct, the coulter terminates in a sharp point, beneath the horse's neck are three leaves, and the two last A's in CÆSAREA are not cross-lined.

NOVA CÆSAREA.

1788. My researches, pursued with equal zeal, in relation to this issue, have been rewarded by only four additional types, which are as follows:

No. 6. This is very curious, rough and imperfect, and, as a whole, a peculiar piece of workmanship. The horse's head is spirited, the eye placed in a regular oval socket, and the mane exhibits three large plaits, reaching down to the lower line of the neck. The plow is large, badly executed, and the legend is punctuated thus: ✣ NOVA CÆSAREA.

No. 7. This type may be determined by the horse's ear being large and open, six small braids turning inward, forming the mane, the mouth and nostrils well formed, the plow peculiar, being a mere skeleton, the handles two curves, long and slim down to the foot-board, the beam thin and straight, the coulter placed much in advance of its true position, and the legend thus: NOVA ✣ CÆSAREA ✣.

No. 8 bears the general appearance of the preceding, but not quite as well executed; the horse's ears are small, mouth bad, mane thin and short, the plow varying in being stouter, but nearly of the same form, and the date placed differently.

No. 9. In this, the horse's head and plow larger than in any of the preceding types; beam of the plow large and thick, no singletree, the handles large and very near to each other, and the legend thus: NOVA CÆSAREA ✣.

TRANSLATIONS

OF

LEGENDS APPEARING UPON COINS &c., IN THIS WORK.[1]

CRESCITE ET MVLTIPLICAMINI. Increase and be multiplied. — Plate VI., Figure 13.

DENARIUM TERRÆ MARIÆ. Maryland Penny. — Plate VI., Figure 16.

SIT NOMEN DOMINI BENEDICTUM. Blessed be the name of the Lord. — Plate VII., Figure 3.

NON DEPENDENS STATUS. Independent of position. — Plate VIII., Figure 13.

NOVA CONSTELLATIO. New Constellation — assemblage or group of fixed stars, emblematic of the American States. — Plate IX., Figure 5.

IMMUNE COLUMBIA. Free America. — Plate IX., Figure 5.

VOCE POPOLI. By the voice of the people. — Plate IX., Figure 7.

AMERICA INIMICA TYRANS. America hostile to Tyrants. — Plate IX., Figure 11.

QUARTA. DECIMA. STELLA. The fourteenth star—referring to Vermont in the American constellation. Plate IX., Figure 12.

VERMONTS RES PUBLICA. The Republic of Vermont. — Plate IX., Figure 13.

VERMON. AUCTORI. By authority of Vermont. — Plate IX., Figure 15.

AUCTORI. CONNEC. By authority of Connecticut. — Plate X., Figure 4.

INDE ET LIB. Liberty and Independence. — Plate X., Figure 4.

AUCTORI. PLEBIS. By authority of the people. — Plate X., Figure 2.

NOVA CÆSAREA. Now New Jersey. — Plate X., Figures 11 to 21.

---

[1] We give the legends as they appear upon the coins, without reference to their critical correctness.

TRANSLATIONS OF LEGENDS.

NON VI VIRTUTE VICE. I have conquered by virtue, not by force. — Plate XI., Figure 1.

NEO. EBORACENSIS. New York. — Plate XI., Figure 1.

NOVA EBORACA. Columbia. Excelsior. — Plate XI., Figure 2.

NEW YORK. Columbia, paramount or greatest.

NOVA EBORAC. New York. — Plate XI., Figure 4.

VIRT ET LIB. Virtue and Liberty. — Plate XI., Figure 4.

LIBER NATUS LIBERTATEM DEFENDO. Born free I defend liberty. — Plate XI., Figure 5.

EXCELSIOR. More lofty, higher, more elevated. — Plate XI., Figure 6.

SALVE MAGNA PARENS FRUGUM. Hail, mighty mother of production! — Plate XI., Figure 16.

REUNIT PAR UN RARE ASSEMBLAGE LES TALENS DU GUERRIER ET LES VERTUS DE SAGE. He united in himself the rare combination of a talent for war and the virtues of the sage. — Folio 140.

IN UNITATE FORTITUDO. In union there is strength. — Folio 142.

"——— Manus hæc, inimica tyrannis,
Ense petit placidam sub libertate quietem."

——— This hand is hostile to tyrants,
And seeks with the sword for peace under liberty.

SYNOPSIS

OF

INTRODUCTION AND MASSACHUSETTS CURRENCY.

INTRODUCTION.

A Coin an index to a people and their state of civilization... PAGE	11
Lost history revealed through the agency of coins. Earliest money transactions on record..................	12
Positive coins imputed to the Greeks	13
Romans issued a silver coinage 281 B. C., gold 207 B. C.	15
Gauls used for money gold and iron rings	15
Coins issued by the British prince Cunobeline...	15
Emperor Claudius subjugated Britain in the 42d year of the era of Britain, and the Roman coinage soon after gained the ascendant	15
Saxons succeed the Romans in Britain, with money totally different...	16
Saxon Heptarchy — kings of Kent from the accession of Ethelbert, A. D. 568.	16
Coins of the kings of Northumberland..	17
Dignitaries of the Church strike money and enjoy the profits of mintage...	17
Coins of the Saxon and Danish sole monarchs of England...	17
Anglo-Norman kings. No improvement in coinage	18

COINS OF THE ENGLISH SOVEREIGNS.

Henry VII., A. D. 1485 to 1509	19
Henry VIII., A. D. 1509 to 1547...	19
Edward VI, A. D. 1547 to 1553	20
Mary, A. D. 1553 to 1558..	20
Elizabeth, A. D. 1558 to 1602	20

COINAGE OF SCOTLAND BEFORE THE UNION.

Earliest coins attributed to William the Lion, A. D. 1165; to the princes of the Hebrides, Donald VIII., A. D. 1093; Alexander I. 1107 .:...	20
Alexander II. and III., Baliol and Bruce..	20
Mary, A. D. 1542 to 1587	21
James VI., A. D. 1587 to 1625	21
Scotland merged in the United Kingdom, &c.	21
Coinage of James I., A. D. 1602 to 1625...	21
Charles I., A. D. 1625 to 1649...	22
Coining down the plate of the colleges...	23

SYNOPSIS OF INTRODUCTION, ETC.

Siege pieces, 1644 and 1645	23
First Scottish coinage in this reign by Briot	24
Irish money ordered to be abolished	24
Commonwealth, A. D. 1648 to 1660	24
Pierre Blondeau perfected the stamping of coin by the mill and screw, and was invited to England	24
Charles II., A. D. 1660 to 1684	25
First milled coinage, 1663	25
Coinage of William and Mary, and William III., A. D. 1688 to 1702	26
Anne, A. D. 1702 to 1714	27
George I., A. D. 1714 to 1727	27
George II., A. D. 1729 to 1760	27
George III., A. D. 1760 to 1820	28
Bank-Tokens sanctioned	28

MASSACHUSETTS CURRENCY.

Roger Williams' description of the money of the New England Indians, 1628	46
A Mint decided upon, and the court enacted laws for its government, 1652	49
First emission of coin, 1652	50
The court concludes that John Hull, the Mint-Master, has too lucrative a position, and desires his resignation. His daughter's marriage, dower, &c.	51
The Mint an important institution. Endeavors made under the administration of Governor Andross to have the Mother country legalize it	52
Interesting incident—in relation to the oak-tree coins—of Sir Thomas Temple, Governor of Nova Scotia, and Charles II., 1662	52
The Colonial government called to an account relative to the Mint	53
A diplomatic operation to soothe the wounded prerogative of the king, 1666	53
The Mint continued its operations	53
More diplomacy, aimed at the gastronomic proclivities of his majesty, 1677	53
Free-Mint suggested, 1680	54
Still more diplomacy contemplated through agents of the colony bound to London, 1681	54
Officers of the London Mint opposed to the Boston Mint, 1685	54
Long-established form of the Colonial government departed — the Mint survives, and another attack is made upon it by the Lord High-Treasurer of England, 1686	54
Country-pay still permitted, 1687	54
Report of the condition of the Treasury, 1688	55
Petition to William and Mary for permission to renew Mint operations	55
The colonists resort to paper-issues, 1690	55
Governor Hutchinson's congratulations relative to the condition of the Treasury, 1774	55
An emission of paper authorized, 1775	55
Massachusetts agrees to the articles of Confederation, 1777	56
Massachusetts Bank chartered, 1784	56
The Confederated government of the United States enter into a contract for the coinage of copper, 1786. See "First United States Cent."	56
The erection of buildings for the second Massachsetts Mint authorized, coin described, &c.	56
The second Mint ended in 1788	57

INDEX

TO

MATTERS CONTAINED IN PARTS I. TO V.

ABORIGINAL COINS OR MONEY .... PAGE   36
Annapolis Shilling, 1783 94
"   Six-pence, 1783 94
"   Three-pence, 1783 95
Auctori Connec, 1785 102
"   "   1786 104
"   "   1787 105
"   "   types and varieties of 107–110
"   "   1788 110
"   "   types and varieties of 111
"   Plebis, 1787 112

BALDWIN & Co., California, coinage of 225
Bars, F. D. Kohler, California 226
Bermuda Islands 58
Bone money 39
Boulton, Mr., of France, machine for coining invented by 35

CALIFORNIA COINS 223
Carolina Half-Penny, 1694 70
Casting, Monsieur, his invention for milling 35
Castorland Half-Dollar, 1796 136
Cent, 1794 202
"   1795 203
"   1796 204
"   1808 209
"   1816, 1817 211
"   1839 216
"   Feuchtwanger, 1837 235
"   First United States, 1787 126
"   Liberty-cap, 1793 201
"   Massachusetts, 1787 127
"   New York, 1796 134
"   Nickel, 1858 220

Cent, (Pattern) 1851 233
"   (Patterns) 1853, 1854, 1855, 1856 234
"   (Pattern) 1858 235
"   (Patterns) 1792 230–231
"   Ring-, (Pattern) 1850 233
"   Wreath-, 1793 200
Chain-Cent, 1793 199
Cincinnati Mining and Trading Co., California, coinage of the 224
Coal and Lignite 37
"   specimens of money of 38, 39
Coinage 33
"   steam-, 1836 235
Coins 32
"   of the United States 145
Columbia Copper 143
Confederatio Copper, 1785 98
Connecticut Coins 102
"   "   types and varieties of 107, 108
Continental Currency, 1776 86
Copper coinage of the U. S. Mint 245, 246
"   money 44
Cuneator 33

DE DANSK AMERIC, 1740 143
Degrees of Rarity of Coins of the United States.. 237
Dime, 1797 178
"   1837 192
"   1838 193
"   (Pattern) 1792 230
Dollar, Gold, 1849 170
"   "   1854 173
"   Gold, (Pattern) 1836 231
"   Gold-Ring (Pattern) 1852 233
"   and Half-Dollar (Pattern) 1839 232

INDEX.

Dollar, (Pattern) 1836	231
" " 1838	232
" Piece, North Carolina	222
" " California	226
" Silver, 1794	175
" " 1795	176
" " 1798	179
" " 1836	191
" " 1838	193
" " 1840	194
" Silver-ring (Pattern) 1852	233
Double-Eagle, 1849	169
" " (Pattern) 1849	232
Dubosq & Co., California, coinage of	225
Dunbar & Co., " "	225
EAGLE, 1795	155
" 1797	156
" 1798	157
" 1838	165
Encrinite Lily	42
Extended hand an emblem, &c.	41
FEUCHTWANGER CENT, (Pattern) 1837	235
Fifty-Dollar Pieces, Moffatt & Co., California	226
First United States Cent, 1787	126
Five-Dollar Piece, North Carolina, 1787	222
" Pieces, Baldwin & Co., California	225
" " Cin. Min'g & Trad'g Co., Cal.	224
" " Dubosq & Co., California	225
" " Dunbar & Co., " "	225
" " Mass. & Cal. Co. " "	225
" " Moffatt & Co. " "	224
" " Mormon, Utah	225
" " N. G. & N., California	223
" " Oregon Exchange Co., Cal	223
" " Pacific Co., California	224
" " Shultz & Co., " "	225
Florida Piece, 1760	81
GALENA MONEY (Aboriginal)	43
Georgius Triumpho, 1783	93
Gold Coinage of the United States	155
" " " Mint	241, 242
" Dollar, (Pattern) 1836	231
" Money (Aboriginal)	43
" Ring Dollar, (Pattern) 1852	233
" " Half-Dollar, (Pattern) 1852	233
Good Samaritan Shilling, 1652	63

Granby Coppers, 1737, 1739	79
Groat, Lord Baltimore, 1659	64
HALF-CENT, MASSACHUSETTS, 1788	127
" " 1794	202
" " 1795	203
" " 1797	204
" " 1800	206
" " 1809	209
" " 1828	213
" " 1840	216
" Dime, 1794	176
" " 1797	178
" Dollar, 1794	176
" " 1801	180
" " 1808	184
" " 1837	192
" " 1840	195
" " Castorland, 1796	136
" " and Dollar, (Pattern) 1839	232
" " Gold, California	226
" " Gold-Ring, (Pattern) 1852	233
" " (Pattern) 1858	234
" " Washington, 1792	138
" Eagle, 1795	155
" " 1798	157
" " 1808	160
" " 1834	164
" " 1838	165
" Penny, Carolina, 1694	70
" " Liverpool, 1791	138
" " New England, 1694	72
IMMUNIS COLUMBIA, 1787	121, 123
Index of Dates, Degrees of Rarity, &c., of the Gold, Silver, and Copper Coinage of the U. S.	237
Ingots, U. S. Assay, Moffatt, & Co., California	226
JANUS COPPER, 1776	87
J. S. O., California, coinage of	224
KENTUCKY COPPER, 1791	126
" " 1796	135
LIBER NATUS LIBERTATEM DEFENDO, 1787	124
" " " " 1787	125
Liberty-Cap Cent	201
Lignite and Coal pieces	87
" coin-like mass of	33

INDEX.

Lignite coin	38
Liverpool Half-Penny, 1791	138
London Half-Penny	70
Lord Baltimore Groat, 1659	64
" " Shilling, 1659	63
" " Six-pence, 1659	63
" " Penny	64
Louisiana Copper, 1721, 1722	73
" " 1767	83
MARYLAND CURRENCY	63
Massachusetts and California Co., Cal., coinage of	225
" Cent, 1787	127
" Coppers, 1776	88
" Currency	46
" Half-Cent, 1788	127
Measure	30
Miners' Bank of San Francisco, coinage of	224
Moffatt & Co., California, coinage of	224
Moneyer	33
Mormon coinage, Utah	225
NEO EBORACENSIS, 1786	122
New England Half-Penny, 1694	72
" Pattern Shilling, 1650	59
" Shilling, 1652	59
' Six-pence, 1652	59
New Jersey	112
" Coppers, 1786, 1788	112
New York	122
" Cent, 1794	134
" Coppers	123
" Gold Coin, 1787	122
N. G. & N., California, Half-Eagle	223
Nickel Cent, 1857	220
" " 1858	220
Non Dependens Status, 1778	89
North American Token, 1781	144
North Carolina Five-Dollar Pieces	222
" " Gold Coins	220
" " One Dollar Piece	222
" ' Two-and-a-half Dollar Pieces	221
Nova Cæsarea, 1786	112
" " types and varieties	115, 117, 121
Nova Constellatio, 1783	90
" " 1785	91, 92
Nova Eborac, 1787	123
OAK-TREE SHILLING, 1652	60
" Six-pence, "	60

Oak-Tree Three-pence, 1652	61
" Two-pence, 1652	61
J. S. O. — Ormsby — California, coinage of	224
One-Dollar Piece, California	226
" " North Carolina	222
Oregon Exchange Co., California, coinage of	223
PACIFIC Co., California, coinage of	224
Pearls	40
Penny, Lord Baltimore, 1659	64
Pieces, Pattern	231
Pine-Tree Copper, 1766	88
" Shilling, 1652	60
" Six-pence, 1652	60
" Three-pence, 1652	60
Pitt Piece, 1766	81
Processes of Assay of Gold and Silver Coins — U. S. Mint	149
QUARTER DOLLAR, 1831	189
" " 1853	198
" " Gold, California	227
" Eagle, 1796	156
" " 1808	161
" " 1838	165
REED, TEMPLETON, California, coinage of	224
Ring-Cent, 1850, (Pattern)	233
Rosa-Americana Farthing, 1722	75
" " 1723	76
" Half-Penny, 1722	75
" " 1723	75
" Penny, 1722	75
" " 1723	75
" " 1733	76
" types and varieties	76
SCALE OF SIZES, or Measure of Medals and Coins	30
Shell Money	40
Shilling, Anapolis, 1783	94
" Good Samaritan, 1652	63
" Lord Baltimore, 1659	63
" New England, 1650, (Pattern)	59
" " 1652	59
" Oak-Tree, 1652	60
" Pine-Tree, 1652	60
Shults & Co., California, coinage of	225
Sign — an Egyptian hieroglyphic	43
Silver Coinage of the U. S. Mint	243, 244
" Money	43

INDEX.

Silver-Ring Dollar, 1852, (Pattern) 233
Six-pence, Annapolis, 1783 94
"   Lord Baltimore, 1659 63
"   New England, 1652 59
"   Oak-Tree, 1652 60
"   Pine-tree, 1652 60
Somer, Summer or Bermuda Islands' Coin 58
Standard 31
Steam-Coinage, 1836, (Pattern) 235
Sterling 32
Stone Money 42

TABULAR Statement of Coinage of the U. S. Mint, 241
Terra-Cotta Money 41
Ten-Dollar Pieces, Baldwin & Co., California 225
"   "   Cincinnati Mining and Trading Co., California 224
"   "   Dubosq & Co., California 225
"   "   J. S. O., California 224
"   "   Miners' Bank, of San Francisco, California 224
"   "   Moffatt & Co., California 224
"   "   Mormon, Utah 225
"   "   Oregon Exchange Co., Cal. ... 223
"   "   Pacific Mining Co., Cal. 224
"   "   Templeton Reed, California .. 224
Three-Cent Pieces, 1851 107
"   "   (Pattern) 232
"   Dollar Pieces, 1854 172
Three-pence, Annapolis, 1783 95
"   Oak-Tree, 1652 61
"   Pine-Tree, 1652 60
Tin-piece, 1690 69
Tory Copper, 1785 100
Total Coinage of the U. S. Mint 247, 248
Tree-Coins 60
Twenty-Dollar Pieces, Baldwin & Co. Cal. 225
"   "   Mormon, Utah 225
Twenty-five Dollar Pieces, Templeton Reed, Cal. 224
Two-and-a-half Dollar Pieces, Mormon, Utah ... 225
"   "   "   North Carolina ... 221
Two-pence, Oak-Tree, 1652 61

Types and varieties of Auctori Connec, 1785 104
"   "   "   1786 105
"   "   "   1787, 107, 108
"   "   Cents 238
"   "   Half-Cents 239
"   "   Nova Cæsarea, 1786.. 115, 116
"   "   "   1787 .. 117–120
"   "   "   1788 121
"   "   Vermon Auctori, 1788 101

UNITED STATES 145
"   Gold Coinage 155
U. S. A. Copper, 1783 89

VASE, ABORIGINAL 38
Vermon Auctori, 1787 99
"   "   1788 101
Vermont 98
Vermontensium Res Publica, 1786 98
Vermonts Res Publica, 1785 98
Virginia Half-Penny, (Copper) 1773 83
"   "   (Silver) 1774 83

WAMPUM 45
Washington Cent, 1792 131
"   "   1792 134
"   Cents, 1783 95
"   "   1791 .... 128, 129
"   "   1792 .... 131, 133
"   Coppers, 1792 137
"   "   1795 138
"   Half-Dollar, 1792 133
"   Half-Penny, 1791 138
"   Medalet, 1790 137
"   Medalets 140
"   "   1795, 1796, 1799 ..... 139, 140
"   "   1799 .... 141, 142
"   Piece, 1776 85
"   Token, 1795 138
"   Tokens, 1788 95
"   "   Coppers, Medalets, &c. 137
Weight 31
Wreath Cent 200

INDEX TO THE SUPPLEMENT.

Introduction..Page 249

Auctori Connec, 1785............................... 258
"   "   1786............................. 258
"   "   1787............................. 259
"   "   1788............................. 261

Franklin Copper, 1794............................ 255

New England Copper............................... 252
North Carolina   " 252
New York Coppers, 1786........................... 253
Nova Constellatio, 1786........................... 253
Nova Cæsarea, 1786 254
"   "   1787................................. 261
"   "   1788................................. 262

Oak Tree Shilling, 1652........................... 251

Pine Tree Shilling, 1652.......................... 251

Pine Tree Shilling, 1652........................... 251
"   Copper,   " 252

Tory Copper, 1787 254
Types and varieties of Vermon Auctori, 1786... 256
"   "   "   1787... 257
"   "   "   1788... 258
"   "   "   1787... 260
"   "   "   1788... 261

Undesignated by name............................. 255
"   " 255

Vermontis Res Publica, 1785 254
Vermon Auctori, 1786............................. 256
"   1787..................................... 257
"   1788..................................... 258

THE END.

www.ingramcontent.com/pod-product-compliance
Lightning Source LLC
Chambersburg PA
CBHW022044230426
43672CB00008B/1068